What reviewers have said...

"What happened to Canada's 1837 rebels after they were transported to Australia is a story that needs to be told. This book does it in fine style."
Montreal *Gazette*

"There's much stirring material in veteran newspaperman Jack Cahill's research into the fate of Canada's rebels of 1837. Some escaped the gallows by hours, thanks to their wives' desperate pleas – only to be sent in scurvy-laden ships to Tasmania."
Toronto *Globe and Mail*

"Images of cramped, dark, foul-smelling quarters aboard a convict ship where prisoners lose their teeth to scurvy and barely survive long enough to begin their sentences in a harsh and cruel new world are not normally what make good bedtime reading.... The storytelling in this book about Canadian rebels and American idealists who were captured in the rebellions of 1837-38 and shipped off as convicts to an Australian hell-hole is so good this reviewer found it hard to turn off the light at night."
Brockville Recorder and Times

I was the convict
 Sent to Hell,
To make in the desert
 The living well:

I split the rock;
 I felled the tree –
The nation was
 Because of me.

MARY GILMORE,
"OLD BOTANY BAY," 1918

FORGOTTEN PATRIOTS

Canadian Rebels
on Australia's
Convict Shores

JACK CAHILL

Robin Brass Studio
Toronto

The author gratefully acknowledges permission to quote from *The Fatal Shore* by Robert Hughes. Copyright © 1985 by Robert Hughes. Reprinted by permission of Alfred A. Knopf Inc.

The author gratefully acknowledges a grant from the Ontario Arts Council.

Title page picture: Courtesy National Library of Australia, Canberra

Published 1998 by Robin Brass Studio
10 Blantyre Avenue, Toronto, Ontario M1N 2R4, Canada
Fax: (416) 698-2120
E-mail: rbrass@total.net
Website: www.total.net/~rbrass

Printed and bound in Canada by AGMV-Marquis, Cap-Saint-Ignace, Quebec

Canadian Cataloguing in Publication Data

Cahill, Jack
    Forgotten patriots : Canadian rebels on Australia's convict shores

Includes bibliographical references and index.
ISBN 1-896941-07-9

1. Canada – History – Rebellion, 1837-1838 – Prisoners and prisons. 2. Penal colonies – Australia – History – 19th century. 3. Canada – Exiles – History – 19th century. 4. Australia – Exiles – History – 19th century. 5. Prisoners, Transportation of – Canada – History – 19th century. 6. Canadians – Australia – History – 19th century. I. Title.

FC457.P7C33 1998   071.038   C98-932038-3
F1032.C33 1998

To Robert Clark,
Old Asia Hand

Un Canadien errant

Un canadien errant, banni de ses foyers,
Parcourait en pleurant des pays étrangers.

Un jour, triste et pensif, assis au bord des flots,
Au courant fugitif il adressa ces mots.

"Si tu vois mon pays, mon pays malheureux,
Va, dis à mes amis que je me souviens d'eux.

"O jours si pleins d'appas vous êtes disparus…
Et ma patrie, hélas ! Je ne la verrai plus!

"Non, mas en expirant, O mon cher Canada !
Mon regard languissant vers toi se portera…"

Antoine Gérin-Lajoie (1824-82) wrote these words a few years after the events of 1837-38 and set them to a French folk melody. The song, in which a melancholy exile expresses his longing for his native land, became one of the most popular French-Canadian songs. What follows is a fairly literal translation.

A wandering Canadian, banished from his home,
Travelled, weeping, in foreign lands.

One day, sad and wistful, sitting beside a torrent,
To the rushing stream he spoke these words.

"If you see my native land, my unhappy land,
Go, tell my friends that I remember them.

"O days so full of charms, you have vanished…
And my native land, alas! I shall see it no more!

"No, even in death, my dear Canada!
My listless gaze will be turned to you…"

Contents

Maps

Preface

On September 27, 1839, in the early morning, HMS *Buffalo*, about 700 tons and fifteen guns, sailed out of Quebec City bound for the end of the earth. A crew in military uniforms paced the top of her three decks. In a small, dark hold in her lower deck, below sea level, 141 prisoners huddled miserably. Their clothes and bodies were covered in vermin, their cheeks sunken from malnourishment, their arms and legs swollen from recently removed shackles. They were hunched in the four and a half feet of headroom and hardly able to move in the crush of smelly, skinny bodies. They were not sure where they were going.

All but four of these men were French- and English-speaking Canadians and Americans who had taken part in the 1837-38 rebellions aimed at ending British and elitist rule in Canada and attaining some form of democratic government. The other four were common criminals – three murderers and a deserter. Some of the Canadian rebels were men of substance, doctors, lawyers, landowners and ships' captains. Some of the Americans were idealists, anxious to spread their cherished freedoms to the northern part of the continent. Others were adventurers. All of them had been sentenced to hang but had had their sentences commuted to forced transportation to a faraway place, where, the authorities hoped, history would forget them.

Smaller numbers of Canadians and Americans were shipped off in other, similar ships. And, in fact, they were all but forgotten. A few general English-Canadian histories mention their numbers but fail to report what happened to them. Some Quebeckers still regard the Lower Canadians involved as martyrs. Americans seem unaware of their countrymen's fate.[1]

This is the story of some of them...

JACK CAHILL

ix

Acknowledgements

$\mathcal{T}$he idea for this book came from Robert Clark, a recently retired Canadian Broadcasting Corporation producer in Ottawa and former fellow foreign correspondent in Indochina. He sent me two newspaper clippings on Tasmania, written by Canadian travel writers, which mentioned a Canadian connection with the island because it had once been the home of a number of Canadian convicts. Clark suggested there might be a book in this and that I should write it because of my background in both Australia and Canada.

At first it seemed a daunting task. Although I was born and educated in Australia, like most Canadians and Australians I had never heard of any Canadian convicts in the Australian convict system. The travel stories mentioned the convicts were involved in the 1837-38 rebellions in Canada, but who were they? And why were they sent to Tasmania, and how did they get there, and what happened to them? I talked with at least a hundred Canadians and a score of Australians and none had any knowledge of their existence, let alone the answers to the questions. A few Canadian historian friends did know some Canadians had been transported to what was then Van Diemen's Land, and had a rough idea of their number, but that was the extent of their knowledge.

The mystery began to unfold, however, with my first inquiry – to the State Library of Tasmania in Hobart. Assistant Manager Tony Marshall replied with an enthusiastic opinion that a book should be written, offering all possible help, and enclosing a long bibliography that included the journals and narratives of nine of the Canadian convicts, on which the book was eventually based. To my surprise, most of these rare journals and narratives were also available at the Baldwin Room of the Toronto Reference Library, where the helpful librarians seemed to enjoy digging them out for me.

Though based on these old accounts, the book could not have been written, or at least not without much longer research, without the work of three more recent authors: the late William Kilbourn, who commended the manuscript while making some helpful suggestions and whose entertaining and informative book *The Firebrand* (Clarke, Irwin, Toronto, 1956) led to a better understanding of William Lyon Mackenzie and his times; Edwin Clarence Guillet, whose scholarly but anecdotal book *The Lives and Times of the Patriots* (Thomas Nelson, Toronto, 1938) provided much insight into the aftermath of the Canadian rebellions and some facts about the convicts; and Robert Hughes, whose classic on the Australian convict system, *The Fatal Shore* (Alfred A. Knopf, New York, 1987), was consulted regularly.

I owe particular thanks to Desmond Morton, professor of history, author and now director of the new McGill Institute for the Study of Canada, who encouraged the project from the beginning then bestowed an enthusiastic blessing on the completed manuscript. Several Canadians helped me in my research, including Terry Howes, Esther Summers, Janice Wood and Margaret Stawinoga, while, in Australia, Sydney librarian Judy Dallimore found some rare documents for me, journalist and author Alan Gill helped with some research on the French-Canadian convicts and Owen Dooley, an old school friend, spent many hours voluntarily chasing hard-to-find facts with a professional persistency.

Lew Gloin, Toronto editor and wordsmith, read early parts of the manuscript and made some helpful suggestions, and Gerry Hall, my friend and great editor when I was senior feature writer at the *Toronto Star,* helped with his usual guidance, skill and cheerfulness. Journalist and author Anthony Westell edited the manuscript as we circumnavigated Lake Ontario in my boat, visiting many of the places the convicts came from or fought in. He was assisted by the other crewman, Stanley Westall (different spelling, no relation), another fine journalist. My wife, Marie, was encouraging, as always. And the Ontario Arts Council provided a substantial grant from its Works in Progress program.

My agent and friend Beverley Slopen was her usual professional and persistent self and editor-publisher Robin Brass most helpful. – J.C.

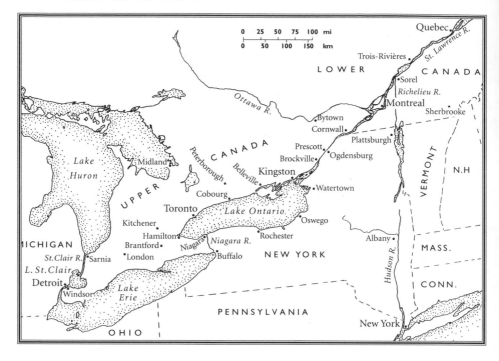

Central Upper and Lower Canada and the adjacent United States at the time of the rebellions of 1837-38.

CHAPTER 1

The Rebellions

Up and waur them a', Willy,
Up and waur them a',
Better brave the tyrants down,
Than let this country fall.

UPPER CANADIAN REBEL SONG OF 1837

*T*he first character in this story, unlike many others to follow, is well known to history. He is a tiny, be-wigged Scot with a bulging forehead, a bristling fringe of white side-whisker, a burning, fanatic eye and talents for oratory and muckraking journalism, a ranter and a raver. A lot of people in his day think he is slightly mad. He is also a natural leader and a radical reformer, much hated by the establishment of what was then Upper Canada and is now Ontario.

He is William Lyon Mackenzie, a printer and publisher by trade, and we meet him on a cold early December afternoon in 1837 when he is forty-three. He looks ludicrous astride a white farm horse in the yard of Montgomery's Tavern on Yonge Street north of Toronto, wearing a thick overcoat not so much to guard against the weather but against bullets because he intends to ride his white horse to war. He is going to capture the city of about 12,000 souls, four miles south of Montgomery's, of which he was the first mayor. As he rides back and forth he is shouting shrill and contradictory orders to a group of seven or eight hundred men in an odd variety of uniforms, some armed with muskets, others with knives or pikes strapped to long sticks or fishing poles.

The diminutive Scot has no military experience whatever. Nor have the vast majority of his followers, normally peaceful pioneering farmers, mechanics and a few professionals. Some of this crowd, and others who later follow their course, are destined to be hanged. Others will suffer a fate they believed to be even worse than death on the gallows. However, the repercussions of the bizarre thing they do on this day will eventually help to alter drastically the nature of government in Canada, indeed the country itself. They will also extend, in ugly retaliation against them and their acts, to the very end of the earth.

This odd, in a military sense preposterous, group has a just cause.

In the 1830s, Upper Canada was controlled by what some people sarcastically called the Family Compact, a relatively small, tightly knit group of men that included the leading members of the administration – executive councillors, senior officials and some members of the judiciary. Its members controlled the machinery of government although the lieutenant-governor had the final say and could overrule them. This Tory establishment in turn made sure that like-minded friends and relations received the lesser appointments throughout the province. So the main Compact spawned little local "family compacts" consisting of sheriffs, magistrates, militia officers, customs collectors and other officials.

The design the Compact sought to impose upon the province was clearly defined and, many argued, well meaning. Indeed, in many ways before the depression of the late 1830s, the province prospered. But the power and advantage the Compact members achieved as by-products of the system were unfair and the means they used were often petty, ruthless and selfish.[1]

The cardinal point in their strategy was that the little pioneer North American community they dominated must remain an integral part of

William Lyon Mackenzie, grandfather of future Canadian prime minister William Lyon Mackenzie King. A printer and publisher by trade and a radical rival of the Upper Canadian establishment, he led Toronto's Yonge Street rebellion in 1837. (Toronto Reference Library)

the British Empire. They had a strong sense of nationality but it was British nationality, not Canadian, and they had no desire for any other. As colonial British did everywhere, they sometimes seemed to be more British than their fellows at home. They regarded the rising tide of democracy in the world, with its best example just across the American border, with fear and contempt. Government did not, in their view, derive its authority from the consent of the governed, but from the King, from history and from religion, providing the religion was represented by the Church of England.

To the Compact, Upper Canada was not a multicultural province, nor was it pluralist. It was British. Yet the population of Upper Canada was overwhelmingly American in origin. Inns and mills were commonly run by Americans and many schools and religious groups were tinged with republicanism.

In a time when religious, class and political identities were closely intertwined, the matter of the Clergy Reserves was a major source of resentment. The government reserved a proportion of the land for the Church of England, the "established" church, which broadly speaking was the church of the English upper crust. But of an Upper Canadian population of about 400,000, about a quarter were officially classed as Anglican. Slightly less than a quarter were Presbyterian. Methodists ranked next with 17 per cent, followed by Roman Catholics (12 per cent) and Baptists (3 per cent). There were also a few Mennonites, Quakers and Lutherans. And there were six Jews, all in Toronto.[2]

So trouble brewed. Mackenzie began to preach rebellion in his newspaper, the *Colonial Advocate*. He was elected to the Assembly as member for York and was kicked out of the chamber several times for his critical harangues, sometimes literally hauled out by the scruff of his neck. He was sometimes a vicious scandalmonger, often inaccurate, and once his printing presses were destroyed by angry Compact members. But he had many supporters, mostly small farmers, tradesmen, mechanics, some of them well-educated. They were known as Reformers.

The basic complaints of these rebel Reformers, as well as some of the more conservative political leaders, were the obvious: that public opinion was ignored in Upper Canada; that the government was in the hands of a small oligarchy that reserved nearly all jobs for its own members or its hangers-on; that this group directed economic development for its own profit, and tried to monopolize much of the public land for the advantage of one religious denomination. Originating political arguments that continued to be unresolved in Canada late in the next century, the Reformers were preoccupied with constitutional reform and their most immediate and tangible target was the Legislative Council, a sort of non-elected senate, composed of Compact members, which had been frustrating the elected assembly for years by rejecting or side-tracking its bills, particularly when the Reformers were in the majority in the representative body. The Reformers insisted there was only one way to make this ancient form of senate responsive to public opinion, and that was to make it elective.

Sparks were added to this smouldering political discontent when a new lieutenant-governor, Sir Francis Bond Head, arrived in the province at the beginning if 1836. His was a very strange appointment – so astonishing, in fact, that many believed he was not really appointed at all, that it was a horrible mistake, as his career in Upper Canada eventually turned out to be. No one was more surprised by the appointment than Sir Francis himself. By his own cheerful admission he knew absolutely nothing about colonial affairs. Nor had he any experience in politics. He was a slight man with a boyish face and a thick mop of curly hair who was born to a family of country gentry and became a military engineer and a bit of an adventurer. At one stage he was engaged to manage the mining of silver by a British company in South America but it went broke. He did achieve something there, however. He became the first Englishman to gallop all the way across the pampas of Argentina to the Andes and back in the space of a week, earning himself the nickname of Galloping Head. He also learned from the gauchos how to throw a lasso, and when he returned to England to become a lowly assistant poor law commissioner, he demonstrated the art before King William IV with such skill the king granted him a knighthood. Bond Head also recommended that the lasso be introduced into the British army as a weapon, but the military authorities saw no use for it.[3]

The question of finding a gentleman willing to exile himself to Upper Canada apparently arose at a British cabinet meeting in November

Sir Francis Bond Head, lieutenant-governor of Upper Canada from 1836 to 1838. He knew nothing about colonial administration when he was appointed and was strongly opposed to any form of democracy. He was known as "Galloping Head" because he once rode across the pampas of Argentina to the Andes and back in a week. He won his knighthood by impressing King William IV with his skill at throwing a lasso. (Toronto Reference Library)

1835, after several men had refused the post. According to one account, someone suggested "young Head," a brilliant thirty-year-old Oxford don who, as Sir Edmund Head, was eventually governor-general of Canada in the 1850s. Or it was possible that Sir Francis's elder brother, Sir George Head, a senior military officer with much experience in North America, was the intended appointee. All that seemed certain was that there was a general agreement in cabinet to the name of Head, and it is possible the messenger sent forth to inform the appointee got the wrong man.[4]

The Head who did come to Canada was an ultra-conservative pseudo-aristocrat who abhorred even the thought of democracy. He believed that his business as governor was to govern and that he alone was responsible. The executive council and the two Houses were welcome to make recommendations but it was up to him to decide whether they should be accepted or refused. Obviously he threw in his lot with the Family Compact, provided its members did what he told them to do. He considered the Reformers a confused, mad, ignorant, disloyal rabble and treated them as such. Naturally, he did not like Mackenzie at all.

After his first meeting with him he wrote: "Mr. Mackenzie's mind seemed to nauseate its subjects.... Afraid to look me in the face, he sat with his feet not reaching the ground and with his countenance averted from me, at an angle of seventy degrees; while, with the eccentricity, the volubility, and indeed the appearance of a madman, the tiny creature raved."

The feeling was mutual. Mackenzie rode the countryside preaching eloquently against Sir Francis and the Compact, causing occasional melees as loyalists and their Orangemen goon squads attempted to break up his meetings. His political machine met at Elliott's Tavern, at the northwest corner of Yonge and Queen streets in Toronto, and, more secretly, in John Doel's Brewery, at Adelaide and Bay streets, where it issued, on July 31, 1837, a Canadian version of the American Declaration of Independence.

Government is founded on the authority, and is instituted for the benefit of a people; when, therefore, any government long and systematically ceases to answer the great ends of its foundation, the people have a natural right given them by their Creator to seek after and establish such institutions as will yield the greatest quality of happiness to the greatest number.

7

At night, in the forests, Mackenzie's "Patriots" tried to drill as military units, using ancient weapons to shoot at pigeons, and pikes forged by village smithies. At these drills the "troops," sometimes comprising three or four hundred men and boys, wore a great variety of uniforms. Some carried as weapons a carving knife at the end of a fishing pole. Others "presented arms" with walking sticks and umbrellas. They were normally peaceful people, but they were frustrated by their political impotence and the corruption among the powerful, and now, as the depression deepened, unemployment rose, poverty worsened and farms and businesses failed, they became dangerously angry. The catchphrase "Liberty or Death" was common among them.

Sir Francis ignored all of this with amazing aplomb. Assuring the British government that the rebels could do no harm, he wrote of Mackenzie: "First he wrote, and then he printed, and then he rode and then he spoke, stamped, foamed, wiped his seditious little mouth and then spoke again; and thus, like a squirrel in a cage, he continued with astonishing assiduity the centre of a revolutionary career." But there was no need at all to worry about Mackenzie and his mob, he insisted.

Discontent was mounting in Lower Canada as well, where the *habitants* were dominated by a *Château Clique* and rich merchants they called the "Aristocracy of Shopkeepers." In the poorer parts of Montreal and the rural villages there was also a similar strong popular reaction to which was added a hatred of British rule, a desire for independence, and a distaste for the ancient French seigneurial or "feudal" system of land tenure, particularly as many of the tenures, and the services and privileges that went with them, had been acquired by English or Scottish settlers.

This anger threw up another odd leader in Louis-Joseph Papineau, himself a *grand seigneur*, who embraced, in a rather casual way, the democratic system of the United States. He was, according to political historian Bruce Hutchison, a confused man – regal in stature, superbly handsome, with noble Gallic face and plume of curling hair – who had

Louis-Joseph Papineau (1786-1871), lawyer, seigneur, politician. A critic of imperial authority and strong advocate of an independent French Canada, he led the Lower Canadian Patriotes until it became obvious they would be crushed in the rebellions of 1837, when he fled to the United States. His career, particularly his behaviour during the rebellions, has been a continuing source of controversy and conjecture. Many of his fellow Patriotes accused him of cowardice. He was granted amnesty in 1844, returned from exile and re-entered politics, advocating annexation to the U.S. (Toronto Reference Library)

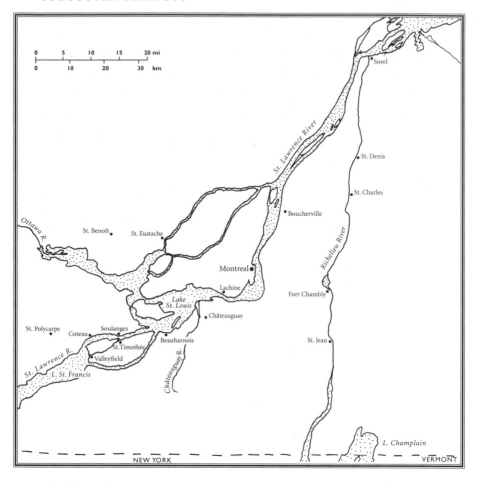

The Montreal area, showing major sites in the uprisings of 1837-38, as well as the villages where François-Xavier Prieur lived.

the natural orator's mortal defect. He could rouse himself and the people, but he never quite knew for what purpose and when it came to action he was impotent.

But Papineau and his *Patriote* followers certainly had a political grievance, worse even than that of Mackenzie and his Patriots in Upper Canada. Between 1822 and 1836 the appointed Legislative Council, comprising members of the *Château Clique*, had rejected no fewer than 224 bills passed by the elected Assembly, in which the French Canadians held a majority. And the British prime minister, Lord John Russell, had authorized the governor to dispose of the province's revenues without the Assembly's consent.[5]

So, sharing similar problems and common anger, the *Patriotes* and those who called themselves Patriots in Upper Canada planned their rebellions in loose collaboration.

The *Patriotes* set up a central committee in Montreal with a semi-military defence wing, *Les Fils de la liberté*, which issued a manifesto that virtually called for an independent "Canadian Nation." Then, late in October 1837, after the government issued warrants for the arrest of Papineau and his lieutenants, a few thousand French Canadians gathered in the small towns and villages of the Richelieu Valley, south of the St. Lawrence River, with whatever muskets and pikes they could find. About 6,000 government troops marched into the valley to confront this ragtag rebel army late in November 1837, by which time Papineau, who did not like even the prospect of violence, had fled to the United States, leaving the *Patriotes* more or less leaderless.

Nevertheless, government troops were briefly defeated at the village of St. Denis on November 23. But two days later they easily captured nearby St. Charles. Then about 2,000 government troops marched on the village of St. Eustache, eighteen miles northwest of Montreal, where two leaders bolder than Papineau, J.-O. Chenier, and a mysterious foreigner, Amaury Girod, had assembled a few hundred followers who were armed only with muskets and alcohol. Girod fled when he saw the long columns approaching and later blew his brains out. Chenier and 200 villagers locked themselves in the church and bravely withstood a brief siege until the soldiers set fire to the building and they were smoked out, killed or captured. Rebels at a nearby village, St. Benoît, decided to surrender. The soldiers set fire to both villages, razing them to the ground, and the first round of the uprising in Lower Canada was over almost as soon as it had started.

In Upper Canada Mackenzie had intended to strike in concert with

The Battle of St. Eustache. In late November 1837, about 2,000 government troops marched on the village of St. Eustache, eighteen miles northwest of Montreal, where a few hundred Patriotes had assembled. Some of the Patriotes withstood a brief siege, but they were eventually killed or captured. (Hartnell, Back View of the Church of St. Eustache and Dispersion of the Insurgents, *Toronto Reference Library)*

the French Canadians on December 5, but there was a mixup, the first of many, that found about seven or eight hundred Upper Canadian rebels gathered at John Montgomery's tavern, on Yonge Street, four miles north of Toronto, armed with blunderbuss, pike and cutlass, just in time to hear the discouraging news of the defeat of the *Patriotes* near Montreal. Mackenzie's followers were also hungry and miserable because, after their long, cold rides from the countryside, John Linfoot, a Tory who had just leased the inn from Montgomery, refused to feed them until he saw the colour of their money. The only real soldier among them, Anthony Anderson, had been killed in a chance skirmish with loyalist Toronto alderman John Powell. So little Mackenzie offered to lead the attack himself.

Now, as we meet him on his white horse, Mackenzie leads his band of rebels down Yonge Street to Gallows Hill, just south of the present St. Clair Avenue, where they are met under a flag of truce by government agents who relay an offer of amnesty from a now-frightened Lieutenant-Governor Bond Head. Mackenzie refuses the amnesty but his troops hesitate and decline to advance farther. Instead they demand dinner. This makes the little man mad. "He went on like a lunatic," one of the participants wrote later. "Once or twice I thought he was going to have a fit." While food is being served to the hungry troops on Gallows Hill, Mackenzie wanders off to a house beside the road and sets it on fire, a bizarre act that worries the rebels so much they begin to stream back to Montgomery's Tavern.

Throughout the rest of the afternoon Mackenzie revives their revolutionary zeal with his oratory and at dusk they march again down Yonge Street, where they are met by about thirty loyalists under Sheriff William Jarvis at a barricade on the town's outskirts. The loyalists fire at the approaching mob then run for their lives. The front ranks of the rebels return their fire, then drop to the ground to reload their muskets and allow those behind to have a clear shot. But those behind think their comrades have been shot and they turn and run back to Montgomery's Tavern, where they continue to wrangle and procrastinate.

By this time, Bond Head has finally understood that there is something seriously wrong in his province. But he has sent his army troops to Lower Canada to deal with the situation there. He arms himself with two double-barrelled guns and two pistols in his belt and allows Colonel James FitzGibbon, a veteran of the War of 1812, to organize a militia of volunteers who have streamed in from the countryside and which, according to a contemporary report, also consists of local "judges, crown officers and most of the other public functionaries, the merchants, mechanics and labourers."[6]

This group of about 1,100 ill-trained loyalist troops marches out of town on December 7 to the music of two bands and the cheers of many of the town's 12,000 people. Two hundred rebels bravely meet them near Montgomery's Tavern but, outnumbered and outflanked, they soon scatter. The loyalists fire cannon balls through the wooden walls of the tavern, causing two hundred men inside to run for the woods. One of the rebels is killed in action. At least eleven are wounded and four of them die later in hospital, while the loyalists are unscathed. The fighting is all over in about twenty minutes and Bond Head, who has followed in the rear of the loyalist advance, orders the burning of Montgomery's Tavern and another house, turning a woman and her four children onto the road. So, as a military operation, the Toronto rebellion fails dismally, as does a supporting movement on Brantford and Hamilton, led by Dr. Charles Duncombe of London, a few days later.[7]

"The yeomen and farmers of Upper Canada had triumphed over their perfidious enemy, 'responsible government,'" Bond Head proclaimed.

The shooting of Moodie, at the Battle of Montgomery's Tavern, December 7, 1837. Loyalists attacked the rebel headquarters at the tavern after the rebels, led by William Lyon Mackenzie, failed to capture Toronto. One rebel was killed in action, and four died later in hospital. (Toronto Reference Library)

Mackenzie escaped across the border, borrowing horses from friends and wading naked, neck-deep across one icy creek, hiding in frozen ditches while government troops passed a few feet away. On the American side of the Niagara River he was welcomed by admiring republicans. With his brilliant, angry oratory he soon gathered a band of about a thousand other Canadian refugees and American sympathizers on Navy Island, in the Niagara River upstream from the falls, within the Canadian boundary. There he formed a provisional government of the new republic of Canada, issued his own money, raised his own flag and planned an invasion of Canada. But the Canadian authorities foiled him. His only source of supply was the little American steamer *Caroline*, which was making a daily trip from the American shore to the island.[8] On the night of December 29, Canadian troops, armed with cutlasses and pistols, crossed the river to reach the *Caroline*, berthed at Schlosser. They hurled the crew and passengers ashore, killing one man in the process, and set the ship on fire, sending it down the Niagara River towards the falls, thus performing an act of war against the United States which was fortunately ignored by the new, mild president, Martin Van Buren.[9]

A few months later, on April 12, 1838, two of the rebel leaders, Samuel Lount and Peter Matthews, were hanged at the Toronto jail (although carpenters at first refused to erect a scaffold for men they regarded as the first martyrs to Canadian liberty). And most general Canadian histories end the story of the rebellions of 1837 at this point.

But that is not where the story ended. For a brief, sparsely recorded period following the rout of the rebels on Yonge Street, most of settled Upper Canada erupted into a cruel and, for many, disastrous wave of vengeance. Bond Head started this repression with a proclamation offering rewards for the capture of Mackenzie and several other rebel leaders, but it was aimed at all Patriots and their supporters. It read in part:

The burning of the Caroline. *Canadian troops set the little American steamer on fire because it was carrying supplies to William Lyon Mackenzie's rebels on Navy Island in the Niagara River. This was an act of war, but it was ignored by U.S. President Martin Van Buren. Most of the ship sank in the rapids above Niagara Falls but some parts went over. The figurehead was found near Lewiston. (City of Toronto Archives)*

In a time of profound peace, while every one was quietly following his occupations, feeling secure under the protection of our laws, a band of rebels, instigated by a few malignant and disloyal men, has had the wickedness and audacity to assemble with arms, and to attack and murder the Queen's subjects on the highway....

  Brave and loyal people of Upper Canada, we have been long

PROCLAMATION.

BY His Excellency SIR FRANCIS BOND HEAD,
Baronet, Lieutenant Governor of Upper Canada, &c. &c.

To the Queen's Faithful Subjects in Upper Canada.

In a time of profound peace, while every one was quietly following his occupations, feeling secure under the protection of our Laws, a band of Rebels, instigated by a few malignant and disloyal men, has had the wickedness and audacity to assemble with Arms, and to attack and Murder the Queen's Subjects on the Highway—to Burn and Destroy their Property—to Rob the Public Mails—and to threaten to Plunder the Banks—and to Fire the City of Toronto.

Brave and Loyal People of Upper Canada, we have been long suffering from the acts and endeavours of concealed Traitors, but this is the first time that Rebellion has dared to shew itself openly in the land, in the absence of invasion by any Foreign Enemy.

Let every man do his duty now, and it will be the last time that we or our children shall see our lives or properties endangered, or the Authority of our Gracious Queen insulted by such treacherous and ungrateful men. MILITIA-MEN OF UPPER CANADA, no Country has ever shewn a finer example of Loyalty and Spirit than YOU have given upon this sudden call of Duty. Young and old of all ranks, are flocking to the Standard of their Country. What has taken place will enable our Queen to know Her Friends from Her Enemies—a public enemy is never so dangerous as a concealed Traitor—and now my friends let us complete well what is begun—let us not return to our rest till Treason and Traitors are revealed to the light of day, and rendered harmless throughout the land.

Be vigilant, patient and active—leave punishment to the Laws—our first object is, to arrest and secure all those who have been guilty of Rebellion, Murder and Robbery.—And to aid us in this, a Reward is hereby offered of

One Thousand Pounds,

to any one who will apprehend, and deliver up to Justice, WILLIAM LYON MACKENZIE ; and FIVE HUNDRED POUNDS to any one who will apprehend, and deliver up to Justice, DAVID GIBSON—or SAMUEL LOUNT—or JESSE LLOYD—or SILAS FLETCHER—and the same reward and a free pardon will be given to any of their accomplices who will render this public service, except he or they shall have committed, in his own person, the crime of Murder or Arson.

And all, but the Leaders above-named, who have been seduced to join in this unnatural Rebellion, are hereby called to return to their duty to their Sovereign—to obey the Laws—and to live henceforward as good and faithful Subjects—and they will find the Government of their Queen as indulgent as it is just.

GOD SAVE THE QUEEN.

Thursday, 3 o'clock, P. M.
7th Dec.

☞ The Party of Rebels, under their Chief Leaders, is wholly dispersed, and flying before the Loyal Militia. The only thing that remains to be done, is to find them, and arrest them.

R. STANTON, Printer to the QUEEN'S Most Excellent Majesty.

Proclamation by Lieutenant-Governor Sir Francis Bond Head offering rewards for the capture of William Lyon Mackenzie and other rebels following the failed rebellion on Yonge Street. (Ontario Archives)

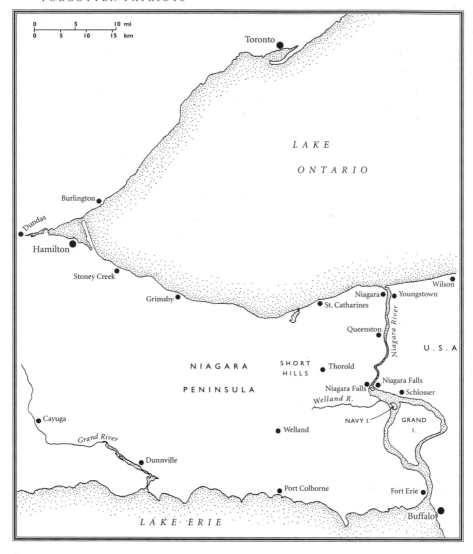

The Niagara Peninsula and western Lake Ontario.

suffering from the acts and endeavours of concealed traitors, but this is the first time that rebellion has dared to show itself openly in the land, in the absence of invasion by any foreign enemy.

Let every man do his duty now, and it will be the last time that we and our children shall see our lives or properties endangered,

18

or the authority of our gracious Queen insulted by such treacherous and ungrateful men. Militia-men of Upper Canada, no country has ever shown a finer example of loyalty and spirit than you have given upon this sudden call of duty. What has taken place will enable our Queen to know her friends from her enemies – a public enemy is never so dangerous as a concealed traitor; and now my friends let us complete well what is begun – let us not return to our rest till treason and traitors are revealed to the light of day, and rendered harmless throughout the land.

The proclamation went on to appeal to "those who have been seduced to join in this unnatural rebellion" to return to their homes and become good and faithful subjects, whereupon they would find the government of their Queen "as indulgent as it is just." But its general thrust seemed to give loyalists licence to seek out, capture and even punish anybody they thought to be a rebel or sympathizer of democracy, and this they did throughout the countryside.

The result was the hanging of many men and the banishment of many more, those forgotten by history, to the end of the earth in chains.

CHAPTER 2

Retribution and Revenge

With loyal bosums beating high,
In your good cause securely trust,
God and Victoria be your cry,
And crush the traitors to the dust.

SUSANNA MOODIE, 1838

In the rampage of repression after the uprisings in Upper Canada, gangs of loyalist militia roamed the land rooting out Patriots and their sympathizers. They burned houses, destroyed farms, looted stores and terrorized people. In one punitive militia march on Norwich, near London, the property of all Reformers was appropriated or destroyed and 500 men were arrested. In this and other parts of the province, ultra-loyal gangs drove away cattle from Reformers' farms and sold them cheaply to friends. Wheat was seized in large quantities. Whatever was not worth stealing was destroyed. Even contemporary writers with strong Tory sympathies admitted that Reformers were roughly treated and shamefully robbed.

Aided by tattletales anxious to protect themselves and long lists of names foolishly left behind by Mackenzie and other lists discovered by the militia after Duncombe had hurriedly buried his papers, the punitive forces charged into houses flourishing their guns, making arrests, and demanding information, food and horses.

Women were not spared. When Charles Durand, a young Hamilton lawyer, who had done nothing more than shake Mackenzie's hand and talk briefly with him during the Toronto uprising, was still in the Toronto area, an armed gang led by a sheriff burst into his Hamilton house, startling his wife and her sister and overturning furniture as they searched for papers that might prove he was a Reformer. They found nothing, but next morning another gang of twenty men armed with muskets and bayonets rushed into the house, cursing and swearing. They destroyed the house's cellar and the vegetables in it, threatened to burn the house and barn down, then left, leaving the two women shaking with fear. That night they came back, rushed into the bedroom where Mrs. Durand and her sister were sleeping, looked under the bed, pointed pistols at the women and demanded candles and water. Next day when Mrs. Durand and her sister tried to go to a friend's house, they were caught two miles from Hamilton and marched back.[1]

Worse occurred to Mrs. William Comfort, whose husband was accused of harbouring Mackenzie during his escape. A contemporary report stated:

The magistrates so brutally treated his wife in the hope of obtaining information she did not possess, to implicate her husband, by telling her among other things he would be hanged the next day, that premature labour was brought on and she and her babe, before that day's sun was set, were in their graves....

The brutality exercised in this case roused the indignation of even some of the Orange tory party; and when [Comfort] begged the authorities to allow him to go out on bail, only to the funeral and to provide some place for his [four] children, he was refused.... They laughed in very derision at the request.... His poor children came to Toronto and sought admittance to their father. Their tears and entreaties softened the heart of the jailer and he took them to the chancellor, Jamieson, whose office it was to grant passes, and begged permission to let the father see them; but it was against the orders of the governor and could not be permitted.[2]

Some women defended their homes from loyalist raids with spirit. One young woman in Pickering Township was reported to have driven away a gang attempting to enter her house by swinging a hardwood sapling and threatening to smash their skulls open. An attempt to arrest a Mrs. Kenny near Ayr failed miserably when she took off, bounding fences and hedges with the leaps of an Olympic hurdler and sprinting across an open field to warn her husband, leaving male pursuers far behind. She and her husband escaped, but apparently at the cost of sacrificing their home.

In the circumstances, thousands of reform-minded Upper Canadians (some reports estimate more than 25,000) sold their farms and homes for about a sixth of their real value and fled to the United States, where many used what small amounts of money they had left to buy land west of the Mississippi River. Others, those who had, in fact, taken part in the uprisings, suffered many weeks of hardship, starving in the frozen forests, before they were arrested or escaped across the border.

The enormous brain-drain from the fledgling province affected its future economy and history. One of the fleeing rebels, for instance, was a tall, tough, semi-literate innkeeper from Vienna, near Port Burwell, named Samuel Edison Jr., who was also known as an exceptional athlete. For months, following William Lyon Mackenzie's instructions, Sam Edison had drilled armed bands in the deep woods of the neighbourhood from which most of them cut their living. When the word came in early December 1837, he set out with his file of armed woodsmen for the revolution in Toronto. However, as they made their way through the deep forests, news of the fiasco on Yonge Street reached them. Worse than that, Edison learned that a force of 600 militia were on their way to battle with his small contingent. As the government troops approached, he dispersed his men in the woods and ran for his home in Vienna. There he said goodbye to his wife and four children and hid for the night in a barn near his father's house.

At dawn the athletic Edison started to run through the woods for the United States border, more than eighty miles away, closely pursued by the King's men with Indian guides and dogs. He ran for two and a half days, stopping only briefly to catch his breath and eat some food, until he crossed the frozen St. Clair River to safety at Port Huron, Michigan.

Sam Edison settled in Milan, Ohio, where he started a prospering shingles business and he was joined there in 1839 by his Canadian wife, Nancy, and their four children. They had three more children but two of them died in infancy. Then, in the dead of winter, on February 11, 1847, when Nancy was middle-aged, she gave birth to her seventh child, a sickly son with fair hair, large blue eyes, a round face and a head so abnormally large the village doctor thought he might have brain fever and the Edisons believed him to be "defective." They named him Thomas Alva Edison. Eventually the amazing inventions of Thomas Edison changed the economy of the United States and the future of the world.[3]

Other escapes were just as daring or dramatic. One man found an old canoe near Oshawa with its bow completely rotted away. He put himself and a heavy stone in the stern and paddled for eighteen hours with the bow clear of the icy waters until he reached the American shore. Others took off by rowboat from the mouth of Factory Creek, near Cobourg. On the night of December 27, 1837, the 100-foot schooner *Industry*, which had been laid up for the winter near Oshawa and was owned by a Reformer, Daniel Conant, slipped quietly from her moorings and sailed close along the shore of Lake Ontario. It was a bright moonlit night but bitterly cold and her owner was deeply concerned about the dangers of navigating Lake Ontario in winter. Every mile or so, when a light flashed on the shore, she backed her mainsail and lay to while a canoe carried a Patriot from his hiding place in the forest. She made about forty stops. Then a fine offshore breeze blew her, sailing wing and wing, sixty miles across the lake to Oswego.

But off Oswego the small ship was met by three miles of ice. The

Patriots and crew tried to force a passage but managed to move only a quarter of a mile before darkness. During the night the wind and the temperature fell and by morning the ship was solidly frozen in. Still the ice was hardly thick enough to bear a man's weight. The men decided to try to walk ashore anyway. They took spars and poles from the ship to help on their hazardous journey but every few minutes one of them fell through the ice and had to be rescued by his companions. Soon they were all chilled and weak, but they continued to stumble towards the shore, where hundreds of Americans had gathered to shout encouragement. Then, when they were just a few feet from the shore, the pack ice started to move out into the lake.

"Already it had parted from the shore streak of ice and left a space of open water now seven feet wide," a contemporary report said. "Jump it they could not, because their clothes were frozen so hard that they could not spring, and besides, the ice on the other side of the open space was not thick enough to hold one alighting after the jump. Their last hope sank within them; death stared them in the face; their wives and friends in Canada would see them no more. Every minute added to the gulf of water between them and the shore ice."

However, by a stroke of luck or amazing foresight, one of the sailors had carried with him a plank instead of a spar. It was just long enough to bridge the open space and he laid it down, calling on the others to follow him or perish. All of them did so, struggling ashore to the cheers of the spectators and their freedom. The *Industry* sank.[4]

Charles Duncombe, the popular doctor who led the London area revolt, made one of the more exotic escapes. He had £500 on his head but was held in such high regard by most of the people of the district he had little trouble finding refuge. After abandoning any hope of success in the rebellion, he assembled most of his men in a Quaker meeting-house at Norwich and advised them to go home. Then, dressed in Quaker garb, he set out himself but immediately fell through the ice in a mill-pond. He was able to scramble ashore and make for the woods on his white horse. He spent the first night with a friendly couple who

Dr. Charles Duncombe, who led
the 1837 rebellion in the London
area of Upper Canada. He
escaped afterwards to the United
States disguised as an old
woman. American-born, he
regarded annexation to the
United States as the best solution
to the problems of Upper
Canada. He was eventually
pardoned, but returned to
Canada only briefly, spending
the rest of his life in Sacramento,
California, where he died in
1867. (Toronto Reference
Library)

placed him between them in bed to avoid detection. After that he spent three days concealed in the woods, subsisting on berries, herbs and roots, while his faithful horse grazed nearby in the open. He became so hungry he was forced to venture into the settled area of Nilestown, where he knocked on the door of a political friend named Putnam. A posse recognized his white horse in the yard and rushed into the house, searching every room. But Duncombe had been put to bed as "grandmother," wearing a nightcap, and the posse ignored him. A friend named Douglas sheltered him the next night. His house was burned to the ground a few hours after Duncombe left.[5]

Eventually the doctor, who had also been member of the Assembly for his district of Oxford, sneaked to the home of his sister, Mrs. Shenich, near London, where he remained in a hay loft for several weeks. His sister and friends then disguised him as "Aunt Nancy," using the sister's old clothes and even a curl of her hair. "Aunt Nancy" set out in a sleigh for the west and was not stopped as she approached the frontier. From Sarnia she crossed over on the ice to the United States. Gallant members of the militia who had helped escort the old lady across were astounded when she shouted in a deep masculine voice from the American shore: "Go back and tell your commander you have just piloted Dr. Duncombe across the river!"[6]

While all of this was going on in the first half of 1838, Americans in the border states, with their dreams of manifest destiny, were organizing a network of secret societies aimed at liberating their oppressed neighbours. These societies, usually involving masonic ritual – the Canadian Refugees Association, the Sons of Liberty, the Hunters' Lodges – recruited their members from passionate republicans, refugee Canadian Patriots, the unemployed and adventurers, who were promised a cash bounty and a grant of land in a new Canadian republic. They had the tacit support of state authorities, met only mild opposition from the federal government, and firmly believed that the oppression of the people of Canada would lead to a mass uprising in support of republicanism.

Between January and June they made several raids into Canada, on islands off Detroit, on Pelee Island in Lake Erie, across the St. Clair River, and across the Niagara frontier, but they were killed, captured or repelled by Canadian forces. Anticipating such aggression, the Upper Canadian authorities passed a special act in January 1838 "to protect the inhabitants of this province against lawless aggression from subjects of foreign countries at peace with Her Majesty." The act provided that persons involved in aggressions (meaning Americans) should be tried, like Canadians, before Canadian courts martial or regular courts.[7]

The result of all of this internal upheaval and external aggression was that by August 1838 there were 885 persons in jail, including 422 from the Home District (Toronto), 163 from London, 90 from Gore (Hamilton), 75 from Midland and 43 from Niagara. The Niagara prisoners included many captured at the brief battle of Short Hills in June.

Of this total of 885, 3 were eventually executed, 14 escaped, 27 were sentenced to transportation (but 13 of those were subsequently released),

20 were banished, 12 sentenced to the penitentiary, 140 pardoned, and the rest – the majority – were acquitted or dismissed from custody.[8]

However, they all had a rough time in prison. One of the prisoners, Robert Marsh, an American, described the Toronto jail:

We were put into a hall that was occupied during the day by thirty or forty, and at night all locked in different cells – from five to eight in a cell. The jail was crowded full; some crazy, some for murder, some for stealing, some for desertion, and various other crimes.[9]

This old jail, as well as all others, was alive with vermin. It is out of my power to describe this place, and our feelings at our entrance and during seven weeks confinement in this horrible place. Our rations were hardly sufficient to keep us alive; what there was was more filthy, if possible, than any before. Bullocks' heads, boiled with a very few peas that the rats had been among – and I declare it was impossible to tell, many times, of what our scanty meal consisted, – it appeared to be their intention to poison us here. The bullocks' heads were boiled with brains, teeth, and often the hair was so thick in the broth, together with the effects of rats and mice, that we could not stomach it; we came to the conclusion that our days would be ended here.[10]

In the second half of the year the Americans, aided by a few Canadian refugees, made two more invasions, more ambitious and in greater numbers than before, but they were just as badly led and organized and suffered even worse results. These invasions were made by members of the Hunters' Lodges, an elaborate secret organization with more than 1,100 branches and 80,000 members, thought to have received its name either because members pretended to be hunters when drilling with their weapons, or because the first lodge was organized in Vermont by Dr. James Hunter, a refugee from Whitby, Upper Canada.

Early in November 1838, the Hunters' Lodges massed about 1,000 men at Ogdensburg, intent on capturing the Canadian village of

Prescott on the other side of the St. Lawrence River. They had been assured by their leaders that 90 per cent of ordinary Canadians and 75 per cent of Canadian troops would rise to their support, but this support did not materialize. Nor did the courage of the leaders. The original leader of the expedition, "General" John W. Birge, who wore an elaborate, braid-encrusted uniform, had second thoughts about his role while on the way to Prescott in the steamer *United States* with an advance guard of about 200 troops. He retired to his cabin with a bellyache.[11]

The other leader, a river pirate named Bill Johnson, who styled himself "Commodore of the Navy of the Canadian Republic" and walked about with his belt crammed with pistols and Bowie knives, decided it was his duty to remain with his "fleet" rather than land on Canadian shores. As a result Nils Szoltevcky Von Schoultz, a Pole with some military experience, found himself casually elected leader of an armed invasion after the troops had landed.

This tall, handsome and well-bred young man led his dazed little army to a stone windmill near the river bank, hoping its three-foot-thick walls would provide a fort-like protection. And it did. Cannon balls fired by a large contingent of Canadian troops bounced off its circular walls for five days while Von Schoultz and his men fought bravely back with muskets and a few cannon, waiting for their promised reinforcements. But no reinforcements arrived. At least twenty of the invaders were killed. Some escaped and made their way back to the United States. Those that remained ran out of ammunition and in desperation loaded their cannon with nails, hinges and buckles from their belts. In the end they had no food or water and after five days Von Schoultz surrendered.[12]

Of the 157 prisoners thus captured after the Battle of the Windmill, 140 were tried by court martial at Kingston. Eleven, including Von Schoultz, were eventually executed and sixty were sentenced to transportation for life.[13]

The Hunters, undeterred by this disaster, struck again at Windsor a month later. On December 3 a group of them marched through Detroit

Nils Szoltevcky Von Schoultz, who was elected leader of the Patriots after the original leaders failed to land with their troops near Prescott in the Battle of the Windmill. He was captured and hanged at Kingston. (Ontario Archives)

About 200 Patriots, mostly Americans, landed at Windmill Point on the Canadian side of the St. Lawrence River in November 1938, expecting thousands of rebel Canadians to join with them and put an end to imperialism, but no Canadians did. The Patriots occupied the stone windmill which gives the point its name and fought bravely against a large contingent of government troops for five days, then surrendered. Americans gathered on their side of the river to cheer the battle as if it were a modern-day sporting event. (Toronto Reference Library)

Colonel John Prince, leader
of the loyalist militia when
Patriots invaded Windsor.
He took no prisoners. "I
ordered [them] shot upon
the spot and it was done
accordingly," he reported.
(Toronto Reference Library)

without interference and took possession of the steamer *Champlain* as she lay at anchor in Detroit Harbour, locking the crew in their quarters. In the dark hours of the next morning the *Champlain* crossed the river amid floating ice and landed 135 men on a farm about three miles from Windsor, a village of a few hundred people.

The Hunters were poorly armed. Some had no firearms at all and carried long poles with some kind of lance on the end, but they marched on a barracks, on a site later occupied by the Windsor Town Hall, which contained a garrison of twenty-eight men. The garrison opened fire on the invaders, killing an officer and wounding several men, whereupon the Hunters set the building on fire and shot some of the garrison while they attempted to escape. Others were burned to death.

The invaders then moved to the centre of the village where their leader, L.V. Bierce, a lawyer from Akron, issued a proclamation to the citizens of Canada, invoking the names of the rebels hanged after the 1837 uprising: "The spirits of Lount, Matthews and Moreau are yet unavenged. The murdered heroes of Prescott lie in an unhallowed

grave in the land of tyranny.... Arouse then, soldiers of Canada! Let us
march to victory or death!"

Canadian soldiers did not do this. Instead, after the Hunters set fire
to a ship and burned down several houses to the cheers of about 5,000
sympathizers on the American side of the river, the Canadian militia,
under Colonel John Prince, routed them in a brief battle. Prince's official report of the battle said "of the brigands and pirates, twenty-one
were killed, besides four who were brought in at the close and immediately after the engagement, all of whom I ordered shot upon the spot,
and it was done accordingly." An eyewitness said Prince, wearing his
hunting clothes, made some of the rebels run the gantlet. "He gave the
captured rebels a running chance for their lives; they were all to start
from a line, and any that got over the fence and clear into the country
were to go free. I believe there was not one who got clear over the
fence." Another forty-four were listed as captured and the rest escaped
into the woods. Four of the militia were killed and four wounded.[14]

The forty-four prisoners, mostly Americans, but with six Canadians,
three Scots and two Englishmen among them, were tried in London later
that month. One man was acquitted and the rest were convicted of "hostile invasion of the province" and sentenced to death. Six, including two
Canadians, were executed, eighteen had their sentences commuted to
transportation, and of the others, one eventually escaped, two informers
were set free and sixteen were deported to the United States.

In November 1838, shortly before the Battle of the Windmill, rebellion
broke out again in Lower Canada, this time in the Eastern townships,
close to the border over which support from the Americans was supposed to flow. But no support came for the *habitants* and after a few
skirmishes their uprising crumbled within a week in face of 7,000 government troops and batteries of artillery.

This time 850 prisoners were taken and charged with treason. Most
were eventually discharged or released on bail, but 108 were tried by a
court martial in Montreal, which opened on November 21, 1838, and sat

for five months. By the time it had finished its work, the court martial had acquitted only nine and sentenced ninety-nine to death. In the end, twelve of these were hanged, fifty-eight had their sentences commuted to transportation, two were banished, and twenty-seven were released under bond for good behaviour.[15]

All the French Canadians sentenced to transportation suffered that fate, but this was not the case for all the Upper Canadians. John Montgomery, for instance, the jovial, reform-minded owner of the Yonge Street inn where the Mackenzie-led uprising was plotted and fought, was sentenced to death, then had the sentence commuted to transportation for life. While he was imprisoned at Kingston's Fort Henry, he and other prisoners learned from a friendly Orangeman, who was employed at the fort, of a subterranean passage under a casement adjoining their cell, leading to the yard outside which was surrounded by a twenty-eight-foot wall. The Orangeman, John Orgen, also smuggled to them a short pointed piece of bar iron and a spike.

For weeks Montgomery and his cellmates hacked away at the wall of their cell. They burned the loosened mortar in their stove or carried it outside during exercise periods and buried it in a woodpile. They hid the stones they removed under their beds and placed a piece of furniture over the hole. To drown the worst noise of the digging, two men played the drum on the stove, beating it as hard as they could with a poker while their cellmates laughed uproariously. Montgomery pretended he was reading the Bible and shouted demands for peace and quiet, thus adding considerably to the cacophony. On the night of August 5, 1838, Montgomery and fifteen others crawled through the hole in the wall, carrying a scaling ladder made from the boards of their beds. They found the secret passage, emerged in the yard, climbed over the giant jail wall and were free. Montgomery fell into a ditch and was so badly injured he could not walk. He begged the others to leave him, but they carried him with them and eventually all but two reached the American shore.[16] Montgomery settled in Rochester, where he ran a boarding house frequented by Patriot refugees and sympathizers.[17]

When Montgomery was found guilty of high treason in Toronto, and Chief Justice John Beverley Robinson had asked if he had anything to say before sentencing, Montgomery had replied: "I have. I have not had a fair trial. There are witnesses here who have sworn my life away.... These perjurers will never die a natural death; and when you, sir, and the jury shall have died and perished in hell's flames, John Montgomery will yet be living on Yonge Street."

Montgomery's prophecy proved true. He was pardoned in 1843 and returned to Toronto, where he again became an innkeeper, at first in the centre of the city and then on the site of his old tavern on Yonge Street. One of the men who testified against him shot himself and another slit his own throat. By the time he died in 1879, within a few weeks of his ninety-sixth birthday, he had outlived the judge and all the jurors, witnesses and prosecutors at his trial.[18]

Another key character in the Upper Canadian drama of 1837-38 also escaped. Sir Francis Bond Head, whose Conservative snobbery and ignorance had caused much of the troubles, was recalled to England in disgrace. He was originally scheduled to make his way to Halifax and then to New York by British warship because he was afraid refugee or American Patriots might kidnap him if he travelled through the United States. Then he became convinced there was a plot to murder him on the way to Halifax so he changed this plan at the last minute. He left Toronto by steamer on March 24, 1838, supposedly bound for Montreal. However, he left the ship at Kingston disguised as the valet of a local Tory judge. They made their way in a small boat to Cape Vincent on the American shore of Lake Ontario, and then by stage coach to Watertown. But this was an awful mistake because Watertown was a gathering-place for Canadian refugees, the very people he was trying to avoid. The most prominent Patriot leaders, including even Mackenzie himself, were staying at the town's Mansion House.

So the former lieutenant-governor, now a gentleman's gentleman, shook severely in his buckled shoes when, on arriving for breakfast, he found the lobby of the hotel filled with his enemies. He sneaked away

33

Sir George Arthur, lieutenant-governor of Van Diemen's Land (1824-36) and Upper Canada (1838-41). He was regarded as a moderate, even occasionally merciful administrator by the Canadian establishment, but a cruel tyrant by many Australians. (Toronto Reference Library)

and hid near the hotel's stables, huddling in a wheelbarrow which almost concealed his small frame. An Irish-Canadian rebel, Hugh Scanlon, noticed that the valet was missing and went looking for him. He found him in the wheelbarrow and, recognizing the lieutenant-governor, courteously invited him to breakfast to meet his late subjects.

"I assure you," said Scanlon, "you'll receive every courtesy due to your rank." Obviously Bond Head was not at all keen about this, but there was nothing he could do but accept the invitation. He was therefore surprised and greatly relieved when the Patriots did, in fact, treat him in a friendly way, even assisting in his arrangements for departure and cheering him, gleefully and mockingly, as he left town in a coach and four.[19]

Bond Head was replaced as lieutenant-governor by Sir George Arthur, who is described in most Canadian histories as a moderate bureaucrat. According to *The Canadian Encyclopedia* he was appointed to the Canadian post "after an undistinguished military career and two minor colonial appointments."

But the last of those "minor" colonial appointments was a dozen years as lieutenant-governor of the penal settlement of Van Diemen's Land, the little island now called Tasmania off Australia's southeast corner, and Australians have a different view of the man. In early Australian history Colonel George Arthur is a bureaucratic ogre who sent hundreds to the gallows, and the builder of the notorious Port Arthur jail, the Australian icon for cruelty. In what would be regarded today as blatant conflict of interest, he made a fortune from land speculation in areas where he knew roads and bridges were to be built by the convicts he controlled. And he was responsible for the extermination of the Tasmanian aborigines.[20]

Arthur was a tough man sent to Upper Canada to clean up the mess left by the ineffective Bond Head. His appointment helps explain that strange sentence of transportation that was imposed on so many rebels – why so many Canadians and Americans were made to suffer the unusual punishment, for their continent, of dismissal in chains to the end of the earth, where the bloody lash ruled over the sweating, shackled, miserable hordes of the banished of the British criminal class.

CHAPTER 3

A Remarkable Woman

And now that the rebellion's o'er
Let each true Briton sing,
Long live the Queen in health and peace,
And may each rebel swing.

UPPER CANADIAN SONG OF 1838

*B*enjamin Wait, a young Upper Canadian Reformer, went to the end of the earth the hard way but it could have been worse for him. He was rescued from the gallows even as the hangman prepared the noose for his neck and only because he had a remarkable wife. Twenty-four-year-old Wait, who was born in Markham, near Toronto, had become a sawmill operator at the small community of York, on the Grand River, about halfway between Caledonia and Cayuga in southern Upper Canada. Then, when his business failed, he worked as a teacher at Willoughby Township, a clerk at Port Colborne and a labourer. He was once jailed briefly for debt and he had a reputation as an agitator. According to Lieutenant-Governor George Arthur, he was "a bold and intelligent man." Shortly after the affair at Montgomery's Tavern in December 1837, Wait left his Haldimand County home to join the reform forces in the western part of the province, but when he arrived at London on December 13, he found the reformers under Dr. Duncombe had scattered. So he fled to Navy Island, where Mackenzie was planning his invasion of Canada, and then, when the island was evacuated, to Coneaut, Ohio, and subsequently to Schlosser, on the American side of the Niagara River.[1]

Wait was one of the Patriots aboard the steamer *Red Jacket* when it moved quietly on the dark night of June 11, 1838, towards the Canadian shore near Navy Island in the Niagara River to drop off twenty-six Canadian refugees and American supporters, carrying fifty stand of arms. Their aim was to gather more Canadian supporters at the Short Hills, an area rife with Reformers in the interior of the Niagara Peninsula, then go about liberating the province from British rule.

They set up base in the Long Swamp, managed to avoid loyalist patrols searching for them, and gathered many Canadian recruits. Then, on June 20, the Patriots, now numbering almost 200, marched the twelve miles from their base in the swamp to capture St. John's (now Thorold), the major village in the Short Hills. There they discovered that a party of ten mounted troops, sent in investigate rumours of a rebel invasion, were sleeping at Overholt's tavern. The rebels attacked the tavern. Awakened by a sentry, the loyalist troops responded and kept the rebels at bay.

In about half an hour of shooting, one attacker and two defenders were wounded. Then James Morreau (sometimes spelled Morrow), a thirty-two-year-old tanner from Pennsylvania, who was the main rebel leader, ordered his men to pile straw around the building and burn it down. The loyalist commander, a Sergeant Bailey, sensibly decided to surrender. He and his men were marched into the woods, stripped of their food, arms and horses, then released.[2]

This was the Patriot raiders' only victory. As in so many other episodes of the rebellion, their small and amateurish invasion was soon easily repulsed. However, the incursion caused rumours to spread that a huge force of Americans had poured across the border into the Short Hills to launch a full invasion. Sir George Arthur called out the militia to resist the rumoured thousands of Yankees, but the citizen-soldiers soon found that they had to contend only with a small band of mainly Canadian rebels. In face of the overwhelming force of the militia, the rebels tried to slip back over the American border, but most failed to make it. Wait and Morreau were among sixteen captured the day after the skirmish at Overholt's tavern. Within a week, thirty-six rebels were captured in a manhunt that lasted a month and eventually rounded up seventy-five of them.[3]

Arthur personally visited Wait in the Niagara jail and offered a free pardon and money if he woud give information about his fellow rebels. But Wait refused and was told by Arthur, he claimed, that "for your obstinacy, in refusing to make reparation to the country for the injury you have done it, you shall feel the rigor of that power you affected to despise and be hung despite every effort to the contrary."[4] Wait did not have much of a chance at his trial anyway. The judge was one Jonas Jones who had been involved in a bitter land dispute with Wait's friend and his wife's guardian, the radical politician Robert Randall. On August 11, Wait was sentenced to hang for high treason two weeks later, along with Samuel Chandler, a forty-eight-year-old wagon maker from St. Johns and Alexander McLeod, a carpenter, aged twenty-four, from East Gwillimbury, north of Toronto, who had taken part in the attack on Toronto led by William Lyon Mackenzie. James Morreau, the leader of the raid, had already been sent to the gallows.[5]

In pronouncing the sentence on Wait, Judge Jones, said: "You, Benjamin Wait, shall be taken from the court to the place whence you last came and there remain until the 25th of August, when between the hours of eleven and one, you shall be drawn on a hurdle to the place of execution, and there hanged by the neck until you are dead, and your body shall be quartered. The Lord have mercy on your soul."

Wait resigned himself to his fate. He had personally attracted the wrath of Sir George Arthur. He was one of the leaders of the raid. There was no appeal from the sentence. He had no hope. However, he did have this remarkable wife.

Nothing is recorded about the looks of Maria Wait, a Canadian girl, but she must have been of determined appearance. She was born Maria Smith, but apparently was brought up in the home of Robert Randall and well educated before she married Wait in October 1836. She was an elegantly dressed and intelligent woman, who, like her guardian, the longtime radical member of the provincial legislature, brooked no nonsense.[6] She had absolutely no fear of people in high authority and a bitter contempt for some of them, particularly Sir George Arthur. She was mentally and physically dauntless and when her husband was sentenced to hang she was only in her early twenties and the mother of an infant girl, Augusta.

Maria Wait was not only horrified by the prospect of the hanging but also by the imminent quartering of her husband's body. She moved with her baby to a house close to the jail and visited him every day, bringing food and clothing. Often the jailer forced her rudely away from the gratings. Once, by order of the sheriff she was detained at the gate of the yard by an armed guard, who pressed a bayonet into her breast and drove her back. But she persisted in visiting her husband, occasionally catching a glimpse of the same "Jack Ketch" who had hanged Lount and Matthews in Toronto and was forced to wait about the Niagara jail for his next jobs.[7]

Maria was breast-feeding her baby girl, but almost immediately after Wait was sentenced she decided to leave the child with a friend and somehow, though she had no money, make the arduous 700-mile journey to Quebec City to plead with the newly arrived governor-general, Lord Durham, for her husband's life. She asked her husband's attorney, Alexander Stewart, for his help but he did his best to discourage her. You'll make matters worse, he warned her. Going over the head of Lieutenant-Governor Arthur with an appeal to the governor-general would just make Arthur angrier and more determined than ever to carry out the executions, he said. Others whose help she sought said much the same thing, adding warnings that her child's life would be endangered. They told her that because the time remaining before the hangings was so short (two weeks), she would perform much more useful and sensible wifely duties by remaining at her husband's side and consoling him as best she could.[8]

Maria took no notice of any of this advice and also decided to try to win a commutation for Samuel Chandler because he had such a large family (a wife and ten children). She suggested to his eldest daughter, Sarah, who was nineteen, that she accompany her on the long journey to plead for her father and, after consulting with her father's friends, the young woman agreed. But these friends also did their best to dissuade Maria from going. They argued that the two appeals could prevent the possibility or either being effective, and his Lordship would more likely be impressed by a young girl asking for the life of her father, than by a wife asking for the life of her husband.

Maria would have none of this. She was not put off when letters of introduction were obtained for Sarah Chandler, but not for her, and when money was collected for the young girl while she remained almost penniless. She went to the prison surgeon to beg him, if she failed in her mission, not to dissect her husband's body, but even he, a kindly man, told her he was afraid he'd have to do as he was ordered. And he also begged her not to go to Quebec City because she would only further exasperate the government and make matters worse, if that was possible.

"Still I was not to be deterred from my object; confident in the rectitude of my course, I feared no evil," Maria wrote later. "I passed immediately to the place of embarkation, where I found Miss C. with some of her friends, who were there to see her safe on board. James Boulton, Mr. C.'s attorney, was to accompany her to Toronto, who had taken occasion to use very ungentlemanly language in his efforts to persuade me not to think of going ... for I would ruin the cause of his client and finally prevent the government from doing anything for the 'unhappy prisoners,' as he was pleased to term them."[9]

She was also met on the dock by a Judge Butler, who said he too felt a deep interest in the success of the mission but "wondered how a woman, who, he had been informed, manifested a good degree of sense on ordinary occasions, could thus be so mad-brained as to persist in exciting the still greater fury of the Government, by personally seeking their mercy, despite the advice and opinion of all her friends."

But still Maria Wait would not listen. When she boarded the steamer for Toronto with Sarah Chandler, she saw her companion introduced to the captain and offered special privileges while she wasn't. Feeling hurt and worried about money, she went ashore again, because the boat was not due to sail for an hour or so, and sought the home of Jesse Ketchum, a prominent businessman, politician and philanthropist whom she had once seen at her guardian's house. After she told Ketchum and his wife her story, the three sank to their knees and prayed together while Mrs. Ketchum wept. The Ketchums gave her ten dollars and she returned to the boat, where she insisted, more confident now, on seeing the captain, who then treated her with the same kindness and attention as he did the Chandler girl.[10]

They reached Toronto that day and Kingston, in a smaller steamer, the next, then continued by boat through the Thousand Islands to the head of the Long Sault, by stage to Cornwall, by boat again to Montreal, then again by small boat to the village of Sorel farther down the St. Lawrence River, where the former lieutenant-governor of Upper Canada, Sir John Colborne, was based. Sarah Chandler had a letter from friends to Colborne's son asking him to persuade his father to use his considerable influence in Quebec. The son, an army major, gave Sarah a letter to the aide-de-camp to Lord Durham, a Colonel Couper, but the young woman refused to introduce Maria Wait to him.

"I begged Miss C. to introduce me; but she declined, either from excessive bashfulness, or some other reason unknown to me," Maria wrote later with some charity. "Consequently I was still left without a line of introduction, recommendation, or anything, save my own determination to effect the object if possible, let the obstacles be what they might."

They reached Quebec by steamer about nine the next morning and went immediately to the Castle St. Louis, where Lord Durham lived. There the aide-de-camp, Colonel Couper, agreed to meet them and Miss Chandler handed him her letter while Maria Wait apologized for having no letters of introduction and begged that she might be allowed to present a petition anyway "on behalf of a youthful and suffering husband under sentence of death." Couper said he thought there was no chance, in the circumstances, that Lord Durham would meet with her. Besides, His Lordship was suffering a headache and some other physical problems. However, he took the Chandler letter to the governor-general and returned in a few minutes to state that Durham could not deal with the matter at that time but might be able to reply to both appeals by ten the next morning.

The two women spent an anxious day and night on the ship that had brought them to Quebec, then returned to the castle at exactly 10 a.m, only to be told by Couper that Lord Durham had not yet decided on the matter.

"Sir," replied Maria Wait, " I certainly trust his Lordship will do so today, because if I don't leave Quebec tonight with the boat, when I do reach Niagara I'll find my husband a mangled corpse." She said she knew Durham was a merciful man because he had already ordered the release of many prisoners in Lower Canada. She was confident, she said, that he would extend this clemency to the Patriots of Upper Canada and especially to her husband and Chandler. The aide-de-camp said he hoped an answer might be available by four that afternoon and asked the women to come back then.[11]

The two women rode around Quebec City in a caleche all day and returned to the castle at four only to be told by Couper that he had had no reply from Durham, although he still hoped to receive one before the ship sailed that evening, whereupon he would relay the response to them on the ship.

Sarah Chandler burst into tears. Maria Wait put her foot down. "If you'll permit me I'd rather wait here," she said. "Any further delay is the equivalent of a refusal by Lord Durham to grant a commutation and that means we'll get back to Niagara just in time to embrace the bodies of our loved ones just before they are laid in their tombs. In the circumstances I can't leave here until his Lordship listens to me."

"Couper's humane countenance," she reported, "glowed with compassion. He ordered a glass of wine and water for me and left the room; while with our agitated hearts raised to God, we awaited his return in almost breathless suspense; and thanks to our heavenly Father, we were not long thus to suffer."

As soon as Couper reappeared, Maria Wait knew the crisis was over. He wore a broad smile. He told the women that although Lord Durham, as governor-general, could not grant free pardons to their husband and father without an investigation of their cases, he would nevertheless order a commutation, or at least a stay of execution, until the documents concerning them could be sent to him for examination. In the meantime, he said, Durham would give them a letter to Sir George Arthur requesting him to delay the hangings and would also send a special messenger with them bearing a private letter to the lieutenant-governor.[12]

The two were, of course, ecstatic as their boat left Quebec City. But it was now less than a week to August 25, the date of the hangings. They doubted if they could reach Niagara in time. They wondered if they could find Arthur in the meantime. And even then, would he act before the nooses tightened? Then they had a lucky break. At Montreal they met on the boat an MP from Lower Canada, a Mr. Simpson, who told them Arthur was visiting the parts of the country they were to travel through and at every stop Simpson enquired on their behalf about Arthur's whereabouts and assured them they had not yet passed him. He also gave Maria twenty dollars, which she shared with the Chandler girl.

When they reached Coteau-du-Lac, just a few days before the hanging date, they found the steamboat that was to take them to Cornwall was waiting for the arrival of Arthur. He boarded the vessel next morning and Maria Wait pounced immediately the ship left its moorings. Through the captain and Arthur's aide-de-camp, one of his sons, she arranged a meeting with Arthur in the ladies' cabin.

The meeting was cold and formal. Maria recorded what happened in a letter:

Sir G., after seating himself, remarked, "You wish to see me, madam?"

"I do," replied I, "and am happy of the honour, as I have brought a letter from Lord Durham to Your Excellency touching cases of vital importance, both to myself and Miss Chandler," on which I presented the letter, and watched the countenance of the Governor while perusing the same, the dark changes of which indicated no good to our cause if His Excellency could prevent it.

He seemed exceedingly annoyed and said, "You have appealed to Lord Durham in the case of your husband, under sentence of death for *treason*; and you for your father," addressing Miss C.

"We have," I replied, "and Your Excellency will doubtless admit that the importance of the case is a sufficient apology for making any exertion that might be in our power," to which he reluctantly assented, scarce knowing how to express his displeasure that the victims had indeed been wrested from his deadly grasp by his superior, who had thus been induced to exert his authority beyond the limits of Lower Canada.

"But Madam," said he, "I cannot accede to the request and prevent the due course of the law upon offences of this nature."

"*You can not accede to the request!*" Maria Wait shouted back. "Permit me to say, sir, I left Quebec with an assurance from Lord Durham that the life of my husband should be spared, at least until his Lordship, as *Governor General*, could investigate the matter."

"The state of the country, madam," said Arthur, "demands that examples should be made and most especially of such *obstinate and heinous offenders*," alluding to Mr. Wait's positive refusal to give any information that would implicate others, which he had sought personally, with an offer of pardon.

"And had," said I, "the force of example, as Your Excellency is pleased to call these sanguinary measures, and the blood that has already flowed from the gallows, told happily upon the country, I should not now be under the painful necessity of pleading for the life of a beloved husband."

"But, madam," he inquiringly remarked. "what am I to do with the repeated applications from the west [Upper Canada], imploring me to adopt some measures that may put a stop to these frequent attacks from which Her Majesty's faithful subjects are suffering the loss of life, property and so forth?"

"Permit me to ask Your Excellency in return," I said, "Will the execution of these men restore to the people of the west the lives and property which they have lost by previous aggression?"

"By no means," he replied, "but the example may deter others from similar transgressions."

Maria Wait did not like this at all. She turned angrily on Arthur and delivered a political diatribe:

"If Your Excellency will allow me, I do most sincerely think that no example could go further to pacify excited feelings, and have a more salutary influence upon the country at large, than a general extension of mercy and pardon to political offenders; for well do I know that the people of this country have been goaded on to rebellion by various and repeated acts of legalized oppression.

"I crave Your Excellency's indulgence, and beg leave to say further, that my friends, even my own family, have been special objects of this oppressive persecution, the effects of which I have felt from my infancy up to this moment; and no longer since than last autumn, my unfortunate husband was told by several members of the bar at the Niagara assize, at which he had a suit, that it was useless for him to seek redress, as he was known by the Court to be a *reformer*, and alone, Your Excellency, to these sad truths may be attributed the present lamentable state of Canada, a resistance to which has placed my husband in his present melancholy situation.... Now may we hope that Your Excellency will think favourably of our request?"[13]

She reported in her letter that Arthur refused to agree and brusquely left the cabin. So she decided to send a message to Durham, with the messenger who had accompanied them, stating that Arthur was determined to frustrate his order for mercy. "As I was sealing and addressing this communication," she wrote, "the Governor returned bringing with him Mr. Macaulay, his private secretary, whom he introduced, saying that he had brought his secretary to note down, if we would give it, the substance of the verbal communications we had received in Quebec, which we readily gave."

Maria Wait then told Arthur she had written a letter to Durham stating the results of her interview with Arthur, and that she intended to forward it immediately to Durham. She waved the letter aggressively in front of him and according to her letter, Arthur backed down, his lips quivering with rage:

> "Oh, I wish you to understand me, madam, before you communicate my answer to Lord Durham. I have granted a respite to your husband and (addressing Sarah Chandler) also to your father. But there must be more executions...."
>
> Sir George left us [Maria wrote]. Mr. Macaulay asked if I was a native of Canada, and being told that I was, he regretted much that I should have been involved in circumstances of so grievous a nature, and hoped that I might be reinstated, and yet happy in the country of my birth. I thanked him and he bade us good morning.

But Maria did not trust Arthur. When the ship reached Cornwall and the messenger left for Quebec, she sent her letter to Durham anyway so he would at least know of the disrespect Arthur had shown for his authority.

(Left) Benjamin Wait. Convicted of treason and rescued from the gallows at the last minute through the efforts of his wife, Maria, he was transported to Van Diemen's Land. There are no pictures of Maria Wait, who must have been as modest as she was courageous. (Welland Historical Society)

(Right) Samuel Chandler, a prosperous farmer from St. John's (now Thorold) on the Niagara Peninsula, was a leading rebel. He was also saved from the gallows by Maria Wait and sent to Van Diemen's Land. (Welland Historical Society)

The two women travelled by coach to Prescott, then Toronto, then by ship to Niagara, where they landed on August 22, three days before the execution date. As they rushed to the jail, they saw the gallows being prepared, and when they told the jailer of the stay of execution he would not believe them. They had no official papers with them, he pointed out, and he had orders from the sheriff, who was away in Kingston, to have everything ready to carry out the executions to the letter.[14]

Maria Wait saw her husband briefly and tried to convince him a respite would come. He told her their baby, now with her grandmother about twenty miles from Niagara, had been dangerously ill. So now she had another difficult choice to make. She desperately wanted to see her baby, who might be dying. To save the life of her husband, she knew she would have to return to Toronto to find out why the official notice of the respite had not arrived. She chose the journey to Toronto and left by ship at eight the next morning.

In Toronto she did not really know what to do. She hired a carriage and told the young driver to take her to the home of the chief justice. She pounded on his door but he was not home. She tried to find the attorney-general, but could not. In desperation she drove to Parliament House, where the executive council was sitting, and where she was told by officials there had been no communication from Arthur about any respite for the Niagara prisoners, but if what she said was true, she could trust Sir George and a notice of the commutation might arrive at Niagara by the mail boat due at eleven the following morning. She called on Anglican Bishop Jacob Mountain, of Montreal, who was visiting Toronto, and begged him to appear before the council to ask them to stay proceedings until they heard from Arthur. He promised to do what he could. Then she rushed to the docks and scrambled up the gangplank of the steamer to Niagara just before it pulled away.

Next morning she was allowed to hand her husband his breakfast through the iron bars of his cell. She told him the official message from Arthur was expected at eleven. The boat came but there was no message. Nor was there any message on the evening boat at six. The executions were scheduled for between eleven and one the next day. Now the only chance for reprieve had to be an official document carried personally by the sheriff, who was expected to return in the next few days from Kingston, but no one knew exactly when. He arrived in the governor's boat at 12.30 on the morning of August 25, six hours before the bodies were due to drop. He told a clergyman who met him on the dock that the reprieve was official. The clergyman told the prisoners.[15]

Benjamin Wait said he learned that the sheriff had asked the lieutenant-governor in Toronto for the order of reprieve, but Arthur had delayed until after the last boat had left for Niagara before giving it to him. The sheriff then obtained the use of the governor's own boat, but only "after considerable altercation."

Arthur's purpose, Wait asserted, was to ensure, through delay, that the executions were carried out, while he would be in a position to satisfy his masters in London by laying the blame on some petty officials, including the sheriff, who had failed to deliver the reprieve in time.[16]

The sentences of Wait and Chandler were commuted to transportation for life. As soon as the reprieves were officially announced, Maria Wait rushed to her baby, twenty miles away. She found the health of the little girl much improved and was able to carry her on a pillow back to Niagara.

CHAPTER 4

Uprisings and Invasions

Let our victorious banners fly,
And give our bugles breath,
Forward! And let the battle-cry
Be Victory or Death!

But what is yonder darking cloud?
And what in bold array?
THE BRITON'S COME! lord: what a crowd!
GOOD GOD! LET'S RUN AWAY.

FROM YANKEE SONG OF TRIUMPH, PRINTED
IN THE TORONTO PATRIOT, MARCH 2, 1838

*S*ix weeks after the sentences of Wait and Chandler were commuted, on October 6, 1838, the jailers rivetted fetters to their legs and
led them, along with Alexander McLeod, the twenty-four-year-old carpenter from the Toronto area, and Jacob Beemer (or Beamer), a
twenty-nine-year-old innkeeper from Oakland, near London, to the
Niagara dock for the start of what became a long journey.

Maria Wait was, of course, at the jail with her baby to say goodbye
to her husband. She packed what clothes he had and a few of his favourite books. He kissed the baby but apparently only "wrung the hand
of her whose affectionate care I fancied I was no more to experience"
before he was moved, chains clanking, to a steamer that took the four
of them to a bug-ridden jail in Toronto and next day to Fort Henry at
Kingston.

At Fort Henry they found several dozen other prisoners who had been involved in the uprisings at Toronto, London and Niagara, and who were being guarded heavily because of the recent amazing escape by Montgomery and his fifteen comrades. According to Wait, the treatment was not bad. The prisoners were allowed to make handicrafts and he and four others formed a "literary society" to while away the long, lonely nights.

Maria braved a hazardous winter voyage on Lake Ontario to visit her husband in early November, but when he hugged her delightedly he found her to be thin and wan – "but a shadow of mortality." "Unusual exertion, combined with deep mental distress, had made sad havoc of youth and of health, though the spirit was yet whole and the mind firm," he wrote. She was allowed to visit him for fifteen minutes a day, and she brought food and clothing, but the visits lasted only for four days, until November 9, when the sheriff came to the cells, accompanied by Maria Wait, and announced that twenty-three of the prisoners, including Wait, were to be moved immediately to Quebec "for safekeeping during the winter."[1]

The Waits were allowed to say goodbye in a storeroom filled with the clothes and baggage Montgomery and the other escapees had left behind, and the soldier guarding them turned his back briefly to give them some privacy. Wait mentioned the possibility that he would be sent to London, England, on the way to somewhere else. Maria said she would follow him to England, making personal appeals for his freedom, and then literally to the end of the earth, if necessary.

"You can't do that," Wait insisted, "not all that way, alone and unprotected."

"Why not?" she replied. "I travelled a long way through many embarrassing circumstances to appeal to Lord Durham and that was successful."

"There's a big difference," he argued, "between an inland journey of fourteen hundred miles, surrounded by sympathetic people, and an ocean voyage, unprotected and surrounded by strangers."

51

"God will protect me," she said.

"But what about the baby?" Wait asked.

Maria Wait hesitated but only for a moment.

"God will look after the baby too," she said. "If I'm unsuccessful with my petitions to the Queen and even if you're sent on to Van Diemen's Land I'll follow you there and share your exile. I'll leave our child in the hands of the orphans' God."[2]

Wait knew it was no use arguing further. A feeling of great love swept through him. He could not get over the calmness he felt as he was led away and chained, hand and foot, to J.G. Parker, one of the two Toronto rebels who had been recaptured after the escape from Fort Henry. Wait, Parker and the twenty-one others were hustled onto the deck of the steamer *Cobourg*. Wait could see Maria in the distance, waving a kerchief.

As the prisoners were moved down the St. Lawrence towards Quebec, by land sometimes, but mostly on the decks of a series of ships, still chained together in pairs, unfed for days at a stretch and shivering in wind-driven snow and sleet, they passed by the burning homes of the French Patriotes, set afire by the troops of Sir John Colborne in the repression of the second wave of revolt in Lower Canada. As Wait recalled:

A shudder, a feeling akin to horror shot through my frame as my eyes were first directed to the yet smoking ruins of a proscribed Canadian's homestead. Every building that might have afforded the slightest shelter to man or beast was burned to the ground. Every tree cut down, and every particle of food destroyed or carried away. We soon swept past this mark of a tyrant's displeasure to the view of another scene still more heartrending; it appeared to have been the residence of a person of considerable wealth, for numerous piles of smoking embers were observed which, from appearances, betokened the building to have been of no slight magnitude. Though all had now vanished but the ashes, and the poor, forlorn, destitute beings who had once made their roofs echo with the sounds of gladness, perhaps of sacred worship, had just ventured from their hiding place and were apparently hunting about the premises if perchance the remorseless incendiaries had left undestroyed one morsel whereby a raging hunger might be appeased. There stood a mother of five children, vainly weeping over the ruins of her home, as if their tears could restore what they had lost....

We touched at Beauharnois, a small village formerly containing several hundred houses, but now only filled with smouldering ruins, exhibiting the traces of the demon of destruction. Here, but the day before, under the eye of Colborne, every excess had been perpetrated; houses reduced to ashes; property of every description, and furniture were broken up and strewed in the streets.[3]

Among those captured with Wait, Morreau and the others after the Short Hills raid was a tall, thin, handsome youth of about twenty named Linus W. Miller from Rochester, New York. He came from a well-to-do family and was well educated, having spent a few years at law school. He believed, almost fanatically, that it was his duty to see that Canada was a free country, as was his beloved America, even if the effort cost him his life. He talked in big words and flowery language, giving the impression to comrades that he was of superior class and a fully-trained lawyer. He referred to black Canadians as "niggers," regarding them as little better than animals. These days he would be regarded as both a racist and a bit of a smartass.

The day after he was captured he was marched, with about forty others, to a hotel for a hearing before a bench of magistrates who were to make out warrants for their commitments. He was one of the last to appear before the bench and this is how he described the encounter:

Two of the magistrates were elderly, respectable-looking gentlemen; but the third was a young, green-looking fellow evidently full of a sense of his own importance, with but little wit, and less judgement, and in every respect unfit to perform the stern duties in which he was engaged. Without any reference to his seniors he commenced with, –

"Well, what do you have to say for yourself?"

"That depends altogether upon what *you* have to say; as yet I see no occasion for saying anything."

"Your present circumstances appear to have sharpened your wits; but I had forgotten; you are a lawyer; gentlemen, we must proceed in due form…."

"My profession is a matter of perfect indifference; my misfortunes are, possibly, less serious than you would insinuate."

"Be they light or heavy, you are charged with a very serious and heinous crime, for which, if convicted, you must answer with your life; and of your conviction there can be no doubt. You can make any statement you choose, which will be taken down in writing, and read as evidence on your trial. I give you this caution that you may not, unguardedly, say anything to commit yourself."

"You are very kind! but, as the simple truth will answer my purpose, your hint will be lost upon me."

"Damn your impertinence, sir; how dare you answer me, a magistrate of Great Britain, in this manner?"

"I am quite sensible of your importance, though your magnitude may appear somewhat less to me than to yourself. As for impertinence, the charge comes with an ill grace from your worship."

"By heavens! I'll have you punished."

"I am punished already!."

"How?"

"By being subject to the caprice of a magistrate who is unfit for his business."

"You damned Yankee blackguard!."

"Thank you sir, for your compliments."[4]

Linus W. Miller, a brash American law student captured after the rebel raid at Short Hills in the Niagara region, told a magistrate at his treason trial he was "unfit for his business." (Welland Historical Society)

The hearing, according to notes written by Miller some years later, went on in this unusual courtroom manner for some time. It may or may not have happened quite the way he recalled it, but probably his account accurately reflects the attitude of the brash young American. And of course, it did not do him any good. Eventually he signed a statement and went back to jail, charged with high treason.

Miller was just as aggressively obnoxious at his trial at Niagara on July 14, 1838, where he appeared before the same Judge Jonas Jones who had sentenced Wait to death. When he was asked for his plea of guilty or not guilty, he refused to enter any plea because, he said, he was not prepared for his trial. And he insulted the jury by calling them "mere tools of the government, pledged to render a verdict of guilty, and prepared in their hearts." All of this, he reported later, almost sent Judge Jones into apoplexy and caused one juror to protest: "My lord, are we, honest men, to be insulted and abused in this manner?"

But Miller was right on his point of law. He was entitled to time to prepare a defence and, after calming himself, Judge Jones sent him back to jail untried, and called the next case, that of the rebel leader James Morreau, who was found guilty of treason and hanged a few days later.

When Miller was eventually tried on August 1, he was represented by a lawyer, who argued that Miller had joined the rebels while suffering a short period of insanity as a result of studying too hard for the law. The argument presumably impressed the jury, who found him guilty with a "recommendation of extreme mercy," which was virtually an acquittal, but the judge, Miller claimed, angrily refused to accept this verdict, and then another verdict with a simple recommendation of mercy and yet another with a recommendation that his youth be taken into account, until the jury finally came back with a simple verdict of guilty.[5]

So he went to Fort Henry then on to Quebec City with Benjamin Wait and the other prisoners from the Toronto, London and Niagara area uprisings.

A few days before Wait and the other Upper Canada convicts touched briefly at Beauharnois on their way to Quebec City, François-Xavier Prieur and about 200 other French-Canadian *Patriotes* fled from the village as Sir John Colborne's troops advanced.

Prieur, who wrote a detailed journal of his adventures, was typical of the few who rose against British rule and the dominance of the *Château Clique* in Canada's original experience with French-Canadian nationalism. He was born on May 9, 1814, the son of Antoine Prieur, a farmer in comfortable circumstances, and his wife, Archange, who lived in a modest cottage at Soulanges (present-day Les Cèdres) in southwest Lower Canada. Antoine and Archange were devout Roman Catholics with a strong love of their native soil. Antoine was the fourth and Archange the third generation born in Canada so little François-Xavier could claim, even though the nineteenth century was just beginning, and Canadian confederation still half a century away, to be a fifth-generation Canadian, at least on his father's side.

Less than four years after the birth of François-Xavier, his parents moved from Soulanges to the forest country of Nouvelle Longueuil, where a new settlement called Saint Polycarpe had been established and where the *habitants* made their living mainly by logging and carrying furs, trapped in higher regions, to the coast in bark canoes. The children of the riverside settlement learned to swim as soon as they learned to walk and their favourite amusement was riding the logs as they floated down towards the St. Lawrence.

François-Xavier revelled in the log rolling games. He also did well at school. He was fair skinned and blue eyed and he spent a lot of time helping his parents and caring for his younger brothers and sisters, rocking them to sleep with the songs and tales of old France he had learned from his mother. He was the pride and joy of his parents. In his teenage years he remained slight and short, measuring only five feet four and a half inches, not robust enough for the rigors of life as a logger or trapper. And he didn't want to be a farmer, so, on the advice of the parish priest, his parents found him a job in the main general store in Soulanges.[6]

This store was the meeting place of the old hands of the district, and as they gossiped young François-Xavier learned about local history and, more interesting to him, about the details of the British conquest of Canada. He also mastered the arts of buying and selling so that after six years, in 1835, he was able to set up his own business in the nearby village of Saint Timothée, which he built into a successful store. One day, in the course of business, he wrote to Fabres bookshop in Saint Vincent Street, Montreal, which also happened to be the headquarters of an organization that was attempting to foster a spirit of nationalism among the French Canadians. This led to young Prieur's acquaintance with the great orator Louis Papineau and other leaders of the nationalist cause. So when the troubles broke out in 1838, and others refused the job, he was sworn in as *Castor* (French for beaver) of *L'Association des chasseurs*, whose aim was to drive the hated British out of the country. And he became leader of the rebels for the village of Saint Timothée.[7]

Despite his ardent nationalism, François-Xavier Prieur was not all that enthusiastic about an uprising, particularly as the church, to which he was strongly dedicated, opposed any such act. And he had, of course, no military experience whatever. Nor did the farmers, professionals and mechanics who were his troops. Their only intelligence was some underground information that reached them from time to time from other parts of the country promising an imminent insurrection and urging them to prepare. Their armoury consisted of about a hundred sporting guns and six small iron-bound, wooden cannon, along with a few hundred cartridges and a small quantity of powder and lead.

The first act of rebellion by this odd and isolated rebel band was the capture of the steamer *Henry Brougham,* which plied between Lachine and the cascades near Beauharnois and which might, the rebels thought, be used by the government to transport troops into the area. As soon as it tied to the wharf in the early hours of November 4, Prieur, with fifty men in his command, led the vanguard of the assault on this small ship. He found only two British officers on board, who were on harmless business, and hordes of panicky passengers running about in their nightgowns. The courteous rebels made sure they were comfortable in the local inn.

Soon news arrived from different directions and it was different news: Dr. Robert Nelson, who became the supreme rebel leader after Papineau fled the country, had ordered the Beauharnois contingent to get ready to march against government troops; and from Châteauguay came information that the rebel leaders there had been arrested by fellow French Canadians who regarded their threatened insurrection as dangerous and hopeless. Prieur had to calm many of his troops who, in the circumstances, were anxious to desert the cause. Then, on November 7, a third messenger arrived from a rebel camp nine miles away on the banks of the Châteauguay, asking for help because an attack by 800 government troops was expected. Two hundred of the Beauharnois group, led by Prieur and a young Montreal lawyer, the Chevalier de Lorimier, reached the camp next evening and placed themselves under the overall command of Dr. James Perrigo, a veteran of the militia of 1812.[8]

The government troops did not attack until the morning of November 9 and, surprisingly, the rebels, totalling about 500, charging and shouting "Hurrah" and "Victory," drove them back across the ploughed fields and fenced paddocks, killing several, until Dr. Perrigo, fearing a bayonet charge in retaliation, ordered his amateurs to stop. This fear of retaliation pervaded the rebel camp for the next two days, heightened by news of the defeats of other rebel groups nearby, with many taken prisoner. In the end the rebel leaders decided that those not deeply involved should return to their homes, that others, under the Chevalier de Lorimier, should make for the United States border, almost forty-five miles away, and that Prieur should return, with his company, to Beauharnois to see what was happening there.

Prieur found 240 men still under arms at Beauharnois, but they were demoralized and the rest of the rebels had gone home to their families. He thought of abandoning the whole thing. After all, there was a total absence of organization, few arms, and the probability that

Sir John Colborne, lieutenant-governor of Upper Canada from 1828 to 1836 when he was placed in command of British forces in the Canadas. He personally led his troops in suppressing the 1837 insurrection in Lower Canada. (Toronto Reference Library)

they were the only rebel group still in action. But then a messenger arrived with news that a government army corps of about 1,200 men had crossed the river at the foot of Lake St. Francis, a few miles away, and was marching on Beauharnois. He organized his troops behind a strong stone wall in the path of the attackers. He recorded in his journal:

> The weather was cold; night was already beginning to fall. There we were on our knees on the frozen soil, guns on our hips, telling our beads, after having repeated the litanies together. Already could be heard the noise of the heavy vehicles and of the cavalry which were advancing slowly and heavily upon the hard road, when Captain Roy came to me, and, addressing himself to us all, told us it was madness to wish to make any sort of attempt with this handful of ill-armed men, that to begin an impossible resistance was merely to spill blood uselessly, and to bring down on our parishes the vengeance of a powerful and implacable enemy; he proposed that we should abandon all idea of attacking the troops.
>
> I could not refuse to admit the justice of his argument.... My comrades and I began to ask ourselves, "What are we going to do?" I was more deeply involved than any of them, but I had no family. I proposed crossing over into the United States. All the others replied that they must watch over their families while at the same time they advised me to set out for a foreign land. We shook hands with aching hearts, and full of apprehension ... we scattered so that we should run into less danger, and also because we had to follow different routes.

Thus ended the military career of François-Xavier Prieur. On the way to the border he had to pass through St. Timothée, where he found the still-smoking ruins of his new home. Friends in the village fed him but he could not stay long for fear of incriminating them. He wandered through the forests but he was not much of a bushman. After several days he found he had completed a circle and was back where he started.

He slept in barns and friends fed him as he wandered, but other former rebel friends betrayed him on the promise of immediate pardons if they revealed his hiding place, and on the morning of November 20, as the army approached a house where he was hiding, he gave himself up so as not to compromise his hosts.[9]

In the same historic week in Canada, while Beauharnois was burning, while François-Xavier Prieur and his men were fleeing from Colborne's troops and Benjamin Wait and his shackled comrades were freezing on the open deck of a small ship bound for Quebec, another young man, an idealistic American, was fighting for his life on the Canadian shore of the St. Lawrence, near Prescott.

The people of Cape Vincent, across Lake Ontario from Kingston, thought Billy Gates was a fine young fellow. He was honest, religious, devoted to his close family and his country, and there was in him a firm Christian belief that he should help others whenever he could.

At school, where he had done well, he had learned over and over of the greatness of America and its system in which all men were free and equal, a lesson he believed more than many others at the time because he was strongly opposed to slavery. He was so well drilled in the benefits of the American way and so charitably inclined, he considered it a duty to bring to others this enlightenment, this new culture, this manifest destiny.

But young Billy Gates was also capable of hate. As Canadian refugees from the troubles of 1837 trickled through his little port town he was horrified by their tales of repression. "These worthy citizens, suspected by those in power," he was to write later, "were compelled to flee the Provinces to ensure their lives; leaving not only their property to be confiscated, but their families to the merciless protection of the jackals of royalty." He grew to despise British royalty and those at the helm of a government just across the lake who were "frightened by the royal whelp [and] vying with royalty itself to crush the rising of the oppressed for liberty's sake."[10]

In November 1837, William Gates, aged twenty-two, joined the Hunters' Lodge at Cape Vincent. And a year later, on November 4, 1838, after some training in military matters, he set out with six others, under orders, for Sackets Harbour, to join a force that would invade Canada at a time when a Patriot uprising was expected near Kingston. "The armies," he wrote, "were to press forward and form a junction; when, with the numbers that would flock about the triumphant standard of liberty, we might put at defiance whatever force Britain might send against us."

Right from the start it did not work out that way. When Gates and his colleagues reached Sackets Harbour, they found a hundred others there on the same mission, but the steamer *United States*, on which they were to embark, did not show up. So they went home again. Then a few days later, Gates and some others set out for a place known as Millen's Bay, near Oswego, where they found a schooner with a hundred men on board. This time the *United States* did appear and took the schooner in tow along with, another mile or so down the river, another schooner with another hundred men aboard and lots of provisions, arms and ammunition.

"It was a bright moonlit evening and we were indeed a happy band," Gates wrote. "We had full confidence in our cause as a just and noble one. We believed we were about to do our neighbours a deed of charity, such as the golden rule inculcates when it teaches us to do to our fellows as we would they should do to us.

"We believed our Canadian neighbours to be struggling for that freedom which we were enjoying and with a little aid they would be successful in securing. Was it therefore wrong that we should stifle our feelings and refuse to act out of sympathy? For one, I can place no credit in that charity which does not exhibit itself by its works.... It was indeed hard to part with my parents, brothers and sisters; yet I felt impelled by a sense of duty for the good of others, to assist in securing for them the same blessings which I was myself enjoying."[11]

The odd flotilla arrived off Prescott the following afternoon, when the schooners were detached. The one carrying Gates ran aground while trying to make a wharf, but soon cleared and was able to travel down the river about a mile to Windmill Point. She carried some more men who had been on the *United States*. The other schooner also ran aground but some aboard and some of her armaments were ferried ashore despite attacks by Canadian ships.

Bill Gates scrambled ashore with about 100 others and took possession of the circular stone windmill, four storeys high, which gave the point its name, and three stone buildings nearby. Soon they were reinforced by about 100 more men, but none of their supposed leaders. So they held a meeting and conferred full powers of command on the handsome and dashing young Pole, Nils Szoltevcky Von Schoultz. Then Gates saw "an innumerable host" of loyalist soldiers marching along the road from Kingston and others pouring out of the nearby woods until the fields around the windmill "appeared alive with redcoats." There was no sign of any Canadian Patriot army to support the invaders.

A big crowd of spectators gathered on the American shore of the river to watch the battle, waving scarves and small flags and cheering as if they were at a later-day football game.[12]

Gates was stationed away from the windmill behind a stone wall when the Canadian militia opened fire. For a while the Canadians were driven back with many losses. Then they charged, firing, with bayonets fixed. Gates fired back until his gun jammed from lack of cleaning. A young man next to him behind the wall rose to fire and was shot in the forehead. He dropped dead at Gates's feet and Gates took his rod to clean his own gun barrel, finally succeeding in loading his gun. But when he rose to fire he saw his comrades retreating towards the mill, leaving him entirely alone with scores of the enemy between him and the windmill. He threw away his gun and fled to a barn, then across about seventy-five yards of open land to the windmill. Bullets hit rocks around him. One passed through the top of his cap and another grazed the waistband of his pantaloons, but he made it to the windmill.

The royalist troops brought up heavy cannon and bombarded the stone building, destroying its rotating wings and demolishing the roof. One ball entered the mill obliquely through a window and ran round and round its circular walls while the Patriots cowered in the middle, watching in horror. There were many wounded among them, but no medicines or bandages, so Von Schoultz called for four volunteers to try to escape to the American side of the river and return with the necessary supplies. It was madness, of course, but Gates stepped forward. So did Daniel George, Charles Smith and Aaron Dresser.[13]

There was a dilapidated rowboat, half-filled with sand and water, on the beach about 500 yards below the mill. There were also a few loyalist troops stationed about 200 yards from the boat to prevent any invaders from attempting to cross the river. Gates and his colleagues crept unseen on their stomachs to the boat. The soldiers eventually saw them as they tried to float the old wreck and ran towards them, firing their muskets. Finally the boat floated. The four men paddled frantically with boards because they had no oars and soon they were out of range of the muskets, but the crew of the steamer *Cobourg*, berthed at Prescott, saw them and the ship set out to intercept them. She fired two balls that passed high over the little boat, then two charges of grapeshot, which missed. By this time the ship was close enough for her crew to fire muskets. Bullets began to pepper the rowboat and she started to sink. So the four Patriots uncovered their heads as a sign of surrender and were hauled on board the steamer.

As soon as Gates reached the deck a black man hit him on the head, knocking him unconscious. When he came to, men were laughing. "We'll fix you," one said. "Let's walk them around the deck as targets for the militia," said another. Next day they were taken in handcuffs to Kingston, then across the bay to Fort Henry, where they were locked in the cells that Benjamin Wait and his Canadian and American colleagues had just vacated. Two days later they were joined in the prison by Von Schoultz and 152 more prisoners from the Battle of the Windmill.[14]

CHAPTER 5

Rough Ships
and Prison Hulks

Come all you young Dukes and you Duchesses,
Take warning from what I do say:
Mind it's your own what you toucheses,
Or you'll end up in Botany Bay.

OLD COCKNEY SONG

The heavy leg irons Wait and his comrades from Fort Henry had worn for almost all of ten days, now tearing deep into their flesh, were removed when they reached the old City Jail in Quebec City. French-Canadian sympathizers brought them reasonable food to replace the inedible oatmeal gruel of the prison. And the sheriff brought news that they would be going to England if a passage could be found for them so late in the season.

This news caused great consternation among nine of the prisoners, who had taken advantage of an odd *"ex post facto"* arrangement under which they had agreed to transportation without a trial of any sort in order to avoid the possibility of a death sentence. They had thought they would not be "transported" very far, perhaps to the United States or another part of Canada; when England was mentioned they were upset and angry and they engaged an attorney to plead their case, but he failed to have any effect.[1]

Wait, on the other hand, was quite keen to go. He had no idea that he might be going farther than England and he and the others who were tried at Niagara were sure they would receive more justice in appeals under English law than they would in Canada. Also Wait had developed great confidence in the persistence and abilities of his remarkable wife, who would no doubt petition everybody of influence in England, even bursting in on the Queen in her palace if necessary.

So he was delighted when the sheriff, a Mr. Sewell, announced on November 22 that a ship had been found, that they would be sailing that day and that "the quarters designed for your accommodation have been examined by a board of magistrates, who pronounced them 'proper and comfortable,' and so they ought to be too, for the owner gets twenty-five pounds per head for taking you 'home' and furnishing you with provisions." He also warned the Upper Canadians that eleven French felons of the worst class, convicted of serious theft, burglary and highway robbery, were to travel with them.[2]

A yawl took them to a small barque lying in the harbour. She was the *Captain Ross*, under Captain Digby Morton, owned by two brothers named Frost, one of whom lived in Quebec, the other in Liverpool. She had been loaded at Montreal with pine and oak lumber, now covered, as her decks were, with ice as the result of winter storms. She was like a floating ice block and was the last ship bound that season for England. Her Quebec owner had concluded that thirty-four humans would not weigh as much as the lumber they replaced and, at £25 a head, would be much more profitable. So he had had a hole about twelve feet square cut through the frozen deck in the mid-ships, and used the removed boards to build narrow bunks in the dark hole below. It was by no means the "proper and comfortable " accommodation promised by Sheriff Sewell.

When we first went below into that hole of darkness [Wait wrote in a letter], the damp chill atmosphere seemed to strike through my whole person; creating in every joint and vein indescribably painful sensations; and emotions of the mind that a frigid desolation alone could produce. The blood appeared to curdle; and trembling, shuddering, palpitating, shrunk back to the heart and left the body cold and chill, benumbed and inanimate; obviously labouring vehemently to regain natural perspiration – sensations that I cannot better portray than by supposing a person, when in free pulsations, plunged unprepared into bitter cold water. A considerable period elapsed before the body could return to its natural feeling. After a few days, this dreary chillness gave way to an oppressive humidity – a suffocating warmth caused by the air being so repeatedly inhaled; and by which it became so vapid and putrid that I cannot but wonder how humanity could endure it.[3]

The prisoners were not allowed on deck for the first fifteen days of the voyage. They were stuck in the cramped, alternatively cold and hot airless hole. Two common buckets were provided for toilets, and as the ship lurched the buckets tipped over. There were not enough bunks for all the prisoners so some had to sleep on the floor of the hold, where they were soaked in the buckets' ugly contents. Those on the lower tier of berths, and those on the floor, were doused, when the wind and waves were high, with rushes of icy ocean that poured through the newly-cut hole in the deck above, which was covered only by a tarpaulin. Ice melting from the lumber cargo dripped through the deck onto the upper berths, so that the bedding, a narrow straw mattress and two blankets for each man, was constantly wet and cold. Some of the bunks were so narrow that their occupants, still chained together in pairs, had to lie head to toe or take turns in them.

The storms washed constantly over the little ship so that the decks, lines, and spars were covered by ice and one part or another was constantly breaking under the weight. Some of the crew, trying to repair the damage, suffered such severe frostbite they were rendered, according to Wait, "cripples for life." The convicts' meals consisted of oatmeal and gruel for breakfast and supper and for dinner a pail of "scouse," made of putrid salt beef and biscuit, boiled together. Most had to scrape up the mess with their hands but a few had brought their own knives, forks, spoons and dishes. Some had also managed to bring some provisions, which the captain allowed the cook to prepare separately provided the result was shared with the crew.

Off Newfoundland, the captain suspected the convicts were planning a mutiny and that Wait and Parker were among the leaders. He ordered the light chains that bound the two men replaced by heavier ones, weighing about fifty pounds. Parker chose to stand next to their shared bunk most of the time, while Wait lay on it. This meant Wait had to bear the chain's full weight on his ankle. He was in constant pain and his whole leg swelled. About ten days away from England the heavy chain was removed, the light one refitted. The weather moderated and the convicts were allowed on deck for an hour at a time so that their health improved. After twenty-five days, the *Captain Ross* entered the Mersey in gloomy mist and fog.

The vessel dropped anchor in the river three miles from Liverpool on December 16, 1838, just thirty-eight terrible days after Wait and his fellow rebels had been escorted from Fort Henry. Now a small steam lighter took them, handcuffed, to the big city docks, and carriages carried them to Liverpool's immense old borough jail, capable of holding more than a thousand prisoners, but occupied at the time by only 300 men, 200 women and about 200 boys under the age of ten.

This jail seemed more like a palace to the Canadian convicts. The jailers were kind and the food not too bad. A homely, warming fire was set for them in a big hall and beer offered, although many refused because they were "temperance." Magistrates visited frequently to ask if there were any complaints and when there were – about the quality of food, for instance – the situation was improved. Clergymen comforted them and dignitaries visited, offering help and advice. Elegantly clothed women came too, especially to visit Wait because they had heard about his wife's heroic efforts in Canada. They promised to support any further efforts she might make if she came to England. Most importantly, influential London Whigs and lawyers, in particular

Joseph Hume and John Arthur Roebuck, offered their assistance and appointed solicitors to plead their cases.[4]

Roebuck, the most prominent of the lawyers, travelled to Liverpool to hear the convicts' stories and was enthralled. He told them he had no doubt he could convince the Queen's Bench they were all being held illegally. But then, when he was talking to Parker and Wait, Parker mentioned the obvious fact that the nine "ex post facto" prisoners, of which he was one – those who had not even been tried because they had decided that agreeing to transportation was better than a possible hanging – would have a stronger case than the others. The lawyer at once agreed and took Parker aside to discuss his suggestion.[5]

Subsequently many of the prisoners blamed Parker for the fact that the "ex post factos" eventually received special treatment before the English courts. But Wait supported the friend who had been chained to him for so long:

I have been thus particular in relating these incidents, for my companions from Niagara were inclined to charge the exclusive proceedings that followed to the designed misrepresentations of Parker, and a fear that his success might be jeopardised by a too numerous participation in the benefits of inquiry; but I saw, at once, the occasion for it.

The nine men, among whom he was numbered, had been treated more palpably illegal than those of us who had received a trial. Their sentences were given under an "ex post facto" law, directly opposed to the British code, that nominal "bulwark of British liberty," viz: the "Jury Act." Ours, too, was illegal and unjust, but truly not so undisguised; for, by the time we were captured, Sir George Arthur had become somewhat more way-wise, and began to think a little more plausibility was requisite in dealing with the Canadians, than with the Tasmanians, whom he had hung up with impunity.

In any event, only the nine "ex post facto" prisoners and three others, Linus Miller, the brash law student from Rochester, John Grant, a Canadian wheelwright, and William Reynolds, a Philadelphia saddler, apparently chosen at random as test cases, had their cases reviewed by the British courts.

The twelve were taken by train to London and housed in the notorious Newgate prison. However, they found that the prison did not live up to its grim reputation. They were confined in two large, airy rooms, allowed to walk in the yard once or twice a day, were well fed and provided with comfortable beds. They also found the prison officers kind, and the governor, a man named Cope, was, according to Miller, "a jolly old gentleman, fond of fun, and always wore a smile on his countenance."[6]

Their trials, in January, before a bench of gowned and bewigged judges at Westminster Hall, with Lord Denham presiding, were well argued and in the true tradition of British justice. Even Linus Miller was impressed. The crown was represented by the attorney general, Sir John Campbell, and the solicitor general, Sir F. Pollock, while three highly-skilled lawyers, Matthew Davenport Hill, John Arthur Roebuck and Thomas Falconer, appeared for the prisoners.

Hill and Roebuck pleaded eloquently for writs of *habeas corpus,* especially for the nine who had agreed to transportation instead of trial, arguing that they were not even convicts because they had not been convicted and therefore could not be sent to a convict colony; that what the lieutenant-governor of Upper Canada (Sir George Arthur) had done was equivalent to granting a pardon to a thief providing he agreed to have his right hand cut off; and that every man, upon incarceration, was entitled to be brought to trial at the earliest opportunity, whereas these men had been punished by a year's imprisonment without seeing a judge, without a sentence of a court, without a trial or even an arraignment.

In the end, the nine who had been transported without trial were released while the sentences of the other three, Linus Miller, John

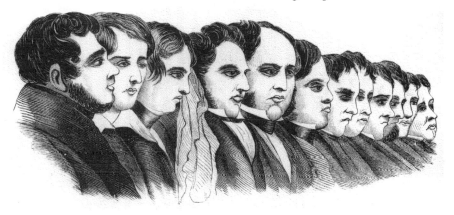

The "Canadian state prisoners" on trial at Westminster Hall, London, England, in 1838, portrayed in a drawing in the London Sun. *Left to right: Paul Bedford, Linus Miller, William Reynolds, Finlay Malcolm, John G. Parker, Randal Wixon, Leonard Watson, Ira Anderson, William Alves, James Brown, Robert Walker, John Grant. (Toronto Reference Library)*

Grant and William Reynolds, were confirmed. However, Reynolds was later set free as a result of petitions from the American ambassador to Britain, who pleaded that he was only eighteen years old (although he was actually over twenty). Most of the ten released men sailed from Liverpool to freedom in North America on the *Wellington* on July 27.[7]

While the trial was pending, the eleven North Americans left behind in Liverpool jail were transferred ominously to the prison hulk *York* in Portsmouth harbour. Their voyage was memorable, even for men who had experienced a rough Atlantic crossing in the icy, dark hold of the *Captain Ross*. At dawn on January 4, 1839, they were driven in carriages through the city to the Liverpool docks and comfortably berthed in the bow cabin of a small steam frigate, the *Meteor*. Officials came aboard with them to report to the ship's officers that they were men of extraordinary character and to bid them a happy passage and speedy release. Then the little ship got under way about 6 p.m. against a strong headwind that twice forced them back up the Mersey before they finally made it to sea. This wind was a warning of much worse to come.

By next morning, off Cork, the wind increased to a gale so strong that all attempts to make the harbour for shelter failed although the captain continued to try until dusk. He then headed for Holyhead but dared not enter without a pilot. When he signalled for one in the early morning, lights flashed back at him warning him to keep away. So he decided to run back to Liverpool. Now the wind howled to hurricane force and one of the worst storms in English maritime history developed. Waves with crests of white spume reached tremendous heights. The packets *Pennsylvania* and *St. Andrews*, bound for America, filled with emigrants and passengers, went aground near Liverpool and broke to pieces. Two other packets, *The Brothers* and *Lockwood*, were washed ashore at the entrance to the Mersey Channel with the loss of nearly all their passengers and crews. The horrible storm that tore at the *Meteor* and her convict cargo swallowed scores of other smaller craft, with all hands. Hundreds perished. The east shore of the channel was strewn with dead bodies and debris, while ashore chimneys and church steeples toppled and houses were blown away.

The *Meteor*, with the convicts thrown about and seasick in the dark bow cabin, rolled, broached and shuddered in this maelstrom. The engine was swamped and stopped. The tremendous waves, breaking awesomely at their towering crests, crashed down on the little ship and swept away her wheelhouse, bulwarks, binnacles and compasses and shattered her lifeboats. The howling wind shredded her sails to ribbons so she ran for Liverpool under bare poles and one small remaining sail. When they were off the entrance to the channel about midnight on January 7, they found that the lightship had been driven ashore and not a single light, buoy or channel mark was left to guide them. The commander, Lieutenant Pritchard, who had sailed with Nelson and had sabre scars on his face to prove it, took the wheel himself and drove desperately for the mouth of the Mersey. He was guided by wrecks lining both banks of the channel, illuminated by flashes of lightning. He could hear the cries of hundreds of voices screaming for help from the wrecks, but he ignored them.

"I was compelled to pass by unregarded," he told Wait later, "for, had it been in my power to have saved them, I should not have dared to do it. By rendering them assistance, and endangering your lives, and risking your escape, would have been placing my commission, my freedom, and even my life, and thereby the support of my numerous family, in jeopardy." Miraculously, he brought the *Meteor* to anchor in calm waters opposite the city.[8]

> During the three days and two nights we were thus "riding the gale" [Wait wrote], our cabin was utterly darkened; the large skylight being canvassed over and battened down; which however, did not exclude the water that at every succeeding wave poured down upon us in torrents, and not only drenched us, but set our beds afloat, the cabin deck being our only berths. Not a man among us was free from violent sea sickness. Our situation can be easier imagined than described; and it may readily be conceded that we needed, or, at least, received no food during these days of misery. It is, indeed, hard to conceive the wretched appearance we made when we first emerged from that sink, and the horrid stench that arose from the cabin when the skylight was first unbattened. The marines who did it swore they never had experienced anything half so nauseous.
>
> Yet no blame could be attached to the commander or any of the officers; for it would scarcely be supposed that they could pay much regard to us when the whole ship, lives, and everything, were in such imminent jeopardy. Much credit is even due to them....

The storm blew over and the *Meteor* made a peaceful voyage to Portsmouth. The convicts wrote a note to Pritchard expressing their admiration of his general humanity and particular heroism during the storm. "I will long retain it, as a memento of more value than the applause of the rich or the powerful," the gallant captain told them. He also promised to see what he could do about a request that they be housed apart from the common criminals on whatever hulk they were sent to. The admiral in charge of the hulks happened to be Sir Philip Durham, a brother of the Earl of Durham, the recently resigned, liberal governor-general of Canada, and Wait was introduced to him as "the man whose life had been saved by the unparalleled conduct of his wife, who had made a journey of seven hundred miles to present, personally, her petitions to his Lordship, the Earl of Durham." Pritchard also described the Canadians as "mostly men of property, respectability and family ... and all their conduct on board my vessel warrant the highest encomiums; and I would add, they are intelligent, *praying*, men."

In the circumstances, Sir Philip Durham promised he would keep the Canadian prisoners apart from his other charges, whom he described as a "set of infamous wretches, whose immorality, obscenity, and common vicious propensities could not be held in too great ab-

Prison hulks in Portsmouth Harbour (oil painting). Overcrowded jails forced English authorities to imprison criminals, both petty and serious offenders, in the rotting hulks of old ships in many harbours. Canadian Patriots spent months on the hulk of the York at Portsmouth. (National Library of Australia, Canberra)

horrence, and which must inevitably reflect disgrace on every associate."[9]

The Canadian prisoners were taken aboard the rotting hulk of the *York*, where they were stripped, washed, their beards and heads shaved, and clothed in coarse prison garb marked with broad arrows. Large, rusty iron bands, weighing about four pounds, were attached to their right legs, but they were given accommodation apart from the common convicts in what had once been a hospital ward.

The prisoners spent two months on the hulk, cold at nights, covered in vermin, semi-starving on prison gruel, but relieved of the hard labour ashore the criminal inmates had to endure. Lawyers appointed by John Arthur Roebuck visited them frequently and kept hopes alive that they might be released. Their number was reduced to ten when James Gemmell became ill and was taken to hospital, and then to nine when Jacob Beemer, believed by the others to be a traitor, feigned an illness and was also taken ashore for treatment.[10]

They were joined at one stage by fifty boys, all under ten years old, who had been condemned to seven, ten or fourteen years in Van Diemen's Land. Wait recorded his conversation with one sprightly lad, aged seven years and five months:

He surprised me by saying he had been tried for picking a gentleman's pocket of a purse containing nine guineas and thirteen
shillings with a few "harporths." But how in the name of common sense could you pick a man's pocket? Why you could scarce
reach his waist. But, "oh, I didn't frisk his pocket. I was in a stall
where they sells rings – he come'd in, and picked out one that
suited him. Just as he was going to pay for it, the shopman called
him over to t'other end of the room, and I whip't up his purse
and run'd away with it; I meets my sister close by the door and
slips it into her apron, and she goes right home and guv it to
mother but I run on til a "trap" nabbed me because I was running. The gentleman come up and said I stole his purse, they
frisked me and couldn't find it; but he swore I took it; so I got
lagged for seven years. Mother keeps the money, tho', and I'm
sorry I couldn't have the bit o' plum puddin she promised me if I
would get her a good swag that day.

"Have you done anything before?" "Oh, yes, I picked up a
handkerchief and two testers the day before and mother gave me
a penny bun and harporth of yale." "Have you got any brothers?"
"Yes, George was transported with father to V.D.L. for taking
plate from the Duke's house; and I've got two sisters, one in the
house of correction, and one at home, who goes every day for
mother's quarteen of rum and pot of yale."[11]

The Canadian prisoners witnessed many lashings, usually for smug-
gling tobacco, with the victim strapped to the mizzen mast and the cat
o'nine tails dripping with his blood. They saw other scrawny offenders
confined to small, dark solitary cells for as long as a week or ten days.
But they were, in general, treated better than the others. Officers recognized them as men of some intelligence and liked to talk with them,
to hear their stories of America, where some wanted to emigrate. So,
with the frequent visits of lawyers, hope remained with them until
March 10, when a big "Bay ship," the *Marquis of Hastings*, dropped an-

chor ominously at Spithead. With almost no warning, the Canadians were escorted in heavy chains to a lighter, which took them to the convict ship for a 16,000-mile journey to Van Diemen's Land.

They were jostled below on the *Marquis of Hastings*, heavily chained by their right legs, and were crushed tightly into a single, large hold, packed with about 230 felons guilty of every crime imaginable. There were murderers and con men, burglars and highwaymen, gamblers and especially pickpockets, who could make the North Americans' meagre rations of "skilly" and ship's biscuit vanish in front of their eyes. They were assigned four to a small bunk. Vermin crawled over all of them as the big ship (about 600 tons) was driven back from the Bay of Biscay to the coast of Ireland, then in fair winds past the Azores, where more gales blew her towards the American coast. She spent several days trying to round Cape Horn without success, then changed course and headed in rough seas and more high winds around the Cape of Good Hope.

Scurvy struck in the tropics with its symptoms of discoloured spots over the surface of the body, swollen legs, putrid gums, violent rheumatic pains, jaundice, extreme lassitude and fainting after the smallest exertion. Thirty convicts died and were consigned to the sea. Most of the others lay still in their bunks, afraid or unable to move [12]

The Canadian convict John McNulty caught it. So did Benjamin Wait, whose head, face and limbs swelled so horribly the surgeon put him in the ship's hospital and drew a large amount of blood from his body. This helped reduce the symptoms of the disease, but Wait's right arm suffered an ugly, painful infection that spread down his right side. He discovered later that the lancet used to withdraw the blood had not been sterilized after it had been used, a few hours before, to open a putrid swelling on the knee of a man who died soon afterwards.

After a four-month voyage as horrific as any in the history of the convict ships, the *Marquis of Hastings* pulled in to Hobart, Van Diemen's Land, in mid-July 1839, where its half-dead human cargo filled the local hospital.

Benjamin Wait thought he would die. His head, face and limbs were grotesquely swollen from scurvy. His whole body turned red then purple. His veins seemed to be filled with balls that rolled continuously to his extremities and his nose bled. As the anchor chain rattled, the ship's surgeon was about to amputate his right arm, putrid as a result of the foul, unsterilized lancet used to relieve his condition. But the doctor changed his mind and Wait was taken ashore immediately to the Colonial Hospital, where he spent eight weeks. The surgeon got five guineas for each convict delivered alive. He had lost a lot of money on the voyage and did not want to lose any more.

John McNulty, who had taken part in the fiasco at Montgomery's Tavern before being captured in the Short Hills raid, and who had been struck by scurvy along with Wait, died in the hospital four hours after the *Marquis of Hastings* dropped anchor. And Alexander McLeod, a fine-looking man who had also taken part in the Yonge Street debacle and was the captured later at Niagara, was also rushed ashore, suffering from galloping consumption. He was lucid in the hospital ward for only five minutes and died within forty-eight hours.

Wait reported:

He was taken, as he expired, stripped naked, put in the "man box," and carried to the dead house, and there stretched upon a table. Five days afterward a body of prisoners, who had come in the *Marquis of Hastings*, were sent to the hospital to carry away and bury the dead. They arrived and found the body on the table in the ward cut in many pieces, with its entrails lying beside it. They gathered the pieces together and put them in a coffin of rough boards, and behold it was poor McLeod, whom they all knew, and respected. The scene was revolting, but there was no alternative; they carried him away and laid him in a "strangers' grave," without ceremony or one mark to distinguish the spot from the thousands of "felon mounds."[13]

As Wait struggled against death in the large ward, "old hands" around him died in their beds if they had one, or on the floor if they did not, often crying with their last breaths for a sight of "home." Wait was treated with some kindness by a friendly surgeon, who gave him narcotics for his pain and sometimes extra food and wine for his skinny, shaking body, and he began to improve. Samuel Chandler, who had been saved from the gallows at Niagara with him, was admitted to the ward for ten days. Garrett Van Camp, who was captured with Wait in the Short Hills raid, was brought in also, having ruptured and otherwise injured himself hauling a cartload of wood. He died in the ward three weeks after landing. So now, of the nine Canadians and Americans who came on the *Marquis of Hastings*, only six remained.

Altogether, in the first week after she sailed into Hobart's harbour, twelve of her convict cargo died and a year later only 103 of the total of 240 were still alive. On her return voyage to England, the *Marquis of Hastings* sank with all hands off the coast of China. [14]

Meanwhile, in England, the brash young law student Linus Miller and John Grant, who had failed in their bid for freedom in the London courts, were transferred from Newgate prison to the *York* hulk, arriving there in mid-July 1839, just as the *Marquis of Hastings* was unloading its wretched human cargo at Hobart. Miller was actually sorry to leave Newgate. He wrote:

> Strange as it may appear, a confinement of six months in Newgate had actually produced an attachment to its old, gloomy walls; and every object in the room I had occupied with my companions, had become dear to me through familiarity, local associations both pleasant and painful, and the recollection that it had been to me a habitation, a kind of resting place in my weary pilgrimage, where I had found repose while drinking from the bitter cup of anxiety, suspense, expectation, hope deferred, disappointment and despair so strangely intermixed. [15]

Miller and Grant were reunited on the hulk with Gemmell and Beemer, who had been left behind when the *Marquis of Hastings* sailed because of their real or feigned illnesses. After six months the four of them were herded aboard the *Canton,* with about 240 common criminals, for their journey to the end of the earth.

The *Canton,* compared to other Bay ships, was more like a luxury liner. There was six feet eight inches of headroom in the convicts' hold, which was kept spotlessly clean. Two large, iron-grilled hatchways provided plenty of ventilation. The food was not bad and wine or lime juice was served at each meal to prevent scurvy. The surgeon, Dr. John Irvine, R.N., a kindly Irishman, visited the prisoners daily to hear any complaints and in many cases he acted on them.

However, Miller found something to complain about:

But to me the prison was a floating hell! The most horrid blasphemy and disgusting obscenity, from daylight in the morning until ten o'clock at night, were, without one moment's cessation, ringing in my ears. The general conversation of these wretched men related to the crimes of which they professed to have been guilty, and he whose life had been most iniquitous was esteemed the best man. I tried to close my ears and shut my eyes against all, but found this a difficult task.[16]

There was some seasickness and a few squalls but mostly the weather was fair and the *Canton* dropped anchor at Hobart on January 12, 1840, after a voyage of 16,000 miles in sixteen weeks. Only two convicts had died on the way.

CHAPTER 6

The Voyage
of the Buffalo

There's whores, pimps and bastards, a large costly crew,
Maintained by the sweat of a labouring few,
They should have no commission, place, pension or pay,
Such locusts should all go to Botany Bay.

FROM BOTANY BAY: A NEW SONG (1790)

$\mathcal{A}$s the *Captain Ross* set sail from Quebec City for England in November 1838, with its frozen complement of Upper Canadian and American prisoners, François-Xavier Prieur was marching from St. Timothée to Montreal with fifty-two other French Canadians, chained together two by two, escorted by a Scottish regiment, his ears assaulted all the way by the foreign screech of bagpipes. Shouts of "Shoot them! Hang them" from hostile mobs greeted them when they reached the fringes of the city. Then Prieur was crowded with a large number of other rebels in a shed erected inside the Montreal jail. The windows of the shed were boarded up and its latrines were not connected to any sewer. Trials were in progress and the sentences, almost invariably, were condemnation to death.[1]

Prieur reported:

On the 19th of December one of our guards told us that Joseph Cardinal [a thirty-year-old lawyer and father of five from the

Parish of Châteauguay] and Joseph Duquette [a law student, aged twenty-two, unmarried, from the same parish] had been notified to prepare themselves to mount the scaffold within the next two days. That aroused in us the hope that others (already condemned) at least would meet a better fate.

It was on the 21st December, at nine o'clock in the morning that our two unfortunate comrades mounted the scaffold, erected above the door of the wall surrounding the Montreal jail; they were supported by Father Labelle, then parish priest of Châteauguay, their confessor. Some hours after the execution, Father Labelle came to see us and described to us the terrible circumstances associated with this scene. Poor young Duquette endured terrible suffering; the executioner had to hang him twice, the rope in the first instance being badly adjusted and becoming tangled in falling, and he smashed his head against the edge of the scaffold so that it became covered with blood.[2]

Prieur was brought before the court martial in the old *Palais de justice* along with eleven others on January 11, 1839, travelling from the jail in a black maria. Not a word of French was spoken in a trial that spread over ten days, so the accused, who spoke little or no English, had limited understanding of the proceedings. Each day as they were dragged in handcuffs from the black maria to the court a rabble gathered to hurl insults at them. Sometimes as they left the jail they saw the corpses of comrades, fresh from the gibbet, stretched in the snow.

Prieur wrote:

Some of our judges even didn't spare us gross insults; some of them also amused themselves during the sittings, sketching little figures hanging from gibbets, and these coarse caricatures, which they passed to one another before our gaze, appeared to amuse them greatly.

But the accused were allowed defence counsel, who did their best, and even the crown prosecutors went out of their way at times to admit evidence of their previous good characters. They were also allowed visitors at both the jail and the courthouse and priests and family came frequently. Prieur's mother fainted twice as he held her in his arms.

On January 24 all eleven were sentenced to death.[3] They were also graded in the judges' notes in order of culpability. Prieur was fifth in the list of eleven.

The condemned were put in cells in pairs and Prieur ended up with the young Montreal lawyer Chevalier de Lorimier, who was hanged on February 15, 1839, along with Charles Hindenlang, a French protestant, who had served in the military during a temporary residence in the United States before joining the *Patriotes* in Lower Canada.

Families and friends were invited to a feast in a room near the cells on the night before these hangings. In their Gallic way, they drank good wine and a forced gaiety prevailed during the gourmet meal prepared by the jailers under the prisoners' instructions. But de Lorimier would only drink an occasional glass of wine. During most of the repast he walked the corridors with his wife on his arm, talking quietly, and when it was over and the many guests were departing Madame de Lorimier threw her arms around her husband's neck and fainted. He carried her like a child to the building's exit, kissed her brow and gently placed her in the arms of relatives.[4]

In the morning Prieur helped his cellmate dress for his death. As he fixed a little white necktie around his neck, de Lorimier admonished him: "Leave the space necessary for placing the rope." Prieur burst into tears. The jailer and a military escort took de Lorimier and Hindenlang away while Prieur and the others prayed. They were on their knees for forty-five minutes. Then a prison employee, a French Canadian, told them in a flood of tears that their two friends and three others from another block of cells were dead.

They brought the number hanged in Lower Canada since December 21, 1838, to twelve. They were the last of the hangings, however, because orders had arrived from England that enough was enough. So Prieur and the others condemned to death sweated in their cells through a long summer, not knowing what was to become of them. Then on the morning of September 26, there was much opening of doors and clanging of iron as heaps of handcuffs were piled in the corridors. Fifty-eight prisoners were shackled in pairs and marched to the Montreal wharves, where a cavalry escort hustled them aboard a steamer, the *British America.* The steamer left at full speed and reached the harbour at Quebec City next day. There it pulled alongside a sailing ship of about 700 tons. She was a strange-looking craft. Her superstructure towered high above the water, much too high for a man o' war. Yet she carried fifteen guns and men in military uniforms paced the top of her three decks. She was a convict ship. She bore on her transom the name HMS *Buffalo.*[5]

The 157 Canadians and Americans who were captured or surrendered after the Battle of the Windmill at Prescott found conditions in the Fort Henry jail abominable. The main meal was boiled bullocks' heads. The prisoners were crowded in groups of about fifty into cells that measured about twenty by thirty feet. There was little ventilation but multitudes of vermin. The prisoners were hauled away singly or in small groups for quick trials, and every Wednesday the sheriff visited the cells with a bundle of death warrants. Their gallant, handsome leader, Von Schoultz, was first to be hanged, then ten others.

Some of the hangings were not neat. After Martin Woodruff, of Salina, New York, a colonel in the Patriot force, went to the gallows on December 19, the *Kingston Spectator* described the scene:

He was placed on the platform, the cap pulled over his face, and the hangman then fastened the rope to a hook on the beam overhead. The platform fell and a revolting, disgusting and disgraceful spectacle was presented to view.

The knot, instead of drawing tight under the ear, was brought to the chin; it didn't slip, but left space enough to put a hand within, the chief weight of the body bearing upon the rope at the back of the neck. The body was in great agitation and seemed to suffer greatly.

The spectators said it was shameful management and then two hangmen endeavoured to *strangle* the sufferer.

And according to the *Port Ontario Aurora:*

His neck was not broken till the hangman on the cross-tree had pulled him up by the collar and let him fall four times in succession.[6]

William Gates's trial lasted less than an hour. He appeared with three others before a court martial of militia officers. An indictment was read and he was asked if he pleaded guilty or not guilty. "Not guilty," he said. Then a Queen's witness was asked if he recognized Gates. "I do not," he replied. That was the end of the trial and Gates was taken back to his cell not knowing its result but presuming he had been sentenced, like most of the others, to the gallows.

One night a deputy sheriff hinted that his name would be on the list next day, so Gates could not sleep all night. When the high sheriff arrived in the morning, his hand on his sword, escorted by twenty-five soldiers with fixed bayonets on their muskets, the young American's knees shook with fear.

"William Gates," the sheriff shouted, "stand there." He pointed to the centre of the room where he always made those condemned to death stand. He called the names of five of Gates's cellmates and ordered them to stand beside him. He read death warrants to those five men. Then he turned to Gates and handed him a piece of paper. "Here, Gates," he said, " is a letter from your father; go and sit down." Gates could hardly stand. He staggered to a seat. He thought he was going to be sick.

His mother visited him several times, once accompanied by his father, two sisters and three brothers. At these meetings he was hand-cuffed and surrounded by six soldiers and he looked so haggard and filthy the family wept when they saw him. But once his mother managed to slip him some money, which he used to bribe guards to buy him some food. And on her last visit she showed him a petition on his behalf, signed by many of the most influential men in Jefferson County, which she was taking to Toronto to present to Lieutenant-Governor George Arthur. Later he learned that his mother, accompanied by his oldest brother, did receive an audience with Arthur, who praised the respectful wording of the petition but offered no hope.

However, Arthur himself visited Fort Henry a few weeks later. To many Upper Canadians he might have been the impressive and dignified Queen's representative but to Gates he was "so fearful of his worshipful person that he approached us with a drawn sword, supported by a lifeguard with drawn swords, who were backed by fifty soldiers with fixed bayonets."

Approaching Gates, Arthur asked his name. "Gates," said Gates.

"Ah, yes," said Arthur. "Your mother handed me a petition for your liberation the other day." Gates said nothing.

"Did you take an active part in the battle at Prescott?" Arthur asked. "Did you fire at any of the Queen's soldiers? Did you kill or intend to kill any of them?"

"Sure, I fired at them," Gates replied. "And if I didn't kill any of them it wasn't because I didn't try. It was because I missed."

"Why did you do that?" Arthur asked.

"Well," said Gates, "they were firing at me."

"That's enough of you," said Arthur and he stomped away.

A deputy sheriff whispered in Gates's ear. "You're gone," he said.[7]

Nevertheless, according to Gates, free pardons for himself and twenty-four others were drawn up in the next few weeks and sent to the sheriff, a man named McDonald, who decided to hang on to them for a few weeks before taking any action. In the meantime a British officer, for some unknown reason, crossed the border to French Creek in

Jefferson County, where he was captured by Americans, abused and beaten, then sent back to Kingston. When Arthur heard of the way the officer was treated, Gates says, he burned the pardons.

So the summer of 1839 passed miserably. No more of the Patriots were hanged but the heat made Fort Henry's crowded cells more hell-like. The bugs bit more ferociously. The bullocks' head soup seemed thinner. And hope died in Gates's skinny breast until late in September when, surprisingly, he and eighty-two colleagues were told to prepare for a move. They were going to Quebec, the prison guards told them, where they would receive free pardons from the governor-general himself, who was anxious to see them. As they left Fort Henry after eleven months, handcuffed and attached by their ankles to a long chain, most of them sick, their happiness reverberated in song – "Hail Columbia," "The Star Spangled Banner," "Hunters of Kentucky," "Yankee Doodle." "We actually felt highly gleeful," said Gates.

At Quebec they pulled alongside that strange looking ship, the *Buf-falo*. They were hustled aboard and herded into its hold, where they found a large group of French Canadians already aboard.

The *Buffalo* and her crew were accustomed to carrying convicts. For years the small, three-deck frigate had plied her dismal trade between England and Australia with cargoes of criminals from the dilapidated hulks in England's harbours and her overcrowded jails. She was in fact a true convict ship, the only vessel ever equipped with spars and sails produced by prison labour from the timber and flax of Norfolk Island, the cruellest of all of the Australian convict settlements. But she was old now. Her hull was riddled with rot, her rigging and sails frayed and shabby.

The prisoners were herded down to the lower deck, below sea level, into a hold that was about seventy-five feet long and thirty-five feet wide. There was only about four and a half feet of headroom except for one small space aft, where a man could stand upright. The centre of this area, the ship's storeroom, was filled with boxes and packing cases, and its sides consisted of a double-row of compartments, six feet deep, which were the sleeping quarters, four men to a bunk. In between the bunks and boxes, there was an alleyway less than three feet wide where a man, doubled over, could move about. Only a little shadowy light filtered down through two hatches, which were stoutly barred.

On October 2, 1839, four days after she was towed by a steamer from Quebec, and soon after she sailed past Cape Gaspé in the Gulf of St. Lawrence, a terrible storm struck the *Buffalo*. The sky blackened. Blinding spray and rain lashed her ugly hull while huge, foaming waves towered above her crosstrees and crashed on her decks. Down below in their dark hole, the French-Canadian *Patriote* prisoners and the English Canadians and Americans captured in the Battle of the Windmill and other rebel border skirmishes, were hurled about continually, crashing into each other and the sharp-edged crates in the centre of their small space.

All but five or six of them were seasick, vomiting on the deck. Some tried to tie themselves down to bunk posts or the masts, using their belts and clothing. They were forbidden to lie down, under threat of lashings, because, their sailor-guards said, exercise was necessary for treatment of their ailment. So they stood up and slid about in their puke and the brown spillage from slush pails that rolled to and fro, their only consolation the fact that there was very little in their stomachs to bring up.

Soon after the 141 men had been shoved down into the darkness, they had been divided into parties of about twelve, mainly for feeding purposes.[8] Each group was issued one tin plate, one knife, one fork and one spoon. Their rations, which remained the same for the entire voyage, consisted of about a pint of oatmeal porridge for breakfast, then on one day, at midday, a half-pint of pea soup, a quarter pound of pork and about four ounces of biscuit; on the alternate day they were issued the same amount of biscuit, three-quarters of a pound of salt beef, and about six ounces of pudding made from flour and a little lard. In the evening they were given a pint of tea one day and a pint of chocolate the next. The daily allowance of fresh water, for all purposes, was one pint each.

They managed to make palettes from little pieces of wood so they could eat their oatmeal soup but, while waiting their turn for use of the knife and fork, most of them, in their hunger, tore their tough meat apart with their hands and teeth. Until, eventually, aided by scurvy, their teeth fell out.

For a week in the storm most of them ate nothing. Most of those who tried threw it up. When the wind finally died, some were too weak to stand and others tottered around, clutching at bunkposts and each other in attempts to remain vertical. A surgeon was sent from the upper deck, a humane man, according to some of the prisoners, who decided none of the skinny, vomit and vermin-covered cargo would survive very long, a situation that was unsatisfactory not only for them but for him as well, because he was paid an amount for each individual who arrived at the destination alive. He pressured the captain to allow them on deck for two hours a day. So after more than two weeks at sea, they were escorted above, two or three groups of twelve at time, to breathe fresh air and exercise their withered limbs.

The French Canadians, separated from the others on one side of the dark hold, prayed a lot and seemed to bear the terrible privations with more fortitude. The Americans cursed their fate and plotted. By now, the Americans estimated they would be somewhere not far from New York City and they decided to take over the ship and force the crew to sail it to New York or some nearby port. Through several nights they whispered in their bunks, worried that there might be spies among the few of the Upper Canadians who seemed to be not rebels but common criminals sentenced for real crimes.

The plot was simple. Aft on the deck on which the prisoners were allowed to exercise there was a small cabin containing some muskets, already bayoneted, with cartridge boxes hanging near each gun. These were to be seized at a time when the Americans were on deck and the officers and soldiers were at dinner, leaving only three or four sentries. The soldiers would be confined below decks and the sailors compelled to head the vessel towards New York. Even if the sailors refused, the mutineers figured they had enough skill among them to manage the ship. And they surmised the ship could be taken over with little, if any, bloodshed, though they were prepared to kill as many sailors and soldiers as would be necessary.

William Gates wrote:

We had the plan finally arranged, and had set the day when we would be near the latitude of New York. The day quickly came, and nothing yet had occurred to damp our anticipations. Joyfully we mustered for dinner, and for once we ate with glad hearts, imagining the hour of our delivery was near at hand.

But judge of our disappointment when, attempting to go on deck, we found our hatch barred down. We divined at once that our plot was mistrusted, if not known. In the afternoon we were visited by the captain and his officers, who closely questioned us concerning our motives and plans; but we so effectively feigned astonishment, that we quite convinced them that we had not thought of the thing.

Nevertheless, from then on the hatches to the hell-hole were kept closely barred. The prisoners were allowed on deck only for an hour at a time and in small numbers, guarded by an equal number of armed soldiers. And worst of all, under threat of the lash or death, they were forbidden to utter a word between 8 p.m. and 6 a.m. as they lay sleepless on their bug-ridden bedding.

The French Canadians, who occupied the starboard side of the hold, while the Americans and Upper Canadians were on the port side, knew nothing of this plot. According to Léon Ducharme, in his *Journal of a Political Exile in Australia* :

On the 12th [of October] we did not go on deck. We were kept at work the whole day washing and scrubbing our quarters. Just about five o'clock in the afternoon we were alarmed by the sound of firearms on deck, and by the coming and going of soldiers and crew, who in an instant were armed with guns, swords and pistols. We could not explain these movements. Then some officers, coming below with a squad of soldiers, compelled the whole 141 of us to go up to the between-decks where we were packed into a space of about twenty-five feet square. There, without a word of explanation, they locked us up, and after making us give up the keys of our boxes and trunks, went into our quarters, opened our trunks, some with our keys, others with iron tools which forced off the lids. They searched all our clothes, took away our razors, our pocket knives, our scissors and our money, with a little of which we had provided ourselves before our departure; they examined our beds and all the chinks and crevices which might conceal any dangerous weapons. Finally, after searches as minute as they were useless, they came above to where we were; and one of the officers, whose name was Niblett, supported by several others, addressed us in the coarsest way, and told us that he had discovered the dark plot that we had formed to make ourselves masters of the crew, and to set a course for the shores of America; that he had crushed the conspiracy at its birth, and taken the necessary measures to forestall our ill designs. We tried to justify ourselves; we tried to assert that the idea of a mutiny against the crew had never come into our minds; that their – the officers' – opinions could be founded only on false reports; that they should be convinced of this by their searches of our quarters. We were compelled to be silent, even while being treated like dogs.

Ducharme reports that the French Canadians subsequently learned that a man named Tywell, one of the prisoners from Upper Canada, had spread false reports about a planned mutiny in the hope of being rewarded with his freedom.[9] But Gates says he and the other Americans involved in the plot discovered later that one William Highland, another Upper Canadian, was the traitor.[10] Suspicion and distrust was rife among the Americans. In his published narrative, Stephen S. Wright blamed fellow American Orin W. Smith as the "most base, unmanly" traitor.

As the ship sailed down the coast of Africa into the equatorial tropics, the hot sun burned the decks and the dry heat penetrated below so that the air down there was yellow with it. The pitch between the planks of the old ship melted and ran. The salt from the prisoners' diet burned a terrible thirst in their guts, so that when their one-pint of water arrived each day, hands clutching for the pannikin shook like an alcoholic's clutching at a tumbler of rum.

When it rained some water collected in the bottom of the ship's lifeboats where pigs and sheep were kept to provide an occasional meal of fresh meat for the officers. Sailors sold some of this water, dark brown from the dung of the animals, to the prisoners, or exchanged pannikins of it for a prisoner's shirt or pair of trousers. Easing their burning thirst with this stuff, the prisoners became more ill.

One of them, Asa Priest, aged forty, from Auburn, Massachusetts, a quiet family man, died. His body was sewn up in sail cloth. Four cannon balls were attached to it and he was cast into the sea while thirty-six of his comrades watched from the deck and the crew stood at attention, presenting arms. Priest had never claimed to be a rebel. He said he had come to Oswego to get money he was owed for a cow, followed his debtor on to the schooner that was taking Patriots over to Canada for the Battle of the Windmill at Prescott, and had then fallen asleep on board and been forced to land. His friends said it was not just the filth and thirst that killed him. He had pined away from a broken heart.

William Gates, who went temporarily blind from a painful eye-inflammation, recorded:

As we neared the tropics, the heat of the climate greatly aggravated our misery, rendering the atmosphere of our hold more loathsome, and the vermin that yet were our companions, more numerous and active. Confined to a pint of water a day, our thirst was so excessive that to endure it seemed impossible. From this and the effects of so close confinement in the putrid atmosphere, and living on salt provisions, we became infected with disease. Our teeth loosened in our heads, and often were so painful as to quite produce delirium. The doctor's forceps were called into pretty active requisition. In this respect I suffered less than most of my companions, for I lost but three of my teeth. Others lost even eight, ten, and a dozen.

The men were dying. During their short times on deck they stood unsteadily, clutching the gunwale for support, as they watched flying fish skip from wave to wave and porpoise jump. By now they were almost certain they were headed for the penal colony of Australia but for how long and what might happen to them there was still a mystery. They did not care anyway. They were dying from the terrible thirst and the scurvy starting to spread among them. They believed they were not going to make it to anywhere and they wished they were dead.

Two things saved them. First the captain changed course away from the African coast to re-cross the Atlantic in order to find more favourable winds and make a long tack around the Cape of Good Hope. Two months after leaving Quebec City, on November 30, this tack took the *Buffalo* to Rio de Janeiro, which became the only stop on the long voyage. Boats came alongside selling fruit cheaply and, with the help of their guards, the prisoners were able to buy some of it with small amounts of money they had managed to conceal or by bartering what little clothing they had left. The captain also bought some fruit for them with the money he had confiscated. The ill were kept below during the ship's four-day stay in Rio, but the fruit juices rumbled in their dry guts and their health visibly improved.

Yet another bad storm, soon after leaving Rio, turned into a lifesaver for some of the convicts. The bucking and rolling, almost as bad as in the storm in the Gulf of St. Lawrence, caused the old ship to spring a serious leak. All hands, including those prisoners who were able, were

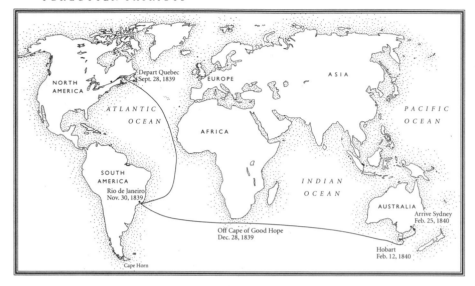

The voyage of the Buffalo *from Quebec to Sydney – almost 16,000 miles in 150 days.*

put to the pumps. The health of these prisoners improved as the exercise drew clean air into their lungs and hardened their withered muscles.

But almost half of them remained horribly ill, unable to leave their bunks even for a short spell on deck. Their condition was so wretched it moved two soldiers to bring some of them a little water in which they had mixed their ration of rum. The soldiers were caught one day in the act. They were hustled immediately on deck and flogged.

In fair winds, the ship rounded the Cape and then ploughed or drifted through the alternate storms and doldrums of the Indian Ocean. And now conditions for the sick convicts improved. As the destination approached they were given a little more water and some lime juice to help stop the ever-spreading scurvy. With some string, a hook and meat-bait, the crew caught some albatross and gave the prisoners small amounts of their meat, which tasted like fish. The surgeon insisted they be allowed on deck for longer periods. They were too feeble and dispirited now to try to take over the ship, he argued. And he was right. The prisoners drank in the sun for several hours a day, heavily guarded, with some mutterings among the Americans of another attempted mutiny, but no strength or will to do anything about it.

One day in the early part of February, a sentry casually remarked to a group of prisoners, "Well, we'll soon be in port."

"What port?" the prisoners asked in chorus.

"Hobart Town, Van Diemen's Land," the sentry replied. Most of the prisoners had never heard of the place.

On the *Buffalo* on February 8, 1840, a shout of "Land ho!" was heard from the masthead and soon the wretched cargo caught a brief glimpse of a mountainous place before a sudden strong wind blew the ship beyond its sight again. For two days it tacked into this wind, trying to make the Derwent River, finally dropping anchor in Hobart's harbour on February 10, four months and twelve days after leaving Quebec City.

Officials boarded the boat and questioned each prisoner closely. What were their names, ages, trades, birth-places, religions, whether married and if so where lived their wives, how many children, their sex and ages, whether their parents were alive, their ages, religions and residences, what amount of education, whether they could read and write, what scars did they have on their bodies and, lastly, for how long were they sentenced?

None of them knew the answer to the last question.

"Put down 'for life,'" the senior official ordered his clerk.

The next day the French Canadians were told they would be remaining on board and eventually taken to Sydney, then somewhere else, while the Americans and Upper Canadians were bundled into a large boat and rowed ashore.

There a large and curious crowd awaited them. "Why, they look just like our men," remarked one astonished woman in a carriage. "They are white, too, and they speak just like our men."

Then roars of laughter erupted in the crowd as the strange "Yankees" stepped ashore and the ground started to heave beneath them, the result of their weakness and long months at sea, and they stumbled and fell and some had to crawl along, too weak to stand on a land that seemed to rise and fall and roll like the waves.

"Come along, come along, you lazy crawlers, creep on, creep on," blue-coated constables shouted at them.

They had not gone far when they passed four scaffolds, with four men on them about to be executed. A little farther along, beyond the town, they passed a gang of about 200 half-naked men, working the road in heavy chains, and then another gang, without chains.

"We thought this was an ominous reception," William Gates wrote in his diary. "Such sights, and the supposition that such might be our fate, served to sink the iron still deeper in our souls." [11]

CHAPTER 7

Botany Bay

From distant climes o'er widespread seas we come,
Though not with much eclat or beat of drum,
True patriots all; for be it understood,
We left our country for our country's good.

FROM "THE RECRUITING OFFICER," AUSTRALIA'S
FIRST PLAY, PERFORMED BY AN ALL-CONVICT
CAST IN 1789

*W*hat sort of place was this where the skinny, ragged, weary men
rolled and staggered off the *Buffalo* to join the few who had arrived
eight months earlier in the *Marquis of Hastings* and one month earlier
in the *Canton*? What could they expect here? Most had no idea. Some
of them had some vague knowledge of Australia, but few would have
heard until a few months before of the small, even more isolated island
off the southernmost tip of the Australian continent, where they stumbled ashore to the sight of chain gangs and gallows. It is likely that none
of these Canadians and Americans had even the faintest idea of the
harshness of the Australian penal system or its beginnings.

The cruel system they now entered suffered its terrible birth pangs
in the tumbledown slums, the class structures, the ignorance of the aristocracy and the filthy, disorganized, overcrowded jails of late eighteenth-century England. There the rich, the propertied, the noble and
many of the merchants lived well under the Georgian roofs of their
London mansions and in sprawling manors on their country estates,

educated enough to read Samuel Johnson and Edmund Burke, healthy enough to ride to hounds, cultured enough to spend a decent part of their earnings or inheritances on the arts.

However, there was another England as described by Robert Hughes in his classic on the Australian convict system, *The Fatal Shore*. Most rural Englishmen were struggling to survive in thatched shacks on farm wages of a few shillings or less a week. Most Londoners lived in tiny tenements on dirty lanes so narrow they seldom saw the sun, where sewers ran into open drains, stank and spread disease. Newfangled machines lowered their already low wages and created massive unemployment. Trade unions were suppressed and there were no wage guarantees so sweated labour was the standard. Men died young with the muck of industry in their lungs or they went blind with it in their eyes. Some old ladies eked out a living gathering dog droppings in the streets and alleys for use in making bookbinding leather. Children went to work at six years of age. They were beaten with straps or sticks if they failed to produce their quotas. Some of the child slaves, considered incompetent or cheeky, had heavy weights hung to their ears.[1]

But gin was cheap. In the middle of the century in England there was a gin shop for every 120 people. To drown their miseries, hopelessness and sense of injustice, the poor drank eight million gallons a year of the potent, white grain spirit, in much the same way that Soviet citizens, two centuries later, drowned somewhat similar disaffections with excessive amounts of vodka.

In the circumstances a great many of these underprivileged English men and women turned to crime and, in a country afflicted by class structures, a criminal class emerged. Patrick Colquhoun, in his *Treatise on the Police of the Metropolis (1797)*, estimated that one Londoner in eight, about 115,000 people, were living off crime in the city and that the city contained 50,000 "harlots" – about 6 per cent of the population.

Because of the unemployment and poverty, this enormous amount of crime was sometimes necessary for survival and often it was easy, because there was no proper police force in England until Robert Peel's

Police Act of 1829 created the "Bobbies." Instead the parishes and wards employed parish watchmen, usually old men too feeble for other work, who were easily bribed with a few pence or a slug of gin to look the other way when a thief was about his business. Other criminals were brought before the courts by paid informers or by "thief-takers" – private entrepreneurs who played both ends against the middle by reaping official rewards for bringing alleged criminals to trial or bribes for not doing so.

There were many hangings, mostly at the gallows at Tyburn in London, and these were attended sometimes by 25,000 to 30,000 people, jostling for the best view, selling from fruit stalls, hawking pamphlets alleged to contain the last testament of the man or woman about to be dangled. Scalpers made small fortunes selling the best seats. In the years 1779-88 there were 1,152 capital convictions in London and Middlesex and 531 executions.

The hangings did not create much more room in the crowded jails. Men and women were packed into these dark holes together, as were hardened criminals and first offenders, young boys and homosexual rapists. Some of the jails were privately owned, by dukes and even bishops, but there was no attempt at reform at all. The prisoners were chained to the floor, with spiked collars around their necks, until they were able to pay a fee for "easement of irons" demanded by jailers, who could load any prisoner with as many chains as they pleased and charge for their removal one at a time.

For a while another cruel custom helped ease the overcrowding a little. Convicts under commuted death sentences, most of them common criminals, were sent across the Atlantic to the New World, where they were put to work on the pioneer farms and plantations. English jailers sold them to shipping contractors, who then sold the rights to their labour to plantation owners. This was the first form of the punishment of "transportation beyond the seas," and in the mid-1700s, 30,000 men and women from Great Britain and 10,000 from Ireland helped ease the terrible overcrowding of their homeland jails by working unpaid, virtually as white slaves, in places like Massachusetts, Virginia and the sugar plantations of Jamaica and Barbados.

But then, in 1775, the American colonies rebelled. The British could no longer send their surplus convicts there. So, as a temporary measure, they jammed them into old hulks of troop transports and men-o'-war in the Thames and other naval ports, like Portsmouth, where the Canadian and American rebels paid their brief visit to the *York*. These hulks were rotting at anchor, falling apart, swarming with rats. On them the worst or most unfortunate of the criminal class rotted too, their bedraggled numbers constantly increasing, marched ashore in the daytime to work in chain gangs on the docks or roads.[2]

Meanwhile almost as far away as possible from all this, in March of 1770, an English navigator, Captain James Cook, was heading home in his ship *Endeavour*, a 106-foot converted Whitby collier, after charting the coast of newly discovered New Zealand, when he was blown by

Prison ship at Deptford, 1826. When the rat- and disease-infested hulks like this one became overcrowded, British authorities started sending convicts to Botany Bay. (National Library of Australia, Canberra)

southerly gales towards a flat, unpromising, previously unknown shore. He anchored in a wide bay and was met by some black inhabitants, whom he described as poorly armed, backward and timid. He also found the shores to be teeming with strange plants and animals, unrecognisable even to the skilled botanist on board, Joseph Banks. Banks and some young colleagues collected 3,000 species of which 1,600 were completely unknown to science. They called the place Botany Bay.

When Cook told the people of England about this hot and dreary place, on the shores of a country now called Australia, Englishmen regarded it as the end of the earth, the most remote place imaginable, an unreal land inhabited by primitive Indians and grotesque animals and covered by weird plants. The strange stories Cook and Banks told when they came home were eighteenth-century science fiction about a place farther away than the sun and the stars.

But the stories created only a brief sensation. For more than a decade, until Pitt the Younger became prime minister in 1783, Englishmen forgot about the desolate, science fiction place. By then the eyesore hulks were overflowing and the rabble was rioting in some of them. MPs from Plymouth and Portsmouth were demanding enforcement of transportation sentences to get rid of the hulks in their constituencies. But Britain's defeat in the American Revolution prevented any more transportation to the New World, and many people pressured Pitt to start new penal colonies in South Africa or Madagascar, or even at the very end of the earth, at the place called Botany Bay, although no Englishmen, apart from Cook and his crew, had ever seen the place, let alone surveyed it for suitability as a settlement for convicts or anyone else.

Pitt's cabinet was desperate. In the summer of 1786, after the African alternative sites had been investigated and found unsuitable, and as more and more skinny, ragged prisoners were being shot and killed in hulk riots, it opted to empty the hulks by banishing their occupants to the unknown, to the Land Beyond the Seas, where the weird animals hopped and the strange plants grew.[3]

About eighteen months later, at three in the morning of Sunday, May 13, 1787, eleven small ships weighed anchor on the motherbank outside Portsmouth Harbour. They were bound for Botany Bay, a journey expected to take eight months. Their cargo of about 750 convicts had already been on board for two months, confined below decks for almost all of that time. They were pale, thin, hungry and hardly alive. Even before the ships sailed, typhus had killed eleven of them and was spreading. The ships had been undervictualled by a crooked contractor, who switched a half-pound of rice for the daily pound of flour per prisoner he was supposed to supply.

Only two of the vessels were naval warships, the rest converted merchantmen, and the largest of the transports, the *Alexander* was only 114 feet long and 31 feet in beam, about as big as one of today's larger racing yachts. Yet their total complement, including officers, seamen, marines, women, children and convicts, was almost 1,500. The prisoners' quarters had no portholes and the headroom in one of the larger transports, the *Scarborough*, was only four feet, five inches, so that a grown man had to bend double to get to a sleeping space of about six feet by six feet for every four transportees.

Pitt's cabinet made an unusual choice for the leader of this convoy. Captain Arthur Phillip, forty-eight, was on the navy's semi-retired list and had been living contentedly as a gentleman farmer at Lyndhurst when he was told he was about to become governor of New South Wales, the name now given to the area around Botany Bay, and that the people he was to govern were all criminals. He was a solitary, self-effacing man and he seemed to believe that at least some of the convicts might be reformed.

He was also a good sailor and he complained bitterly about the lack of space, food and proper equipment and particularly about the conditions on the women's convict ship, the *Lady Penrhyn*. He wrote to his political masters: "The situation in which the magistrates sent the women on board the *Lady Penrhyn* stamps them with infamy – tho' almost naked, and so very filthy, that nothing but clothing them could

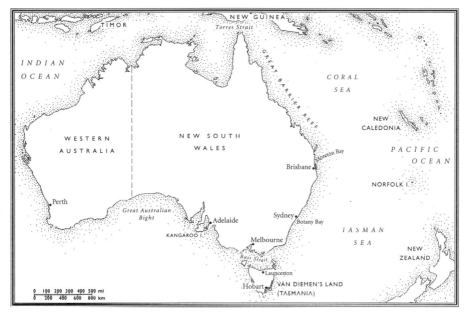

Australia. The state divisions are as they were in the days of the convict camps.

have prevented them from perishing, and which could not be done in time to prevent a fever, which is still on board that ship, and where there are many venereal complaints, that must spread in spite of every precaution I may take hereafter."[4]

The convicts' average age was about twenty-seven but there was a nine-year-old chimney sweep, John Hudson, among them. He was convicted of stealing some clothes and a pistol. Another young boy, James Grace, eleven years old, was sentenced for stealing ten yards of ribbon and a pair of silk stockings. The oldest female convict was Dorothy Handland, eighty-two, a rag dealer who was up for perjury, while the youngest girl was Elizabeth Hayward, a clogmaker, aged thirteen. She had stolen a linen gown and silk bonnet worth seven shillings.

Almost all their crimes involved theft, and many were obviously the result of desperate need. Thomas Hawell, a labourer, was sentenced to seven years for "feloniously stealing one live hen to the value of 2d., and one dead hen to the value of 2d." One Elizabeth Powley, twenty-two,

Captain Arthur Phillip. He commanded the "First Fleet" of eleven small ships that carried about 750 male and female convicts from England to Australia in 1787. The convicts became Australia's first white settlers and Phillip was the colony's first governor. (Mitchell Library, Sydney)

who crept into a kitchen in Norfolk and took small amounts of bacon, flour, raisins and butter, was sentenced to hang but reprieved and shoved onto one of the ships. A hungry West Indian named Thomas Chaddick earned his passage to Botany Bay by sneaking into a kitchen garden where he "did pluck up, spoil and destroy, against the form of the statute" twelve cucumber plants.[5]

There were others on board who had committed less trivial crimes, highway robbery and robbery with violence, for instance, or fencing, swindling and forgery. Most had no training for anything but crime and they were not successful at that because they had been caught, sometimes several times, before their sentences to transportation. There were a few seamen, carpenters, shoemakers and bricklayers among them, but in all they were a questionable lot to pioneer an unknown land.

The prisoners were not told where they were going. Most had never been on a ship or even a small boat before. Except for a few hours on deck on some days, they were chained below in their cramped, hot, airless quarters as the ships went through violent storms where the huge breaking waves of the Indian Ocean towered above the crosstrees and foamed down on the decks. Then, through the humid, tropical doldrums Phillip rationed water to three pints a day and vermin crept out of the woodwork and up from the stinking bilges rolling with dead rats, vomit, dung and urine. The women on the four female transports – *Charlotte, Lady Penrhyn, Prince of Wales* and *Friendship* – could be bought by the marines for a pannikin of rum. Many women were often drunk and unruly and were frequently flogged. Some male convicts were flogged unmercifully as well, but marines who broke discipline were flogged even worse, with up to 200 lashes.

When it dropped anchor in Botany Bay, this small, unlikely armada, which came to be called the First Fleet, had completed one of the great sea voyages of history across more than 15,000 miles of ocean in 252 days without losing a ship. (It stopped in several ports for supplies.) Forty-eight people had died – forty convicts, five convicts' children, one marine's wife, one marine's child and a marine. But in view of the adversity of the voyage and the conditions on the ships, this death rate of a little over 3 per cent was small and a credit to Captain Phillip, the nonentity who was now to begin duty as the first governor of the unknown place. Phillip and his red-coated companions found that Botany Bay was nothing like Cook had described it. The Bay was open and unprotected. Its shore was barren and the startled natives were at first unfriendly, although they soon succumbed to curiosity and to gifts of beads and ribbon. Most of the curiosity centred on the sex of the strange invaders who covered their bodies. The surgeon on the *Lady Penryhn*, Arthur Bowes Smyth, recorded in his diary:

I presented many of them wt. Glass Beads & several Gentlemen put Ribbands & Glass Trincketts abt. their heads but they seemed altogether a most stupid insensible set of beings – they seemed most desirous of Hats from their attempting to seize the Hats of many persons on shore. They seemed to express a Wish to know of what Sex we were and several of the persons onshore satisfied them in that particular. – When they found we were men like themselves they expressed their joy and astonishment by loud Exclamations & grotesque gestures, & immediately shook hands with us.[6]

Even as these first Australian exhibitionists were buttoning their flies on the beach, Phillip decided Botany Bay was no place for a convict or any other sort of settlement. He left with a small party of marines to explore Port Jackson, a few miles to the north, which had been named by Cook, but not entered, as the explorer sailed by in 1770. And there Phillip and his men found one the finest harbours in the world, with hundreds of coves that could anchor a thousand ships, where trees grew thickly along the shores and streams of fresh water flowed. Soon the First Fleet was on its way from Botany Bay, some of the ships colliding as they tacked in a light, adverse breeze, and after a few hours they dropped anchor in the beautiful Port Jackson, or as they would soon call it, Sydney Harbour.

Almost immediately, the male convicts were taken ashore to clear some land at Sydney Cove and build some primitive shelters. But it was two weeks before enough tents and huts were ready for the female convicts. When the longboats finally came for them, those women who had some decent clothes put on all their finery, so that some could even be described as well-dressed.

As soon as they stepped ashore a tremendous orgy erupted. The male convicts chased the women and either seduced or raped them. Some women chased the men as well. At the same time a mighty storm rumbled and lit the scene with lightning. The sailors on the ship demanded an extra ration of rum, then joined the hectic activities ashore. Surgeon Bowes Smyth wrote in his diary:

The Men Convicts got to them very soon after they landed, & it is beyond my abilities to give a just discription [sic] of the Scene of Debauchery & riot that ensued during the night.... The Sailors

in our Ship requested to have some Grog to make merry wt.
upon the women quitting the ship indeed the Capt. himself had
no small reason to rejoice upon them all being safely landed &
given into the Care of the Governor, as he was under the penalty
of 40 pounds for every Convict that was missing – for wh. reason
he complied with the Sailors' request, & abt. the time they began
to be elevated, the Tempest came on –

The Scene which presented itself at this time & during the
greater part of the night, beggars every description; some swearing, others quarrelling, others singing, not in the least regarding
the Tempest, tho' so violent that the thunder shook the Ship exceeded anything I ever before had a conception of.[7]

Thus a great drunken orgy heralded the start of Australia's colonial
history. A long and terrible hangover followed. The First Fleet carried
enough supplies to keep its crew and human cargo alive for about two
years, but it was poor food and had to be strictly rationed. The officers,
sailors, marines and convicts barely survived on the same monotonous
diets of salt meat and tough johnny cakes. At first, the male convicts
got one-third less than their guardians, and the female convicts two
thirds of the male ration, but then Phillip, in face of even more desperate shortage, ordered equal rations for prisoners and guards alike.
There were plenty of fish in the harbour but the Englishmen accepted
this alternative protein infrequently and under protest. The first attempts to grow crops failed. The livestock brought on the ships died.
Only about a third of the convicts could work, as a result of feebleness,
scurvy, age, incurable illness or, because of their slum upbringings, an
absolute ignorance of farming. Women prostituted themselves for a
cupful of flour. Men on the work gangs traded their clothes for food
and worked in the tropical sun as naked as the aborigines. Some punishments for food theft were 300 lashes and six months in chains. One
man drew 1,000 lashes for stealing three pounds of potatoes. He was
literally skinned alive. Wild dogs devoured the chunks of flesh that flew

from prisoners' backs as the lash landed. And the marines suffered almost as much as their uniforms wore away and they went about barefoot. A supply ship, the *Guardian*, carrying a further two year's cargo of food and stores, struck an iceberg and limped into Cape Town, where she was abandoned.

Then in June 1790, almost three years after Phillip had landed in Sydney Harbour, the Second Fleet arrived. It brought little food, however, and four shiploads of misery. Almost a quarter of the more than 1,000 men and women who had embarked had died at sea, the result of brutality or because they were too sick to sail in the first place. The English authorities had used this fleet to rid the hulks and prisons of invalids. Half of those who remained alive were seriously ill and had to be assisted ashore, where they collapsed.

One convict, Thomas Milburn, described the voyage in a letter to his parents, which was later circulated in England as a broadsheet:

[We were] chained two and two together and confined in the hold during the whole course of our long voyage.... [We] were scarcely allowed a sufficient quantity of victuals to keep us alive, and scarcely any water; for my own part I could have eaten three or four of our allowances, and you know very well that I was never a great eater.... [When] any of our comrades that were chained to us died, we kept it a secret as long as we could for the smell of the dead body, in order to get their allowance of provision, and many times I have been glad to eat the poultice that was put to my leg for perfect hunger. I was chained to Humphrey Davies who died when we were about half way, and I lay beside his corpse about a week and got his allowance.

The arrival of the Second Fleet did not help the situation. Nor did the Third Fleet, which landed in 1791, carrying 1,864 convicts, who, wrote Phillip, "were so emaciated, so worn away" that they were unable to work. One man in ten had died on the way.

Somehow the colony survived all this. Sydney grew into a small town as a succession of governors, some brutal, some relatively kind, arrived on the distant shore along with more and more of England's trash, a few political prisoners and the rum-sotted, scarcely trained scum of the British army who were the convicts' keepers.

In time new penal settlements, tougher and even more sadistic, were established at places like Norfolk Island, a tiny, harbourless jungle of huge pines off Australia's east coast, where the French Canadian *Patriotes* were supposed to go, and Van Diemen's Land, where the Canadian and American convicts went.

From 1787 to 1810 about 9,300 men and 2,500 women were transported to this lush but terrible land to suffer the worst of the conditions. About 50,200 convicts, mostly hardened criminals or second offenders, arrived in the next twenty years, and then from 1831 to 1840 a total of 51,200, more than in the previous two decades, were hustled ashore, almost all to remain for the rest of their lives, with men outnumbering women, over this whole period, about six to one.

The system peaked then as the colony developed and free, skilled or semi-skilled settlers arrived, diminishing the value of convicts as slave-labour, so that between 1841 and 1850 transportation to New South Wales virtually stopped while about 26,000 convicts were poured into Van Diemen's Land, jamming the system and creating much new brutality until transportation was eventually abolished there in 1853. Then its ashamed free settlers immediately changed the island's name in the hope of burying its fiendish image. In honour of its Dutch discoverer they named it Tasmania.[8]

CHAPTER 8

The Cruel Shores

Oh! my country, the stranger has found thy fair clime,
And he comes with the sons of misfortune and crime;
He brings the rude refuse of countries laid waste,
To tread thy fair wilds and thy waters to taste;
He usurps the best lands of thy native domains
And thy children must fly or submit to his chains.

FROM A "NATIVES LAMENT," IN THE *COLONIAL*
TIMES OF VAN DIEMEN'S LAND, 1826

*T*asmania hangs from the body of Australia like a heart-shaped pendant, separated from the mainland by the treacherous Bass Strait. Far to the south lies the next mass of land, the frozen, white Antarctica. The first Europeans visited in 1642, almost exactly 200 years before the Canadian and American convicts were thrown on its dismal shore. Two Dutch ships, the *Heemskerck* and the *Zeehaen*, under the command of the navigator Abel Tasman, anchored off a rugged coast which Tasman believed to be a part of a mysterious great southland that had been touched though not explored by a few other Dutch mariners since the start of the century. His expedition had been organized in what is now Indonesia by the governor-general of the Dutch East India Company, Anthony van Diemen, who had instructed him to map "the remaining unknown part of the terrestrial globe." Tasman had not done very well. His orders were to sail from Batavia to Mauritius then south and east until he found the southern land mass. But he sailed too far south before turning east so that he never caught sight of the mainland of what is now Australia. He thought he did, though. He thought this wild coast where the two ships anchored was part of the great southern land, whereas, in fact, it was an island about the size of Ireland off the extreme southeast of the mainland. The wild place did not impress him and his crew. The land looked poor and though there were some signs of habitation, no natives appeared. Tasman wrote little about the place in his journal. But he named it after his sponsor, Van Diemen's Land.

This faraway, unpromising island was largely forgotten until the beginning of the nineteenth century when French explorers began to take a mild interest in the area around it, and American whalers ventured nearby. These threats to British sovereignty, now established at the penal colony of New South Wales on the Australian mainland, caused Governor Philip Gidley King to send, in August 1803, a party of forty-nine freemen, soldiers and convicts to start a settlement on the Derwent River near the southern extremity of the island. They were followed soon afterwards by a group of about 300 convicts, with a few wives and children, guarded by marines under the command of David Collins, a marine officer and former judge-advocate of New South Wales. This group had first been sent to settle Port Phillip Bay, site of the present city of Melbourne, at the southeast extremity of the mainland, but they had almost starved there, living in the end on a diet of lobsters. So they were happy to be ordered to move on to the Derwent.

Their diet did not improve. No food ships arrived at the small settlement they built on the Derwent's banks, which they named Hobart Town. They existed for a time on boiled seaweed scraped off the rocks, which they called "Botany Bay greens." Then they discovered kangaroo meat. The island was full of kangaroos and every man, convict and free, who could use a gun, began to hunt them and eat their tough but flavourful flesh in order to survive. They competed against the native population for the big, bounding animals, often shooting the aborigines instead of the roos. Because the great hunger put guns into the

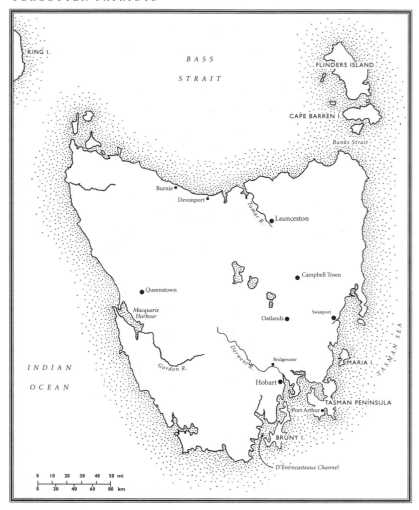

Van Diemen's Land, the island jail now known as Tasmania.

hands of convicts, the settlement became a lawless place. Gangs of vicious men developed who could survive weeks in the bush, eventually to give birth to the tradition of criminal bushrangers. Normal strata and morals of society disintegrated, to be replaced by murder, thievery and prostitution. Van Diemen's Land began as an evil place and remained so for a long time.[1]

To this demented isle, in the next half-century, the British sent tens of thousands of convicts and provided roughly an equal number of free settlers so that on average there was a population of about 30,000 convicts and 37,000 citizens who were "free and without stain."[2]

They survived among tough, natural beauty, in a bracing climate, somewhat similar to England's, with a mountain and lake or river almost always within eyesight. The heavy rains that filled these waterways also created lush grazing and growing land on cleared plateaus a thousand and two thousand feet high. Thick forest originally covered almost all of the island, mostly gum trees, the brilliant yellow wattle, beech and pines. In some parts, where the rainfall was over a hundred inches a year, the tall trees combined with grass trees, tree ferns and horizontal shrubs to make almost impenetrable jungles. When the convicts from Canada arrived in 1840, there were only two towns, the capital Hobart Town at the mouth of the Derwent River in the south, and Launceston in the valley of the Tamar in the north. These towns, about 140 miles apart, were linked by a good convict-built road on which a few villages had sprung up; the most important of these was Oatlands. The population was then about 50,000, about evenly split between free and bond.

Soon after the North American convicts were hustled and bullied ashore, falling down from their lack of land-legs, they found that the lieutenant-governor controlling the colony and their destinies also had North American connections. He was Sir John Franklin, the noted Arctic explorer, whose experience with Australia had started when he sailed in 1801 as a boy in the *Investigator,* captained by his uncle-by-marriage Matthew Flinders, to chart the long coast of the Great Australian Bight at the bottom of the island continent. Subsequently, as a young man he fought gallantly under Nelson at Trafalgar, then in 1819 led a tragic overland expedition across the frozen Canadian tundra that was marred by murder, cannibalism and his own near-death from starvation, but also the successful survey of more than 200 miles of the icy shoreline east of the Coppermine River; and then he made a sec-

Sir John Franklin, the Arctic explorer who was lieutenant-governor of Van Diemen's Land from 1837 to 1843. The Canadian convicts considered him an oaf and referred to him as "Old Granny."
(Toronto Reference Library)

ond, better organized and more productive overland expedition in 1825-27 that resulted in the mapping of 400 miles of Arctic shoreline and a hero's welcome and knighthood when he returned to London.

Franklin's image was different in Van Diemen's Land. He did not seem to be any sort of a hero to the convicts from Canada. To them he appeared as a grossly overweight, indecisive, incompetent oaf, with a halting manner of speech and the ruddy face of a heavy drinker. Two days after they staggered ashore from the *Buffalo,* Franklin paid them a visit at their stockade at Sandy Bay and William Gates recorded in his journal:

> The next Monday we were to be honoured with a visit from his bulkiness, the *great* Sir John Franklin, who once navigated into the northern seas, and came near perishing of starvation. It was about nine or ten o'clock when he was discovered approaching. We were immediately mustered out, duly arranged, and in-structed in mysteries of that etiquette which behoved men of low degree, crushed down to the earth, to observe in the presence of

those who, clothed with British power, have therefore a right to lord it over God's heritage and their fellow men....

The gate of our enclosure was opened and we hailed Her Majesty's Lieutenant-Governor of the island of Van Diemen's Land and its dependencies.... For myself I was amused at the *great* man's appearance, for whether he was great in the mental qualities, he was truly great in all that makes the man, physically – flesh and blubber.

His head was chucked down between his shoulders ... whilst the stomach made equal advances towards the head.

The vital organs were so much encroached that they found it exceedingly difficult to keep the old man in sufficient wind, which came puffing from his brandy bottled nose, like steam from the escape pipe of an asthmatic boat.

After much aheming and hawing, the old man began. I cannot convey any just conception of his speech. He was at least two hours in delivering what any American schoolboy could have spoken extemporaneously in twenty minutes.... The Queen's English suffered not a little – for his words were spoken in half

Lady Jane Franklin, who spent much of her life promoting her husband's hero status and was criticized by the settlers of Van Diemen's Land for her interference in affairs of state. (Tasmaniana Library, State Library of Tasmania)

finished sentences, with stammering pauses between that exceeded the sentences themselves, and his language was excessively poor and tautological.... Whether the great man was a profound scholar or not, I had no means of ascertaining. If he had ever obtained celebrity, the sight of us Yankees must have completely unstrung his faculties, for he made more blundering work of his business than a dullard.

The substance of his harangue seemed to be: that we were bad men – very bad men – were sent there for a very bad crime – rebellion – one of the worst crimes that could be – worse than murder – didn't know what to do with us – guess should put us on the roads awhile – work good for us – should send home for orders – send home to know what to do with us – at present put us on probation – if we behaved well on probation, get rewarded for it.

Even allowing for the natural hostility of a convict to a figure of authority, this was a damning description of the Arctic hero, and the same contempt is echoed, only a little less colourfully, in some of the other convict narratives. The Canadians frequently referred to Franklin as "Old Granny."

Franklin also won little respect from most of the free settlers, who regarded him as a guileless weakling, dominated by his aggressive, intelligent second wife, Lady Jane Franklin, who spent much of her life promoting her husband's hero status. The settlers objected to Lady Jane's constant interference in affairs of state, though many of her contributions to the welfare of convicts and the island's cultural affairs were admirable. Her most notorious initiative was an attempt to rid the island of snakes by offering the convicts a shilling a head for all they could catch and kill. This was highly popular among the prisoners, who captured about 12,000 snakes at a cost to the treasury of £600 before the program was stopped. There were more snakes in the grass than shillings in the coffers.

Franklin was eventually called home in disgrace in 1843 as a result of a brutal condemnation of his administration by his colonial secretary, John Montagu. There, in order to restore his reputation, and despite his fifty-nine years and poor physical condition, he begged for a chance to make another dangerous journey to the Arctic in search of the fabled Northwest Passage through the vast, frozen archipelago that stretches from the North American mainland toward the North Pole. His wish was granted but his ships, *Erebus* and *Terror,* were lost. Not one of the 129 crewmen emerged from the Arctic to tell the story of the voyage, and scores of expeditions have since attempted to solve what has become one of the world's most enduring mysteries. In the six years between 1848 and 1854 more that £760,000, a huge amount in those days, was spent in the search for Franklin and his men, and in 1850 alone a dozen major expeditions were involved in the search. They continue today and are producing evidence of scurvy, cannibalism, and, most recently, lead poisoning.

The writings of the North American convicts in Van Diemen's Land indicate they had part of this great mystery of the missing ships and men solved well before Franklin's last voyage even began. In their minds he was almost completely inept and not physically fit enough to run a penal colony from a comfortable mansion, let alone command a small ship in a dangerous, icy ocean. Some historians go to some lengths to defend Franklin's performance in the penal colony.[3] But the North American convicts in his care so distrusted his administrative and leadership skills that they would not have voluntarily crossed the Derwent River with him in a rowboat.

Franklin was not really in charge of Van Diemen's Land anyway. His predecessor, Colonel George Arthur, by now Sir George Arthur, lieutenant-governor of Upper Canada, still was. His rules remained in force. His officials, including some relatives, were still there, running the place as he had taught them. His monument, the Port Arthur Prison, flourished with a grim severity that was to made it part of Australian folklore. Arthur may now have become the almost benevolent lieutenant-governor of Upper Canada, but his severe, bureaucratic spirit remained in Van Diemen's Land.

The early governors of Van Diemen's Land were an odd lot. The second, after the hungry marine officer David Collins, was Lieutenant-Colonel "Mad" Tom Davey, who ruled the colony from 1813 to 1817 and marked his ceremonial arrival at the Hobart docks by staggering to the ship's gangway, staring blankly at the shore and subjects of his new realm, and emptying a bottle of port over his wife's hat. The third, Colonel William Sorrell, lieutenant-governor from 1817 to 1824, was a good administrator but was personally unpredictable. He abandoned his wife and seven children and, to the shock of the colonial society, installed another woman, a Mrs. Kent, in Government House as first lady. She bore him several more children. It was Arthur, the fourth lieutenant-governor, who stayed longest – over twelve years, from May 1824 to October 1836 – and left the most infamous mark on the inglorious place.

Before his appointment, Arthur managed to persuade the Colonial Office to turn Van Diemen's Land into a colony separate from New South Wales and to frame his commission so that he held almost dictatorial power. He had the title of lieutenant-governor, but was in fact governor because he reported directly to London rather than through the governor in Sydney.

Arthur was tall and stooped, stern-faced, cool and aloof, clad almost always in dark clothes. He seldom smiled and frowned on people who drank or danced or went to the horse races, although he was known to take an occasional glass of port. When he and his wife, Elizabeth, the mother of his seven sons and five daughters, entertained, they did so reluctantly and with tea. There was no jollity. An evening at the Arthurs' was often filled by scriptural readings. In his previous administration in British Honduras (Belize), Arthur had been visited by God, so he was a devout evangelical Christian, who firmly believed he had been put on earth to impose his values on others. His political and social views were extremely conservative and he detested democracy.

During his later incarnation as lieutenant-governor of Upper Canada, some ultra-conservatives regarded him as more or less able, upright and even merciful, but Lord Durham, the governor-general, found him "full of littleness about etiquette, precedence, official dignity etc.," and Durham's successor, Charles Poulett Thomson, described him as "well intentioned, but with the narrowest mind I ever met."[4]

Arthur had had an undistinguished military career, fighting mainly in some successful battles against Napoleon (and being twice wounded) before he was appointed superintendent and commandant of the British settlement on the coast of Honduras in 1814. At first he was popular with the white, slave-owning elite of the small Central American settlement, but his authoritarian manner and the rigid way in which he enforced regulations soon turned the settlers against him. He did show some signs of humanitarianism by trying to provide legal protection for the slaves, and even decided to free some he believed to have been illegally enslaved. But these moves angered the slave owners and led to more opposition to his rule. Arthur responded by dismissing his opponents from office and attempting to make the settlement's system of government less democratic. When he went back to England on leave in 1822, the settlers lobbied successfully against his return. He also lost a court action brought by his military commander, Lieutenant-Colonel Thomas Bradley, whom he had dismissed for disobedience and imprisoned in 1820. Bradley was awarded compensation, and a confidential report from Sir Herbert Taylor, secretary to the commander-in-chief, the Duke of York, criticized Arthur for his "most tyrannical, arbitrary and capricious conduct." Nevertheless, after lobbying hard for the job, Arthur was sent to Van Diemen's Land with almost unrestricted powers.[5]

And he used them. Arthur turned the island into a police state, with police and spies who reported directly to him, a muzzled press and restrictions on free assembly. He kept for himself the right to assign convicts as free or cheap labour and refused to assign them to any settler who offended against his strict regulations. It was all highly bureaucratic and systematic. He set up seven levels of punishment between the extremes of freedom and the noose and allocated them according to good or bad behaviour. They were, in ascending order of severity, the holding of a ticket of leave, assignment to a settler, labour on public works, labour on the roads near civilization, work in a chain gang, banishment to an isolated penal settlement, and penal settlement labour in chains. A convict with a seven-year sentence could apply for his ticket of leave after four years of good behaviour; a fourteen-year convict, after six years; a lifer after eight.[6] But they were still imprisoned because Arthur regarded the whole island as a jail for convicts and freemen alike. He believed criminals suffered some form of mental illness, but could be reformed and that transportation was "the most effective, as well as the most humane punishment that the wit of man ever devised."[7] And he sent many hundreds of men and women to the gallows.

Some historians have argued over the exact number of death warrants Arthur signed during his reign, but a contemporary in Van Diemen's Land, Jesse Morrell, who was for some time the American consul in Hobart, testified:

I was perfectly acquainted with the administration of Col. George Arthur and himself particularly. During his governorship of (almost) thirteen years he signed the death warrants for fifteen hundred and eight persons, only eight of whom were saved from the gallows by being sent to a penal settlement to work in irons. I have seen nine hanging from the same scaffold at the same time, and fourteen in one week.... I also saw two natives executed after a mock trial, in which they had not the least consciousness of what was going on.... These executions took place on a scaffold he had erected in sight of his own dwelling.[8]

Yet Arthur was not wantonly cruel. He was an ambitious, bureaucratic, conservative, pompously pious martinet, who believed he had a tough job to do and did what he could to please his faraway bosses in

London. Convicts were not people to him, but numbers in thick, black-covered ledgers he kept in immaculate order. The hangings of those who broke his rules were part of his duty to London and to God.

Arthur's biggest problem during his long reign in Van Diemen's Land was increasing conflict between the white settlers and the black indigenous population. He solved it in his usual bureaucratic way.

Nobody knows how many original inhabitants of the island existed when the white man came, or where the dark-skinned, broad-nostrilled blacks, who differed in several marked respects from the aborigines of the Australian mainland, had themselves originated. Their number has been estimated as high as 8,000 and as low as 700. Probably there were around 2,000 of them. They may have come over a prehistoric land bridge from the Australian mainland, or by canoes which they destroyed and never learned to build again. Some experts claim they were once Papuans, others say they were Melanesians, still others "Negrito half-castes with the Dravidian Australians." What is known is that they had survived in the hills and forests of the rugged island for centuries, disdaining material possessions, uninterested in agriculture, leading a nomadic life in pursuit of game and shellfish, building no permanent habitations and wearing little if any clothing. Yet studies have indicated they were in no way the intellectual inferiors of those who tried to bring them "civilization."

In their first contacts with the white invaders they were friendly. When treated with respect, they were also respectful. They had a sense of humour, a sense of dignity. They did not like liquor and their women were unwilling to prostitute themselves to the white visitors. They had no idea about the ownership of property, but they were willing to share their food and they liked to sing.

The visitors came from a different context. They came from a world where property and status were of primary importance to some, but the lives of others not of much value; where those considered inferior human beings were treated little differently than beasts, a four-year-old child could be forced to work like a horse in the mines, and a man could be sent away forever for stealing a loaf of bread; where the average lifespan of lower-class city males was twenty. These visitors brought with them muskets, liquor, venereal diseases and their brothers in chains. They were, according to Australian historian Clive Turnbull,

men to whom the mystical operation of running up a flag conferred ownership in all such land around it as they might desire, men to whom all those different in colour and habit from themselves were "savages," and by whom all resisting savages might with justice be expelled....

They prepared to recreate the conditions of their homeland. It was the golden age of imperialism. The spirit of adventure, heavily supported by economic pressure, sent the Englishman questing abroad, nor must these pioneers be denied, whatever the defects of some of them, their general qualities of hardihood and courage. To these men "savages" (foreigners) were obstacles to be overcome, in no way differing from the obstacles of ocean, storm, forest and barren soil; that savages might have rights was no more part of their belief than that oceans and thunderstorms had rights.[9]

When the food ran out in the early days under Lieutenant-Governor Collins, the colonists and their dogs invaded the natives' hunting grounds, looking for kangaroo. While they were at it they also hunted the natives and raped their women. Black men were flogged with kangaroo hide cats, burned with brands and even roasted alive. Women were enslaved, men shot and children destroyed by dashing out their brains. Some bushrangers bound aborigines and used them for target practice. One man named James Carrott killed an aborigine, captured his wife, hung the man's head around her neck and drove her before him as his prize. Some of the colonists were said to have killed blacks for dogs' meat.[10]

In the circumstances the blacks began to strike back, when they could, with spears and stones, so that by the time Arthur arrived in 1824

Governor George Arthur's proclamation to the natives of Van Diemen's Land, ca. 1828, promising equal justice, indicating natives would be hanged if they killed a settler, but a white man would also be hanged if he killed a native. (National Library of Australia, Canberra)

they were an unsettling nuisance. His solution was *apartheid*. At first he tried to persuade the settlers to treat the aborigines with compassion, but this did not work, so he declared martial law against them in the settled parts of the island and ordered them, in a proclamation they could not understand, to leave the settled areas and never "to re-enter such settled districts, or any portions of land cultivated and occupied by any person whomsoever, on pain of forcible expulsion therefrom, and such consequences as may be necessarily attendant on it." The idea was to force the aborigines into the wild outlying areas of the island, where they could survive because there was still plenty of game there. Rewards of five pounds were offered for every native captured in the settled areas and two pounds for every child. But this did not work either.

Arthur then decided to enlist every white man on the island – settlers, soldiers and convicts – in a huge concerted effort to force the blacks from the settled areas and drive them to the lonely Tasman Peninsula, at the southeast corner of the island, where they could be bottled up, with garrisons stationed at the peninsula's narrow entrance to make sure they never escaped. So, on October 7, 1830, what came to be known as the "Black Line" was formed. More than 2,000 men of the military and settlers and about 700 convicts, armed with muskets and handcuffs, stretched in a thin line across the island and surged slowly down towards the Tasman Peninsula, hoping to catch all the aborigines in their human net. But seven weeks later when the Black Line converged on the peninsula, the net contained only one man and a boy. A few aborigines had been seen on the way and two were shot, but the rest, with their sensitivity for the bushland, had slipped away.

So then the God-fearing autocrat tried conciliation. He had already appointed an evangelistic emigrant house-builder from London, George Augustus Robinson, to teach the blacks through kindness and compassion the benefits of the white man's ways and his religion, and now, after the fiasco of the Black Line, he gave him his full blessing. With this strong official support, Robinson went about his business with piety, dedication and daring and also, according to historian

Turnbull, "the zeal of a stupid and presumptuous man." He started in 1829 at Bruny Island, a small place in the D'Entrecasteaux Channel, near Hobart, where he tried with some success to win the sympathies of the small black population. But his real work started a year later when he began his adventurous travels through the wilds of the mainland searching for surviving tribes of aborigines. He took with him a few convict servants and a few friendly blacks from the island, including Truganini, "The Beauty of Bruny."

Truganini was a particularly attractive and promiscuous aborigine woman, about eighteen years old (though she was only about four feet three inches tall and had a bit of a beard).[11] She was the daughter of Mangana, "chief" of Bruny Island. As a child, she had seen her mother stabbed to death by a European. Her sister, Moorina, was carried off by sealers and made a sex slave on Kangaroo Island, off the coast of South Australia. Her stepmother was kidnapped by convict mutineers, who tried to take her with them to China. She was never seen again. As a young girl Truganini visited the mainland of Van Diemen's Land, accompanied by her intended husband, Paraweena, and another native man. Two wood cutters, Watkin Lowe and Paddy Newell, offered to row them all back to Bruny Island. In mid-channel the white men threw the native men overboard. When they grasped the gunwhale in an attempt to get back into the boat, Lowe and Newell chopped off their hands with hatchets. The mutilated aborigines were left to drown while the Europeans raped Truganini. She told her story much later when she had mastered English.[12]

Truganini helped Robinson round up as many aborigines as he could find in the wilds and to lead them, like a pious Pied Piper, to Flinders Island, a sandy, barren place, but with an abundance of game, about forty-five miles long and eighteen wide, off the northeast tip of the colony. There he, and Arthur, considered they could live in peace and contentment and, if possible, respect for a God they would soon learn about.

Robinson arrived at Flinders with twenty-six male aborigines, thir-

The last of the Tasmanian aborigines, Truganini, William Lanney and Bessie Clark, dressed in European finery, photographed by J.W. Beattie in 1866. (National Library of Australia, Canberra)

teen females and one infant on January 25, 1832, and settled them at a place called The Lagoons, on the unsheltered side of the island, where violent winds blew cold rain and sleet, near the sandy shore, behind a stretch of dreary tea-tree scrub.[13] By the next year there were one hundred and thirty blacks on the island and thirty whites to "look after" them. They were given clothes and Bibles and some elementary school-

Sir George Arthur was lieutenant-governor of Van Diemen's land for almost 13 years. When he was recalled in 1836, the people of the prison island lit bonfires in celebration. An editorial in one newspaper, the True Colonist, *declared the misrule of his government had rendered the people "wretched, unhappy, discontented and miserable." Another paper, the* News Register, *was a day late with a similar scathing editorial because its printers got drunk celebrating. (National Library of Australia, Canberra)*

ing, but there was nothing active for them to do, so they went about the business of dying. In all, after five expeditions through the mainland by Robinson and his party, always including key-helper Truganini, two hundred and three blacks, all of the surviving tribes and groups, were rounded up and enticed to Flinders Island. In 1832, five died; in 1833, forty, in 1834, fourteen, and in 1835, fourteen. In 1836, there were only 123 survivors.[14] When Lieutenant Governor Franklin visited the island, accompanied by his wife, in June 1844, there were fifty-four aborigines left to greet them.

In 1847, the new lieutenant-governor, Sir William Denison, abandoned Arthur's final solution to the black problem, closed Flinders Island, moved the remaining forty-four aborigines – twelve men, twenty-two women and ten "young people," some of them half-castes – and settled them in the remains of an old penal station at Oyster Cove, near Hobart. There they vegetated and died, drinking much rum, attracting an occasional curious tourist, and more often white sailors and woodcutters looking for sex.

Billy Lanney, facetiously nicknamed "King Billy," who grew up on Flinders Island and was removed, at the age of thirteen, with the remnant of his countrymen to Oyster Cove, was the last man to die. He had been a poor, ridiculed drunk when alive, but members of the Royal College of Surgeons and the Royal Society of Tasmania, fought over his bones when he was dead. A Doctor William Crowther, F.R.S., C.M.Z.S., later a Tasmanian politician, sneaked into the hospital morgue, cut the skin off the head of Lanney's corpse, removed the skull, and slipped another skull from a white corpse into the black skin. This ruse was discovered, however, and members of the Royal Society were "greatly annoyed" at being deprived of their scientific prize. Body snatching was feared so officials cut off Lanney's hands and feet and guards were placed on the grave after Tasmania's last black man was buried, with Anglican rites, on March 6, 1869. But representatives of the Royal Society managed to exhume the mangled body anyway and dissect what was left of the skeleton. It then disappeared. Dr. Crowther sent the skull by ship to the Royal College of Surgeons in London, but he wrapped it in a sealskin, and the bundle stank so much it was thrown overboard.[15]

"King Billy" was gone, along with the rest of the males of his race who had been shot, or brained, or who had just wasted away from drink, disease or foolish bureaucracy, but Truganini, "The Beauty of Bruny," lived on. As recently as the 1950s, old people in Tasmania could recall seeing her in the streets, a tiny, grizzled old lady with a colourful bandanna around her head. She died on May 8, 1876, and her skeleton was for many years on display in a glass case in the Tasmanian Museum. By 1947, feelings of humanity and political correctness caused her bones to be consigned to the museum's basement. In 1976, the centenary of her death, the skeleton was cremated and scattered on the ocean near Oyster Cove. The long era of the Tasmanian aborigines was over.

There are some excuses for Arthur's administration in Van Diemen's Land, and some recent historians have made them.[16] His bosses in London never seemed to know what they wanted so he often had to make bold decisions without advice. Some of these decisions were sensible and during his long reign the colony's economy improved. But, then, so did his own. When he arrived in Van Diemen's Land, Arthur had nothing but his salary and a huge family. When he left he had a fortune of £3,000 (about $15,000) a year from property investments. He, of course, knew of every colonial project in advance and when he had a causeway and bridge built by convict labour over the Derwent River for the Hobart-Launceston road at Bridgewater, he owned most of the land around it. When he picked the site for a new Hobart wharf, he was accused of boosting the value of property he owned next to it by a multiple of fifteen. He and the "Arthur faction," as his friends, relations and supporters were called, were closely associated with the Derwent Bank, the biggest financial institution in the colony, and some of them were rumoured to be lending money at illegal rates of 15 per cent and even up to 50 per cent. Arthur's successive colonial secretaries, John Burnett and John Montagu, were heavily in his debt. So when Colonel George Arthur went home to England for his knighthood, then on to solve the problems of Canada, he was a moderately rich man.[17]

In all of the towns and villages of Van Diemen's Land, the people cheered and drank and lit bonfires in a riotous celebration of his departure.[18]

CHAPTER 9

Convict Life – and Death

"Surrender now, Jim Doolan, you see there's three to one –
Surrender in the Queen's name, you daring highwayman."
Jim pulled his pistol from his belt and waved the little toy,
"I'll fight but not surrender," cried the Wild Colonial Boy.
FROM "THE WILD COLONIAL BOY"

*T*he one-armed superintendent of convicts in Hobart, Ronald Gunn, was six feet three inches tall, weighed about 200 pounds and, according to Benjamin Wait, had a "rough, dare-devil look and a piercing eye and is wonderfully shrewd." He was also a good man, who took a liking to the rebel from Upper Canada and later to Linus Miller, the American law student, and tried as hard as he could to keep them and all the Canadian state prisoners apart from the evil influence of the English murderers, robbers, pickpockets and other scum who were his main responsibility.[1]

Gunn started his life in the convict colony as a lowly lieutenant in the British army and owed his exalted position of convict supervisor to the fact that he lost his arm in a shooting match with Matthew Brady, then the most renowned bushranger of Van Diemen's Land, whose reign of terror and robbery on the island spurred a strange mixture of fear and adulation in a society split almost evenly between convicts and citizens without stain.

Brady, a Manchester boy, had been sentenced in 1820 to seven years' exile in Van Diemen's Land for stealing a basket with some bacon, butter and rice. He considered the sentence unfair and tried to abscond so many times he was forced into the chain gangs and eventually sent to Macquarie Harbour, the most brutal convict jail of the time. In the first four years of his transportation he was given 350 lashes.

Brady escaped from Macquarie Harbour in a whaleboat in June 1824 with thirteen other convicts, reached the Derwent after a voyage of several weeks and came ashore to rob a settler of his guns. Then he and his followers began to range the bush. They become known as the "Brady gang" and were eventually joined by more "bolters" until their number swelled to about a hundred.

They robbed homesteads, often with the help of convict servants who hid them in barns, fed them and told where the master's guns were kept. They took particular pleasure in robbing magistrates renowned for their orders to flog, and when cornered they always escaped, leaving army or police attackers wounded or dead. Often they selected as their victims settlers who had ill-treated their convict servants. They tied such masters to a tree and ordered the servants to flog them with as many lashes as they had received from them. If the servant hesitated, Brady would turn flagellator himself. But Brady was also chivalrous. He would never harm a woman and when one of his gang threatened to rape a settler's wife he shot him through the hand, flogged him and threw him out of the gang. When he heard about a government executioner and flogger named Mark Jeffries, who had been jailed in Launceston because he had kidnapped a settler's wife and newborn baby, then smashed the baby's head against a gum tree when its crying irked him, he had to be talked out of leading his gang in an attack on the jail to drag Jeffries out and flog him to death.[2]

Colonel George Arthur, newly arrived as the lieutenant-governor of Van Diemen's Land, did his bureaucratic best to catch the gang. He issued proclamations calling on all settlers to join in the hunt for them and to order their convict servants to report whatever information

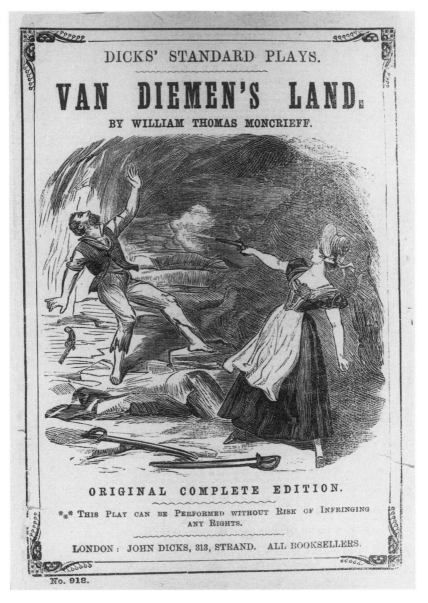

The cover of the play Van Diemen's Land *by William Moncrieff, first published in London in 1831. It depicts a plucky woman shooting a ruffianly bushranger. Bushrangers, convicts who escaped to the bush and preyed on settlers, were the scourge of the prison island, though they were usually gallant to ladies. (Tasmaniana Library, State Library of Tasmania)*

they heard. He posted rewards, first £10 per head for each gang member, then £25. He promised a ticket of leave to any convict who gave information that led to the arrest of any of Brady's boys, and a conditional pardon if he caught the bushranger himself.

But the convicts would rather help Brady or join him. The only result of Arthur's efforts was a notice pinned to the door of the Royal Oak Inn at Cross Marsh:

> It has caused Matthew Brady much concern that such a person known as Colonel George Arthur is at large. Twenty gallons of rum will be given to any person that can deliver his person to me.[3]

Arthur was persistent. He offered new, enormous rewards of 300 guineas or 300 acres of land for free settlers and full unconditional pardons with free passage to England for convicts who caught or helped catch a gang member. He had policemen wearing fetters infiltrate the gang, pretending they had escaped from a chain gang. He enlisted more police and soldiers for the hunt and they began to pick off gang members one by one in bloody skirmishes.[4]

"They were at length surprised by a party of military and soldiers, headed by Mr. Gunn, and nearly all killed or captured," Linus Miller reported in his journal. "During the engagement Mr. G. lost an arm, from a shot by Brady, who generously fired at that limb instead of shooting him through the heart or head, as he might have done had he been disposed. Brady and his comrades were hung, and Mr. Gunn promoted to the important station he has since held."

Before he was hanged at Hobart on May 4, 1826, Brady was celebrated as a hero. Women wept for the "poor colonial boy" who had shown so much courtesy to them and his cell was filled every day with gifts of flowers, fruit and cakes. When his body dropped the common people jeered the executioner and cheered the criminal.

But Gunn was also admired for his bravery and competence and the journals of the Canadian convicts single him out by showing respect, even a liking for him. "He is a man of extraordinary mental powers," Miller wrote. "He has only to see a prisoner once to be able to detect him in almost any disguise for years afterwards. It is said he can call every prisoner in Van Diemen's Land by name when he meets them, tell the name of the ship in which they arrived, the year and day, their original sentences, additional sentences received in the colony, etc., etc; in short, that he never forgets anything."[5]

Gunn assigned the ill and emaciated North Americans from the *Marquis of Hastings* to comparatively easy tasks. Both Samuel Chandler and Benjamin Wait, when he was at last released from the hospital where he recovered from the illness of the voyage, were assigned to the colony's commissary general and sent to his large, lush and lovely farm

A plough gang being whipped at Port Arthur, the toughest of the Australian convict prisons, built by Lieutenant-Governor George Arthur in 1830 on the tip of the Tasman Peninsula in Van Diemen's Land. It was described as an "Earthly Hell" and "an abode of misery." It is Arthur's monument and an Australian icon for cruelty. Some of the Canadian convicts spent time there. (National Library of Australia, Canberra)

near Oatlands, fifty miles from Hobart, where Chandler worked as a carpenter and Wait became a sort of farm manager with considerable responsibilities and teacher to the master's five children.

After the *Canton* arrived, the felons she carried were immediately put to hard labour on the roads, but her four Canadian state prisoners were allowed to idle in the Hobart convict barracks for a few days until Gunn called them to his office; he suggested exercise would be good for them and that they might want to volunteer to sweep the barracks yard for half an hour a day. They all agreed, but Linus Miller, who never knew when he was well off, accepted this gentle treatment in his usual aggressive way. At first he claimed he did not know how to use a broom and then he refused to sweep on Sundays.

It is unlikely that the brash young American could accurately remember a dialogue in detail some years after it occurred, but he wrote in his narrative:

Sunday again came, and after the men were mustered for church, our overseer ordered the four Canadians to remain, as the English prisoners marched off. "Get your brooms," said he, "and sweep the yard." My comrades agreed, but I stood my ground. Bad as the church was, I preferred breaking the Sabbath by going there to sweeping the yard, and the following altercation took place:

"Why don't you go for your broom?"

"I shall not take any half-hour's exercise today."

"The devil you won't."

"Certainly not. It is the Sabbath day, and I can not."

"But you shall, though, by God! I will get you flogged if you don't get your broom at once."

"It is needless to talk upon the subject, for I shall not."

"You will offend Mr. Gunn, who is your friend, if you don't."

"I shall offend my God, who is greater than Mr. Gunn, if I do."

"God Almighty is nothing here compared with Mr. Gunn.

A convict road gang on the way to work in Hobart. Poorly clothed and chained convicts sometimes worked twelve hours a day. (National Library of Australia, Canberra)

Holloa! there, send a constable," shouted the overseer. The constable came and another dialogue similar to the first ensued, which ended in my being ordered to the cells. I led the way and the door being open, walked in. It was a horrid hole, about eight feet long, three and a half feet wide and four feet in height. There was no floor but the mud and filth were more than twelve inches in depth. No nuisance tub was allowed the poor wretches confined there, and sometimes seven or eight were thrust in at a time, to remain from one to three days. No language can describe this dreadful place. I afterwards assisted in cleaning out the same cell, and thirteen barrowloads of filth were wheeled away from it alone.

Such was the place into which I was ordered for refusing to

sweep the yard on a Sabbath day. They closed the door on me and talked together for a few minutes outside, when the constable inquired if I would work, provided they would overlook my offense and not report it to Mr. Gunn, who would certainly flog me. "Fifty lashes," said he, "is the least punishment he ever inflicts for such a crime."

"I shall remain here and take the flogging," I replied. The door, however, was reopened, and I ordered out. "Now," said they, "go to church and be damned to you; but depend on a flogging in the morning," and I went to church.

The next morning I was duly summoned to appear before the great man, of whom the overseer said the Almighty was nobody in comparison. The overseer and constable were there before me.

"I understand you refused to sweep the yard yesterday," said Mr. Gunn.

"I did."

"For which you are liable to be flogged. Have you not read the rules for the guidance of the prisoners here; more particularly with reference to obeying orders?"

"I have read the Bible."

"You are a prisoner and must obey orders or be punished."

"I am a *man* and must not break the commandments of the great Jehovah, who has said, 'Remember that thou keep holy the Sabbath day. Six days…'"

"That will do," interrupted Mr. Gunn. "I understand my catechism."

"I was afraid you did not."

"You deserve a flogging."

"For not working Sunday?"

"For being damned saucy."

"I am not aware that I have given occasion for the use of any oaths."

"Your American independence will not do here. You are in a penal colony and you shall obey orders or be flogged."

"I am sensible of being in Van Diemen's Land, and in bondage too; and it appears there is no Sabbath, no Bible, no God here. Only one week since you told me it was entirely discretionary, with myself and comrades, to work or let it alone. Now, it would seem, we are held as slaves, and required to do the bidding of a depraved wretch, against God and religion. I am in your power; flog me to death if you think proper; I will never work on the Sabbath day; but remember, sir, if you fear not God, that you have superiors, if not here, in Great Britain, who shall hear of this, and who will not, nay, dare not, attempt to justify your conduct. Is it possible that a magistrate, and the principal superintendent of convicts in this colony, will sit in judgement upon, and condemn a man, for refusing to break the commandments of God? Much as I dislike a flogging, I shall glory in it for such a cause. It will cost me pain, but not disgrace."

"Overseer," said Mr. Gunn, addressing that worthy functionary," never ask this man to work again on the Sabbath day, and never show your face here again with any complaint against him." Turning to me, he said, "So long as your conduct continues good, you will find me your friend. Always act conscientiously, and you need not fear anything in Van Diemen's Land."

After this I went regularly to church, but my comrades were always required to get their brooms and sweep the yard.

Miller was soon transferred to Brown's River Station, a logging camp on the Derwent River, where the English inmates were forced to carry huge logs on their shoulders for long distances over rough ground. However, he suffered this hard labour for only a few days before he was appointed to the easy job of night watchman. But again this was not good enough for him. After a month of comparative laziness for the young American, the *Buffalo* arrived at Hobart with its full shipload of North American prisoners, and despite the friendly advice of convict superintendent Gunn, Miller applied to join them. And when he did he removed himself from Gunn's kindliness. Lieutenant-Governor Franklin had received no instructions about what he should do with political prisoners, like these now arriving in his care in large numbers, and it is probable that he eventually overruled Gunn's leniency and ordered that they be treated the same as the felon convicts from England.

In any event, after William Gates and the other American and Canadian prisoners staggered from the *Buffalo* past the gallows and the lines of skinny men working in chains on the shores of Hobart's harbour, they were imprisoned at Sandy Bay Station, a collection of about ten heavily guarded huts a mile or so from the town. Here they were given convict clothing and fed with small rations of meat covered with large maggots.

They were put on probation, the first and cruellest stage of a Van Diemen's Land convict's existence, in which they had to prove through hard labour for the government that they deserved at least a small amount of mercy.

The labour was indeed hard and Gates's job was typical. He literally worked like a horse. His main job was hauling a heavy cart, six feet long, four and a half feet across and two feet deep, loaded with rocks or dirt. He was one of a team of four men attached to the cart by leather yokes and their daily quota was ten loads each drawn for a mile. So they hauled the cart twenty miles a day, sometimes through thick mud and up and down steep slopes. The most difficult part was trying to control a loaded cart while descending a hill.

Gates survived this but some doing lesser labour had serious troubles. Orrin W. Smith, captured in the Battle of the Windmill, a small man who owned considerable property in the States, with the soft

Flogging of a prisoner in Tasmania. Contemporary pencil sketch. (National Library of Australia, Canberra)

hands of one who had never done any manual labour in his life, was forced to swing a heavy pick even after all of the skin from the palm of his hand and inside his fingers vanished. When he was finally allowed to put the pick down, great chunks of his flesh stuck to the handle. Lysander Curtis, another American, also a fighter in the Battle of the Windmill, who had been sick for several weeks, collapsed while wheeling a barrow full of dirt, but a cruel overseer ordered him to work on. He collapsed again after a few minutes and fell on his barrow, unable to move. There he was forced to lie until the end of the shift, when Gates and his team were allowed to haul him back to the camp in their cart. He died two days later in hospital in Hobart. Then, in the third week of this labour, William Nottage, another American, blew himself to bits while tamping a blasting charge.

In the next year Gates was moved, with other North Americans, from station to station in the southern part of the island, specializing in his work as a replacement horse or ox. He worked under some tyrannical overseers, once served seven days in "solitary" – a box about six feet by six feet with no windows – on a daily allowance of a pound of "damper" (a crude, unrisen bread) and a pint of water, and witnessed many lashings, although he, despite threats, suffered none himself. Nor, apparently, did any of the other "Canadians."[6]

Gates, whose treatment was typical of the others', described one flagellation he witnessed at a prison station called Jerusalem:

This man was sentenced to seventy-five lashes for taking to the bush. As the flagellator was tying him to the triangle he remarked to him: "Well, Sandy, you can do your duty to me, for I have no crown nor half-crown to pay for light strokes, and if I had, I don't know as if I should let you have it." This speech rather piqued the man of the cat, who was a fierce fellow to punish, and who had the reputation of being the most cruel flagellator on the whole island. Whilst the man was being stripped for the punishment, I noticed he conveyed a musket ball, which he happened to have, from his pocket to his mouth – for what purpose, at the moment I could scarcely imagine. It was usually the custom, particularly when the prisoner was to be severely punished, that the doctor should stand by and intimate where the strokes should fall. The flagellator seemed to gather up his energies for the task, and truly did he do the tyrant's work most effectually. Never had I seen, of all the flagellations that I had witnessed, one that equalled it in barbarity. Sandy applied the cat with what strength he was able, every blow of which made the blood gush, and as he drew back the instrument at each blow, he would pass the cat through his left hand, from which the blood would drip in streams. The victim's back was a raw, mangled piece of flesh, from which the blood had run in such quantities as to fill his shoes till they gushed over. Yet through it all he never emitted a groan or a word, or even scarcely cringed. At the close of the punishment the bullet dropped from his mouth, compressed and dissevered into several fragments, and when he was unloosed he could not stand, but had to be conveyed to the hospital, where he remained five weeks.[7]

But there were some kindnesses, too. Occasionally, as Gates hauled his cart out of sight of his guards, a sympathetic settler dropped a batch of damper, a few pounds of mutton or a stick of tobacco where he could pick them up and hide them. Sometimes guards allowed him to trap a kangaroo for eating and once a settler gave him a skinny old he-goat which he cooked and hid away in the bush.

An order that eventually came from England kept the Canadian prisoners together and usually apart from the "oldtimers" – the British criminals who stole their clothing and what little else they possessed at every opportunity. Once, when Gates' shoes had worn away and he was hauling his cart over sharp stones with rags wrapped around his bloody feet, a magistrate pulled two half crowns from his pocket and told his guards to buy him new shoes. And one overseer, a reformer named Sherwood, who had been in England during the Canadian rebellions and heard much about them, actually plotted to find a ship on which Gates and others might escape. However, the prisoners eventually talked him out of his plan as it involved too much danger to himself.

So they slaved on. Gates hauled his cart twelve hours a day and sometimes more, his feet still bleeding, his ill-fed body aching as it wasted away.

Under the system imposed by Arthur, the Canadian convicts were supposed to endure this horrible fate for six years, then, if they had good records, be given tickets of leave and assigned to work for settlers for small wages. But on the other side of the world the indomitable Maria Wait was kicking up an awful fuss on their behalf.

As soon as she heard her husband was being sent as a convict to Van Diemen's Land, Maria renewed her vow to join him there. She had no money even for the first stage of the voyage to England, and again she had to face leaving her infant daughter.

"Could I leave my child?" she asked in a letter to a friend. "I could not take her with me and should I join my husband in his exile my heart must yearn for my absent child. Could you, my dear friend, but imagine the heart rending effect of these sad reflections.... I made it subject of prayer to God by day and in the vigils of the midnight hour continued my supplications for guidance and direction while pressing my dear babe to my breast."[8]

At Haldimand, the Honourable William Hamilton Merritt, who had developed the Welland Canal that connects Lakes Ontario and Erie, gave her letters of introduction and $20. The people of Dunnville took up a collection for her and Reform leader Marshall Bidwell, who probably introduced the label "Family Compact" to Canadian politics, and was now exiled in New York, gave her advice and opened his purse. American sympathizers contributed $300. And she bargained for a passage from New York to England for $75, which was $25 less than the usual fare.[9]

In England she organized women's prayer meetings for the convicts. She called on Lord John Russell, who presented a petition to the Queen. She enlisted the aid of the great prison reformer Elizabeth Fry, who wrote to Lieutenant-Governor Franklin in Van Diemen's Land. She tried to see the Queen herself but could do no better than win the support of Lady Barham, one of her ladies in waiting, who "most kindly laid the matter before Her Majesty." Queen Victoria, Lady Barham reported, "expressed herself as being much touched with the circumstances and was pleased to say she would consult her ministers on the subject, when should it be deemed practicable, she would be glad to listen to the application and grant the request though it is most difficult to act in these matters." She again badgered Lord Durham, who was now back in England, and received sympathetic replies to her letters, and she pestered friends of Franklin, including the arctic navigator Sir John Parry, to send letters to him. When the Queen was married that February, she appealed for a special royal pardon for her husband and Samuel Chandler.

"I have besieged the government on every hand, had the best of influence which I think must eventually prevail, if otherwise I will endeavour to reach the land of their captivity and do something for them though I must leave my dear child and friends in America," she wrote.[10]

She ran out of money and went to work as a companion to an elderly widow, Mrs. Ellis. In order to support herself when she got to Van Diemen's Land, she joined the Home and Colonial Infant School Society to learn their teaching methods. Then she received a letter from Lady Barham, stating that nothing could be done at present for the prisoners and that "the Queen regrets her inability to remove the cause of your distress."[11]

This increased her determination to travel to Van Diemen's Land, but the many influential contacts she had made in England tried hard to convince her it would be madness. She would do more good for her husband and child, they argued, if she went back to Canada instead and petitioned the governor-general, Poullett Thomson, armed with the letters of introduction they would give her. They also offered to pay her passage home. So, after ten months in England, she reluctantly returned to America, though she promised, in a letter to her husband, she would still join him, with their child, if she had no success with the Canadian authorities. "Cheer up," she told him. "Rise superior to surrounding circumstances."[12]

Back in Canada she wrote to Governor-General Thomson but received only a verbal reply from an aide. She wrote again and received a reply promising some leniency for her husband and perhaps a ticket of leave, but not the pardon she wanted. So she went to Kingston to appeal to Parliament and to Thomson in person. More than fifty members supported her cause and Thomson received her personally and expressed sympathy. In the end the House asked the government to act on Maria's petitions and a plea was sent by the Canadian government to the British government and the Queen urging them to consent to a pardon for Benjamin Wait.[13]

Nothing happened about pardons, however. Not then, anyway. But gradually, because of her efforts, all the Canadian state prisoners in Van Diemen's Land were given tickets of leave. William Gates and the other almost dead human horses were able to throw off their yokes after only two years of hard labour instead of the usual six. They regarded Maria Wait as a saint. American convict Daniel Heustis wrote in his journal:

Her devoted and heroic services, embalmed in all our hearts, shall be handed down to other generations as a bright example of conjugal fidelity and active philanthropy, worthy of an immortality of honour.[14]

CHAPTER 10

The French-Canadian Convicts

Shall fathers weep and mourn,
To see a lovely son
Debas'd, demoralized, deformed
By Britain's filth and scum.

ANONYMOUS RHYME ABOUT

NORFOLK ISLAND

*W*ith the arrival of the *Buffalo* at Hobart, all 154 Canadian state prisoners condemned to transportation had reached Australia, but the fifty-eight French Canadians still had some distance to go.

These farmers, doctors, lawyers and tradesmen had prayed a lot as the *Buffalo* bucked and wallowed its way through three oceans. According to François-Xavier Prieur, as they awoke after their first night in the dark, almost-airless hold, bruised and gasping for breath, they heard the sounds of anchors being weighed. "With common accord," he wrote, "we went down on our knees and began to say together the morning prayer, a practice that we faithfully observed, morning and evening, throughout the whole length of the voyage."

They had more reason than they knew to appeal for heavenly help. Unknown to them, officialdom had assigned them as far away as possible from the gentle family values and religious fervour of the land they loved. They were headed for the "Isle of the Doubly Damned," that hot and awful place officially named Norfolk Island, where second and third offenders were sent to suffer the worst of punishments, where sadism ruled, sodomy and male rape were normal, and the murder of another inmate and subsequent trial in Sydney the only means of escape.

Norfolk Island, a thousand miles off Australia's east coast, is splendid in scenery, with huge vine-covered pines towering higher than 150 feet over most of its thirteen square miles. It is also a natural jail. It has no harbour, so that visitors must come and go from anchored ships in small boats. Its steep, ragged cliffs are surrounded by reefs on which the long Pacific waves roll and boom monotonously, so that any attempt by an unskilled sailor to leave is just a short voyage to a watery grave.[1]

In the beginning, in the late 1770s, when the British discovered and took possession of this lonely place, they hoped that the huge, straight pines would make spars for ships and the flax plants that grew profusely on its shores would make sails so that Britain's all-important navy and merchant fleet would be independent of foreign suppliers. But the Norfolk Island pines proved to be short-grained and lacking in resin. They snapped like dry twigs. And the convict labour available for a flax industry was unskilled and able to produce only small quantities of coarse canvas. So just one British ship, the *Buffalo*, on which the French-Canadian exiles suffered and prayed, was equipped with these expensive and unreliable products before the island's single industry became the constant infliction of cruelty on a population consisting entirely of convicts.

Over its years as a penal settlement, the commandants of Norfolk Island seemed to be chosen expressly for their sadism. The second commandant, one of the more notorious, was Major Joseph Foveaux, a man with a passion for military correctness, who had been rapidly promoted within the New South Wales Corps, apparently through influence in England. When he arrived on the island late in 1800 he found it swarming with wild and illiterate bastard children, about 200 of them, or roughly a fifth of the population. Most buildings were falling down. There were no decent tools. The master carpenter had been suspended for laziness and the schoolmaster was in jail for debt. Clearly something had to be done and Foveaux went about doing it his way.[2]

He put the convicts to work from dawn to dusk breaking at least five cartloads of stone per man. If they slowed down, complained or broke their poor-quality tools, they were flogged with unmerciful severity. An expression of pleasure spread over Foveaux's face as he watched these almost constant floggings. His head jailer, a transported highwayman named Robert Jones, who had received a conditional pardon, wrote:

The flogger was a County of Clare man, a very powerful man and [he] took great pleasure in inflicting as much bodily punishment as possible, using such expressions as "Another half pound, mate, off the beggar's ribs." His face and clothes usually presented an appearance of a mincemeat chopper, being covered in flesh from the victim's body. Major Foveaux delighted in such an exhibition and would show his satisfaction by smiling as an encouragement to the flogger. He would sometimes order the victim to be brought before him with these words: Hulloa you damned scoundrel, how do you like it? and order him to put on his coat and immediately go to his work.

One prisoner named Joseph Mansbury was flogged so often that his back, according to Jones, appeared quite bare of flesh and he went about his forced labour with his exposed collarbones "looking very much like two ivory polished horns."[3]

In Foveaux's time women convicts were chattels. The island's bellman, named Potter, had acquired the right to sell them as they stepped from the ships that brought them from Sydney. A young, good-looking girl was worth as much as ten pounds when she arrived but she might be sold several times during her sentence, her price decreasing to a gallon or two of rum as her health and looks deteriorated,

A flogging at Moreton Bay, from a pamphlet by William Ross, The Fell Tyrant; or, the Suffering Convict, 1836. Wild dogs ate the flesh as it flew from some convicts' backs. (State Library of New South Wales, Sydney)

which they did rapidly. The sales were held in an old store, where the women were forced to strip naked and run around the room while Potter described their values, like an auctioneer at a cattle sale.

Every Thursday evening a dance was held in the soldiers' barracks where, according to Jones's diaries, the women performed "the dances of the Mermaids." Stripped naked, and with numbers painted on their backs so their admirers could recognize them, and plied with copious amounts of rum, they competed to see who could perform the most obscene gestures.

And they were flogged. Robert Hughes wrote in *The Fatal Shore*:

Women on the mainland or in Van Diemen's Land were rarely flogged, but such punishment was common on Norfolk Island and, indeed, appears to have been Major Foveaux's special treat. "To be remembered by all there," [James] Mitchell [an ex-missionary turned trader] alleged, "was his love for watching women

149

in their agony while receiving a punishment on the Triangle.... It was usual for [him] to remit a part of the sentence on condition that they would expose their nakedness it being part of the punishment. And poor wretches were only too glad to save their flesh and pain." With his pistol in one hand and cutlass in the other, Foveaux would muster the male convicts in a semicircle; the naked woman was compelled to walk past them before she was trussed up to the triangle and the "skinner" or "backscratcher" [Norfolk Island cant for the flogger] went to work. The usual sentences were 25 lashes, the "Botany Bay dozen," but they could go as high as 250. The last Norfolk Island woman to be flogged on Foveaux's orders, in 1804, received such a sentence, but the flogger was squeamish about it; he said he was sick and [chief constable Edward] Kimberley had to take the cat-o'-nine-tails, "upon which," as Jones described it, [he] "cried out that he did not flog women. This reply made the major furious. He then asked one of the soldiers, Mick Kelly by name, to take the tails and go on with the punishment, which he immediately proceeded to perform in such a manner that not one mark was left on her back. This made the Major so wild that he ordered the woman to be placed in the dark cells for fortnight."

Only the soldiers and guards had the company of the convict women, however. For the rest, as more sadistic commandants followed Forveaux, the system nurtured sodomy, then known as "the unspeakable crime." On Norfolk Island, according to some reports, two-thirds of the population were implicated in homosexual activity. At night the male convicts, usually about 800 to 1,000 of them, were isolated in their dingy jail from dusk to dawn, without lights or supervision by officers.

"At night the sleeping-wards are very cess-pools of unheard of vices," reported Thomas Naylor, who was chaplain on the island from 1841 to 1845. "I cannot find sober words enough to express the enormity of this evil.... I watched the process of degradation. I saw very boys seized upon and lost; I saw decent and respectable men, nay gentlemen ... thrown among the vilest ruffians, to be tormented by their bestialities."

Naylor was writing of the time when the religious, naively rural French Canadians were to spend their time on Norfolk. There was a brief period after 1840 when a reformer, Alexander Maconochie, an idealistic Scot, became commandant and tried to bring some civilization to the island, but his influence did not last long and he was replaced by Major Joseph Childs, of the Royal Marines, a vicious, indecisive military hack, whose main order was to stamp out the "unspeakable crimes."

Thomas Rogers, an Irish curate posted to Norfolk Island in 1845 as its sole religious instructor, claimed that Childs had 26,024 lashes inflicted in the last sixteen months of his command. "The ground on which the men stood at the triangles was saturated with human gore as if a bucket of blood had been spilled on it, covering a space three feet in diameter and running out in various directions in little streams two or three feet long. I have seen this," Rogers reported.

But some of the convicts were tough. They were known as "iron men," who expressed their contempt for the lash by suffering the most severe punishments without a flinch. One, in Childs' time, had an order to the "skinner" tattooed on his back: FLOG WELL AND DO YOUR DUTY. So Childs and his underlings devised methods of torture that had more effect on them. These included the "tube-gag," a wooden plug strapped into the victim's mouth so that he could breathe only, with great difficulty, through a small hole in the wood; the "spread-eagle," often used in combination with the gag, in which the prisoner was ironed to three ringbolts, face to a wall, arms fully outstretched, feet together, and left in this crucifixion position for as long as eight hours; the "scavenger's daughter," in which the convict was bound with his head against his knees and left until he passed out from the pain of cramps; and the "water-pit," an underground cell with waist-high salt water, where men were left in darkness for days on end, unable to sleep for fear of drowning.

Such was the place where the fifty-seven French Canadians, and the one unlucky American among them, were going.[4]

After the *Buffalo* reached Hobart and the American and English-speaking Canadian convicts were taken ashore, its sails were hoisted again for the voyage to Norfolk Island, with a stopover in Sydney on the mainland for supplies and further instructions. The winds were strong and favourable and the ship reached Sydney after only four days. And there, soon after the anchor dropped in the magnificent harbour, two men in flowing black robes clambered unathletically up the shipside on rope ladders and, after speaking briefly to some officers, moved down the narrow companionways into the dark hold.[5]

The prisoners gathered around these apparitions while the older one, a stout man wearing small, round, steel-rimmed spectacles, still puffing and panting from his exertions, spoke. "I know each one of you, my sons," he said. "You are my children. You've been torn from the Church in Canada, but entrusted, henceforth, to the care of the Church in New South Wales."

This was John Bede Polding, Bishop of Sydney, who had received letters from the bishops of Canada informing him of the possible arrival of the exiles.[6] His companion was Father John Brady, an Irishman who spoke French fluently.[7] The bishop spoke only briefly, and in less fluent French, but he said he would be back the next day with more priests to hear confessions. He prayed for the bedraggled, skinny group in their threadbare clothes and gave them his blessing. He prayed with even more than his usual fervour, because he knew what the prisoners did not know – that they were on their way to the Isle of the Doubly Damned. Then back over the side he went with Father Brady in tow, the two of them almost toppling several times into the harbour's still, blue waters.

Ironically the church hierarchy in Lower Canada had been supporters, in fact a part, of the establishment against which the rebels had risen, but yet the bond of the faithful had overcome this political tech-

Bishop John Bede Polding, a Benedictine, became the first Bishop of Australia in 1834. His work with Catholic convicts in the colony was credited by the authorities for a decrease in crime and general improvement in law and order. He saved the French-Canadian convicts from a much worse fate. (Mitchell Library, Sydney)

nicality and spread across the far ocean. Some of the French Canadians thought their prayers had finally been answered. "There is no necessity for me to attempt to express the comfort that this holy visit brought us, since these lines are especially intended to be read by my fellow countrymen, Canadians, children of the church, inheritors of

Father John Brady, an Irishman who spoke French fluently, helped Bishop Polding cater to the spiritual needs of the French-Canadian convicts. He later became Bishop of Perth in Western Australia. (Mitchell Library, Sydney)

the piety of glorious ancestors," François-Xavier Prieur wrote in his journal.

Bishop Polding returned the following day with Father Brady and another missionary priest and heard confessions. He also announced that he had received permission from the authorities to celebrate mass and administer Holy Communion in the dark hold that had been the rebels' cell for nearly five months now. So the French Canadians busied themselves constructing a small altar from packing boxes in the one small space in the hold where a man could stand upright. And on the morning of the next day, February 27, 1840, Polding and the missionary priests scrambled up the ladders again, carrying lacy cloth to cover the crate box altar, candlesticks to burn on it, and a golden chalice. They said mass and gave communion. And then, sitting on a box, the bishop gathered the exiles around him. He began to prepare them for the worst and he pulled no punches.

"Bishop Polding told us that he did not believe that he should conceal from us that there was a rumour current to the effect that we were to be sent some hundreds of miles from Sydney, to a little Island named Norfolk, christened in the colony with the name of 'Hell on Earth,'" Prieur wrote. His journal continues with bitter sarcasm:

It seems that certain philanthropical institutions associated with the Canadian Government of the day had created an impression of us as exaggerated as it was vile; that, added to the effect produced by the lying and cruel articles in certain English newspapers published in Montreal, sent out to New South Wales, created the impression that we were personally linked up with bandits ready to attempt anything and to carry out the greatest outrages without a shudder.

The other priests then addressed the French Canadians, imploring them to accept, in God's name, the terrible fate that awaited them. They all prayed together again. Then the grim-faced clergymen clambered down the shipside.

Prieur wrote:

The time of departures of these worthy ministers of religion seemed to us a veritable break; but already, inured to distress and misfortune, and strengthened by the bread of life, we prepared ourselves for the worst, practically certain that we were to be sent to Norfolk Island. We were resigned to everything, in spite of every difficulty in accommodating ourselves to the idea of taking our place amidst the vilest and most corrupt that the three kingdoms could supply.

Bishop Polding was a good priest. He was also a good politician, and with a growing Catholic population in the colony he had some power within the establishment. He had convinced himself, in his talks with the men on the *Buffalo*, and through their confessions, that they were not bad men and that Norfolk Island would completely destroy them. So, immediately on leaving the ship he marched, robes swirling, to Government House, where he demanded to see the governor himself.

The God of the French Canadians must have heard their many prayers because the governor, Sir George Gipps, a hero of the Peninsular War, was a prudent man with a degree of humanity not known in many of his predecessors. He was also, by a strange coincidence, the only Britisher in the colony with an intimate knowledge of the situation in Lower Canada. Shortly before his appointment to New South Wales, he had been a member of a parliamentary commission of three – the others were the Earl of Gosford and Sir Charles Grey – sent by the British prime minister Lord Melbourne to Lower Canada in 1835 to try to discover the basic causes of the discontent of the *Patriotes*. The commission made many liberal recommendations, walking a fine line between sympathy for the French Canadians and support of the colony's anglophone minority.[8] So Gipps knew the problem and the type of person now exiled to his new jurisdiction. And the horrors of Norfolk Island haunted him. Nevertheless, he was loathe to accept this new batch of convicts in Sydney, where the economy was ailing, unemployment among ex-convicts high, and the convict system being phased out and transferred to places like Moreton Bay, near Brisbane, and especially Van Diemen's Land.

Also, the attitude of the Canadian government and derogatory newspaper reports about the Canadian convicts created a political problem for him and he worried that the bishop's contrary judgement of this particular group as mild and decent men might be the result of a bias based on their religion. Still, he agreed to consider the bishop's impassioned pleas.

Meanwhile the rebels sweated on the ship in the harbour, attacked by hordes of mosquitoes of a size they had never seen before, convinced they were about to suffer an evil fate of buggery and brutality, something almost beyond the imagination of men of their religious and family backgrounds.

Officials came aboard and questioned them. Others examined their bodies for identifying peculiarities, opening their mouths to inspect the few teeth they had left.

"Following this second ... inspection, we were again led back into our hell-hole, where we racked our brains trying to guess what it was intended to do with us, as a result of all these proceedings and of this prolonged detention in our floating prison," wrote Prieur. "All this confirmed us in our opinion that we were to be sent to the 'Hell' of which the Bishop of Sydney had spoken."

Bishop Polding went back to Government House several times, finally agreeing with Gipps that he would personally guarantee the good conduct of the Canadians and accept responsibility for any wrongs committed by them if they were allowed to remain in Sydney.

"It was a responsibility extremely difficult to be assumed by this excellent Bishop, who knew us only by the goodwill letters written in our favour by the Canadian prelates," Prieur wrote. "But his charity triumphed over his uneasiness and he saved us from the horrible fate that was awaiting us."

After two weeks in the port, on March 11, an official climbed on board and ordered the exiles to prepare to go ashore. They packed their few possessions in minutes and at last left the *Buffalo*, struggling down rope ladders into a small boat, which set sail to the west end of the harbour and up the wide Paramatta River until at about two in the afternoon they came alongside a jetty at a place called Longbottom.[9]

"There," according to Prieur, " we were conducted under a military escort, about a mile away from the river's bank. Our luggage loaded in carts drawn by oxen accompanied us on the journey. We were so weak, so worn out, and so shaky on our legs that this short mile walk, taken at a slow pace, made us so tired that it gave us all pains in our limbs, pains that persisted with several of us for a few days."

But they were not on the Isle of the Doubly Damned. And back at his manse, when he heard of the Canadians' landing, the Bishop of Sydney prayed his thanks.

CHAPTER 11

Escapes

Was it for this I braved the ocean's roar,
And plied those thousand leagues the lab'ring oar?
Or rather had I stayed, the willing prey
Of grief and famine in the direful bay!
WILLIAM PARSONS IN A POEM ABOUT
CONVICT ESCAPEE MARY BRYANT (1792)

*T*he impatient Linus Miller could not wait for his ticket of leave, even though he knew it would be granted early. He was going to use his Yankee ingenuity, of which he boasted often, to defeat his ignorant jailers and confound the colonial convict system. He planned to escape from Van Diemen's Land and go home. So did some of the other North Americans.

Escape seemed impossible but desperation can drive people to incredible acts of daring or foolishness; there was a long history of attempted flight from the penal system on the mainland, and "bolters" were common in Van Diemen's Land, where they took to the hills and became bushrangers.

Despite the tremendous odds, some actually made it to freedom abroad, but most did not. They perished at sea in little boats or shrivelled up from thirst and hunger on brutal treks across the Australian deserts on the way, some thought, to China, where they would be met by yellow maidens bearing tea and opium.

In 1791, one woman, Mary Bryant, from Fowley, in Cornwall, who had arrived in Sydney with the First Fleet after stealing a cloak, led a group of absconders, including the husband she had married in Australia, her two small children and seven other convicts, on a voyage in a small stolen boat from Sydney to Timor, a distance of 3,250 miles in less than ten weeks. This journey was comparable to that of Captain William Bligh in his longboat after the mutiny on the *Bounty*. Several times the escapees were blown far out to sea, where thirst and starvation almost killed them. When they were washed ashore, half dead, on islands of the Great Barrier Reef, they had to fight with hostile aborigines. On the last leg of their voyage they were chased by cannibals in sailing canoes.

When they reached Timor, the Dutch governor put them in detention until a group of British sailors, whose frigate had hit a reef off New Guinea while pursuing mutineers from the *Bounty*, appeared from the sea in their lifeboats. They clapped the convicts in irons and shipped them in a Dutch East India vessel to Batavia, where Mary's husband and one of her children died of a fever. The survivors were then shipped to Capetown but three of the men died on the way. Mary Bryant, her three-year-old daughter, Charlotte, and the remaining four convicts were put on board a British man-o'-war carrying a marine detachment back from Australia to London, but the little girl died and was buried at sea. And when Mary Bryant finally reached London in mid-1792 she was sentenced as an escaped felon and thrown into Newgate prison to await a transport ship and another trip to New South Wales.

But word spread about her incredible voyage and the popular press trumpeted stories about "the Girl from Botany Bay." The humane writer James Boswell took up her cause and pressured top government officials to pardon her, which they did in May 1793. Boswell then gave her an annuity of ten pounds and she went back to Cornwall, where she vanished from history. Her four surviving companions were also pardoned and one of them immediately enlisted in the New South Wales Corps and set sail again for Botany Bay.

Nobody escaped from Port Arthur. It was reached only by a narrow peninsula guarded by vicious dogs. Here Sir John and Lady Franklin inspect the line of dogs during a visit to the jail. (Mitchell Library, Sydney)

Some groups of convicts hijacked big ships and their crews, occasionally with success. Others stowed away and were dropped off on lonely Pacific islands to end their days as beachcombers.

The most notorious escapee in Van Diemen's Land was a pockmarked little Irishman named Alexander Pearce, who arrived there in 1820 after stealing six pairs of shoes in County Monaghan. He was assigned as a servant but continued to steal from his masters, got drunk and frequently ran away, sometimes surviving in the bush for as long as three months. In 1822, he was sent to Macquarie Harbour on the island's west coast, then the cruellest, most isolated, and most closely guarded of the prison settlements.

On September 20, 1822, Pearce stole an open boat, helped seven other convicts aboard, rowed across the harbour and ran with his companions into the dense bush. The others were Matthew Travers, an Irishman serving a life sentence, Robert Greenhill, a sailor from Middlesex, William Dalton, an ex-soldier (fourteen years for perjury), Thomas Bodenham, a highway robber, William Kennelly, transported for seven years then resentenced to Macquarie Harbour for an escape attempt, John Mather, a Scottish baker who forged a money order, and a man called "Little Brown" whose Christian name is unknown.

They struggled through wild, mountainous terrain where hundred-foot trees sprouted from gaps in steep rocks, ferns and vines clutched at their feet and gales and sleet froze their thinly covered bodies. After a week they had finished the rations they had brought with them. After a few more days they began to straggle and scatter, weak from hunger and cold.

According to later depositions by Pearce, Greenhill first suggested they should kill a man and eat him and the man should be Dalton because, he said, he had been a flogger. There was some argument against this but when Dalton was asleep, about three in the morning, according to Pearce, Greenhill's axe

> struck him on the head, and he never spoke a word after.... Matthew Travers with a knife also came and cut his throat, and bled him; we then dragged him to a distance, and cut off his clothes, and tore out his inside, and cut off his head; then Matthew Travers and Greenhill put his heart and liver on the fire and eat it before it was right warm; they asked the rest of us would they have any, but they would not have any that night.

However they had been without food for four days and they changed their minds next morning. Dalton's flesh was carved into seven portions and doled out.

Brown and Kennelly were the weakest and they straggled behind, afraid they might be next on the menu. Then they disappeared into the forests hoping to make their way back to Macquarie Harbour. Twenty days after their escape, they were found half-dead near the prison camp with pieces of human flesh still in their pockets. Both died within ten days of their return.

The other five trudged on. They took two days to cross the swollen Franklin River and struggled on across the Deception Range and the Surveyor Range, wet and cold and still hungry. Then it was Bodenham's turn. Greenhill split his skull as he slept and he and the others ate him. Towards the end of October they stopped by a little creek, lit a fire and cooked the last of Bodenham. But the mess was so horrible Mather could not eat his share. Instead, he boiled some fern leafs, which made him sick. Greenwell hit him on the head with the axe and chopped him up for food.

The remaining three men headed east but Travers was bitten by a snake, weakened and became delirious. Pearce and Greenhill stayed with him for five days, hoping he would recover, then dragged or carried him through the bush for two more days. Finally Travers begged to be killed and Pearce and Greenhill together used the axe to grant his wish, then carved the best parts from him.

Now there were only two and Greenhill had the axe. They walked apart in fear and distrust. When Greenhill stopped, so did Pearce. Neither slept through several nights and then near dawn, as the two men faced each other across a campfire, Greenhill's head nodded onto his chest and he slumped over in sleep. "I run up, and took the axe from under his head, and struck him with it and killed him," Pearce admitted later. "I then took part of his arm and thigh, and went on for several days."

The pockmarked Irishman began to have some luck. He stumbled on a deserted aboriginal campsite with some game still smouldering in the cooking fires. Then he came across a flock of lambs, caught one and dismembered it. Some Irish convict shepherds fed him for a while. Then he fell in with a pair of bushrangers and sneaked around in the bush with them for two months. But there was a price on their heads and they were caught and taken in chains, along with Pearce, to Hobart, where Pearce confessed the whole story to the acting magistrate, the Reverend Robert Knopwood.[1] Nobody believed him. The authorities thought he was covering for his mates who were still alive in the bush. The two bushrangers were hanged but Pearce was spared and sent back to Macquarie Harbour, where he arrived in February 1823.

At Macquarie Harbour he became a celebrity and a young convict, Thomas Cox, pleaded with him to try another escape. Eventually Pearce agreed and the two men absconded on November 16, 1823. Three days out in the bush Pearce killed Cox and started to eat him. He

Alexander Pearce, the cannibal of Van Diemen's Land. The pencil sketch was done by Thomas Bock after Pearce's execution. (Mitchell Library, Sydney)

was caught almost immediately afterwards and taken back to the jail with about half a pound of human flesh in his pocket. He was shipped to Hobart, tried and hanged. A doctor at the Hobart Colonial Hospital made a souvenir of his head. He skinned it, scraped the flesh away and boiled it clean. The skull has survived and is on display today in a glass cabinet at the Academy of Natural Sciences in Philadelphia.[2]

Though the history of escapes from the penal colonies was written mostly in gore, the North Americans began to plan their escape almost immediately after they were landed on the prison island. In the dark of the evening about May 20, 1840, only three months after their arrival, William Reynolds, Jacob Paddock, Horace Cooley and Michael Murray, all of New York State, sneaked away from Sandy Bay Station, about two miles below Hobart on the Derwent River, where they had been working on a road gang. They hid in the bush for several days, then stole a boat and put out to sea in the vague hope of finding an American whaler heading for home. They were not good planners, nor were they good sailors. Surf smashed their little boat to pieces as they attempted to land on an uninhabited island. They had no food with them and for two weeks they tried to survive on shellfish that clung to the island's jagged rocks. After two weeks all four were starving and Murray was ill and close to death.

They decided to give themselves up to some police who passed the island searching for them. Subsequently they were tried and sentenced to two years at Port Arthur, which had replaced Macquarie Harbour as the cruellest of the convict jails.[3]

Then it was Linus Miller's turn to try. He was now with most of the other Americans at Lovely Banks Station, in a beautiful valley framed by red hills covered by oak forests, about thirty-six miles from Hobart on the road to Launceston. But the natural beauty was a frame for harsh human cruelty. The work building the road was hard and long. The weather was cold and the ground snow-covered for part of most days. Sleet whipped the convicts as they hauled their heavy carts loaded with stone for two miles uphill from a quarry at least twelve times a day. A new issue of clothing was withheld from them and more than twenty worked barefoot, leaving bloody footsteps in the frost. Nearly all were half naked. They were all half-starved. Many were ill or broken in spirit. Those who were not talked of bushranging or death in an escape attempt as better alternatives to their terrible plight.[4]

Linus Miller made his break on the evening of August 29, 1840. Along with Joseph Stewart, a tailor from Pennsylvania, he scaled the outer wall of the prison compound, unseen by a guard only a few yards away. They crept through thick bush until dawn, then slept under cover of a wattle bush. When night fell they set out again, scaling mountains and slipping down dangerous cliffs, resting at times in the warm lairs of kangaroos. The undergrowth and high grass of the valleys was so thick it often took them an hour to travel a quarter of a mile. They decided to risk moving through open country and in the morning hid among rocks on an oak-covered hill and slept.[5]

Miller described in his flamboyant way what happened next:

About 11 o'clock, A.M., I was awakened, apparently by a strange presentiment of coming evil. Raising my head, I beheld a large dog near our feet, and a few seconds discovered to me his master, a middle-aged gentleman of interesting appearance, making directly toward us. He seemed as much surprised as I did chagrin at seeing us, and hastily exclaimed, "What's this? Ah, I see; you are bushrangers …"

"You have stumbled upon a fact, my dear sir," I replied. "We are bushrangers. May I take the liberty to inquire who you are?"

"Oh, certainly. My name is – – – , and I am a district constable."

"I do not wish to insult you, sir, but you will, I trust, pardon me for saying I would rather have seen the face of his Satanic Majesty than that of any district constable on the island. You are most unwelcome to our rude habitation, but please be seated: here are rocks – we can offer you nothing better."

"Oh, you are very polite to a stranger! But I must decline making myself at home until I learn something further of your circumstances and intentions."

"I have not the least objection, sir, to giving you all reasonable information. My own name is Miller. I am a citizen of the United States, and until little more than a day since was a British slave.... Allow me now to introduce my friend Mr. Joseph Stewart. Mr. Stewart, please sit up and make yourself agreeable."

Joe remained motionless and only ejaculated a faint "ahem!"

"Your friend," said our new acquaintance, "seems rather unsociable; but allow me to inquire if you are not the two Canadian prisoners who absconded from the Lovely Banks, night before last?"

"We are the same."

"Indeed! I am sorry, for it is, as you must know, my duty to apprehend you..."

I told him of the horrors to which we had been subjected. He expressed great surprise and much sympathy for our party; and assured me that our wrongs were not generally known or they would have been redressed.

"But," he continued, "it is most fortunate for you that I have fallen in with you today. You have not been absent two days, and therefore will not be punished as absconders. I have influence with the magistrate here, and will insure you a mere nominal punishment, and this indiscretion will be forgotten when your pardons arrive. Come, go with me at once; you will never be sorry for it, and I will even state to the magistrate that you voluntarily surrendered yourselves to me."

"You are very kind, sir, but we can not go with you. We have taken to the bush for the purpose of escaping from the island, and until we have had a fair trial, and failed, shall not surrender, unless absolutely compelled to do so."

"If there was any possibility of your succeeding, I should indeed be sorry to interrupt you, knowing as I do the nature of your crime, and that you have been badly treated here. But, of what am I talking? I am bound by my oath to apprehend you, and must do so.... Nothing can tempt me to break my oath."

Recollecting that I had a letter from a dear sister, received when I was in London, as a last resort I handed it to him, requesting that he would read it. [The letter told of his mother's and sisters' tears for his fate.] He did so but had only read a few moments when I saw a large tear trickle down his manly cheek and another and another followed and soon he was sobbing like a little child....

The stranger rose and offering a hand to each of us, exclaimed:

"God bless you, my young friends, and prosper you in your undertaking. I am a son, a father and a brother, and that letter has brought me to a sense of my duty.... My oath of office is not binding against such men as you. I would not hinder you from going home to such friends for all the world. I could not sleep nights with such a load on my conscience. Should you reach home in safety, remember me to that sister and your aged parents, and tell them there is a man, yes, not one, but thousands in this home of crime who feel for the woes of the unfortunate.... I trust I have not made you so unpleasant a visit after all, as his Satanic Majesty might have done, even though I am a district constable. And now young friends, farewell! and may God Almighty guide you in safety to your homes."[6]

Four days later Miller and Stewart reached Sandy Bay and Miller visited an old man he had befriended when the Canadians were stationed there. He asked the old man to pass along a letter to the captain of an American whaler. The old man called in six or seven constables, who chased Miller through the bush. Miller ran faster and escaped to where Stewart was hiding. They hid under a stone bridge, three miles from Sandy Bay, for two more days, while hordes of constables went back and forth across the bridge searching for them. They were weak and hungry and decided to give themselves up. They had been free for twelve days. After a brief trial they were sentenced to two years in Port Arthur.[7]

Benjamin Wait and Samuel Chandler, whose wife and daughter had made the dramatic trip from Niagara to Quebec City to rescue them from the gallows, were next to attempt an escape. They could not wait for the results of Maria Wait's further efforts on their behalf in England. They planned to get away on an American whaler, although this was virtually impossible because of the bureaucratic competence of former Lieutenant-Governor Arthur. Under regulations he imposed, every ship anchored in the Derwent faced big, automatic fines if it failed to have a twenty-four-hour officer watch. Before leaving port every vessel had to be searched and fumigated with sulphur to drive out stowaways. If a stowaway was found on board, each officer and seamen was fined a month's wages. If two were found they were fined two months' wages and so on. The captain had to pay the fines in full before the ship was allowed to sail. And informers received half the amount of the fine. Nevertheless, many of the ships that called at Hobart for supplies were American whalers and their crews were shocked to learn there were North American convicts ashore.[8]

Wait and Chandler started to plot their escape as soon as they received their tickets of leave in August 1841 and made their attempt a few months later. They were employed on the same farm at Oatlands, fifty miles from Hobart, where they carefully saved most of their meagre convict wages and were able to move about freely. Wait was vague in his description of the escape attempt "for fear of ill consequences to my benefactors, who are again on a whaling voyage, and most probably will visit the same port for refreshment; when should the authorities be aware of the fact, they would be liable to a heavy penalty."

However, Chandler revealed years later that he obtained a ten-day pass to go to Hobart, where he wandered the docks, shaking hands with the captains of American ships until he found one who responded to the secret masonic grip.

This brother mason agreed to pick him up, along with Wait, in the open ocean at the entrance to the D'Entrecasteaux Channel, one of Hobart's main shipping channels. They set a time and date and Chandler returned to Oatlands to tell Wait of the plan, but Wait did not approve. He said there was too much danger; the possibility of missing the friendly ship forty miles at sea was too great. He would not risk it. So Chandler said he would go alone, although he would regret parting with a friend with whom he had suffered so long and so much. This little speech caused Wait to change his mind and he went to a police office and obtained a pass for Hobart, where the two of them "spent Christmas in safe seclusion." Then they disguised themselves as fishermen, hired a small whale boat and set out to the designated spot at sea. They rowed all day and slept in the little boat that night, still in the sheltered channel. Early the next day they moved out into the open sea, where high waves crashed into the boat and drenched them. Neither had any experience of boat-handling, and in their anxiety they had left Hobart earlier than they should have. They tossed about for several days in what Wait described as "danger, destitution and extreme anxiety" and their small amount of food and water ran out. Still, there was no sign of the ship. Hunger gnawed at them and cold sleet stung. They were about to give up and try to row back to Hobart, when a three-master emerged from the haze. Chandler stood in the little boat and gave the masonic sign of distress. Nobody saw it. He stretched himself to his full height and gave the sign again, and then again. The Yankee whaler's sails shook and flapped as she hove to. Soon the two convicts were "afforded comfortable berths in the cabin where we found genuine American hospitality reigning."[9]

They caught some whales and went through gales, storms and a shipwreck that stranded them in South America for a month before arriving in the United States after a seven-month voyage. On landing in July 1842, they learned that another convict, James Gemmell, had escaped from Van Diemen's Land in similar circumstances on an American whaler a month after them, and had arrived in the States a month earlier. In a public announcement Gemmell proclaimed that his good fortune was due to the efforts of Mrs. Wait to obtain his parole.

Chandler went to Maquoketa, Iowa, where his family, including his daughter Sarah, who had pleaded with Lord Durham on his behalf, was waiting for him.[10] And the first officer of the whaling ship, a man from Bristol, Rhode Island, escorted Wait to Niagara Falls, N.Y. There, two years and five months after she had saved him from the gallows, Wait was reunited with his wife, who was teaching school in the town. She held their two-and-a-half-year-old daughter in her arms. A crowd of hundreds gathered at the railway station to cheer their emotional meeting.[11]

CHAPTER 12

The French-Speaking
Slaves of Sydney

On these wild shores Repentance' saviour hand
Shall probe my secret soul, shall cleanse my wounds,
And fit the faithful penitent for heaven.

ROBERT SOUTHEY, IN HIS *BOTANY BAY ECLOGUES*

*I*n the beginning, the French-Canadian convicts were treated as abominably as any others, perhaps worse because the prison stockade at Longbottom, in what is now the Sydney suburb of Concord, was not ready for them.[1]

The bureaucracy in the sleepy convict colony was unable to adjust to the sudden change of plans that had saved the Canadians from the horrors of Norfolk Island. The alternative destination, consisting of four huts, a store room, a kitchen, a barracks and several other small buildings arranged in a square, had not been cleaned by the convicts who had just been moved out and was still plagued with their filth and vermin, mostly fleas and cockroaches. There were no beds or bedding so the new prisoners at the Longbottom stockade had to sleep on the floors of the little huts, with one thin blanket each. The drafts of the cold Australian nights blew through gaps in the walls and up through the separated planks of the floors. The prisoners froze. Meals consisted of a 6 a.m. breakfast of thick soup made from maize or Indian corn flour and an ounce of sugar, a lunch at noon of half a pound of inferior beef or mutton and twelve ounces of poor bread. There was no supper. The supervisor was an ex-army officer named Henry Clinton Baddeley, whom Léon Ducharme described in his diaries as "a veritable tyrant, a man without character, one given to abusing his power in order to ill-treat us every time he could find an opportunity of doing so."

The Canadians were given a day to clean up their huts, which they did as best they could, but the vermin remained. Then they were put to work under armed guards in a nearby quarry, digging and breaking rocks and carrying the results away in wheelbarrows and ox-drawn carts for use on roads, especially on the new main thoroughfare from Sydney to Parramatta, which is now an outer suburb of Sydney. If they slowed in their work, they were threatened with fifty lashes, but they were determined to work hard to show what sort of men they were and there is no record of any lashes being administered. Yet the work was cruel. The soles of the same shoes they had worn on the *Buffalo* soon wore away and the sharp stones cut into their feet so they blistered and bled. The hungry nights on the cold floors with a single, thin blanket were almost unbearable and many became ill.

All this came to an end after a few months, however, when a big fight broke out among their guardians. Baddeley and his police and soldier guards were having a party in the police married quarters and were well into the rum, it appears, when Baddeley, a bachelor, either made a pass at the wife of one of the policemen or stepped in to stop the policeman assaulting the woman. The policeman then attacked his superior, throwing many punches. These seemed to sober Baddeley, who, instead of fighting back, ordered his officers to arrest his assailant and throw him in a dark cell reserved for prisoners condemned to solitary confinement. Then the drunken soldiers and policemen divided into groups, one supporting their chief and the other backing the insulted husband. And a real donnybrook occurred. The French Canadians in their huts heard curses and yells and the sounds of smashing of furniture and crockery.

François-Xavier Prieur reported in his journal:

In the embarrassing position in which he found himself, our Superintendent, forgetting his prejudices and his unjust restriction, rushed towards our little cells, opened the doors and summoned us outside. This we were able to do without any delay, owing to the fact that, by reason of the cold and the lack of bed-clothes, we were lying down, as usual, fully dressed.

Once assembled, which was the work of only a minute, the Superintendent ordered us to arrest all the policemen and all the soldiers and lock them up in one of the sheds, the whole force appointed to guard us. We obeyed, without knowing then a single word about the origin and causes of the quarrel, and without foreseeing what would be the consequences of this extraordinary adventure.[2]

The consequences were quite remarkable. Suddenly Baddeley, who had been bigoted, insulting and despotic, became a friend of the French Canadians. He badgered the government for more blankets and convinced the bureaucrats that the men in his care were harmless, decent folk, who had no need for armed guards (and in his mind, it can be assumed, especially for the sort of armed guards who had ganged up on him).

So the guards were taken away, leaving only Baddeley himself to supervise the prisoners, who were given the duties of cooks, door-keepers, night wardens, and even overseers of their comrades on the work gangs. The cooks found a way to make stews out of the scorched maize flour and meat of the rations, which was a delicacy compared with plain, rotten boiled beef. By grinding and roasting Indian corn, used to feed the working bullocks, they made a kind of coffee, which was not great, but better, the convicts agreed, than plain tepid water. They even managed to make some *tourtière*. And the work gangs, under their compatriot overseers, worked just hard enough to satisfy an occasional

François-Xavier Prieur, a Lower Canadian merchant, who wrote a long account of his sufferings and those of his fellow French-Canadian convicts in Sydney. (From a translation of his journal by Australian historian George Mackaness)

inspection by Baddeley, who did not seem to care much and slept a lot in the daytime.

He had enough energy, however, to organize some of the convicts into special work gangs to cut wood, which he sold for his personal profit. And while the French Canadians kept mum about this fraud, he could hardly complain when they went into private business collecting oyster shells on the rocks and beaches, the only source of lime in the colony, which they sold to passing boatmen for resale to the limeburners in Sydney and Parramatta, pocketing a few pence to supplement their meagre rations.[3]

In the meantime Bishop Polding and Father Brady, who was later to become Bishop of Perth, visited their French-Canadian flock frequently, celebrating mass in a little shed that was officially a stable for the horses but had been converted into a chapel. Its walls were decorated for the masses with large fern leaves and its cloth-covered altar was adorned with holy pictures brought from Canada in the convicts' baggage. Bishop Polding provided a crucifix and two candlesticks.[4]

This general aura of sanctity among the French Canadians (a few of them did not attend mass or prayers) was frequently assaulted by the sights and sounds around them. One of the convicts, François-Maurice Lepailleur, reported in his diary, for Thursday, July 23 , 1840:

During the afternoon we saw a drunken woman, just come from the factory at Parramatta, who began to abuse the woman who lives in the small cabin in front of the gate. After she had sworn a lot, cursed and blasphemed, Mr. Baddeley sent for a policeman. The woman, overhearing Mr. Baddeley, turned her back to us, lifted up all her clothes and showed us her bum, saying that she had a "black hole" there and slapping her belly like the wretch she was. Nothing more vile than that tribe – animals are more decent than they. I would say much more but it would dirty my little journal to go on. It is incredible to see so many drunken women in this country. The roads are full of women drunkards.

And in a diary entry, dated October 3 , 1840:

There was a big disturbance on the road last night. Mr. and Mrs. Sanmorfil [possibly Summerville, neighbours to the stockade] were arrested and put in the lock-up for their bad behaviour and three or four other people were also put in the lockup for the same business. Mrs. Sanmorfil fought with a whore until they were as naked as animals and the whole thing was the result of drink. Until this affair I would have thought that these were respectable people. To see them you wouldn't say that is what they are. They say that the disorder here is much milder than in Sydney. A man or woman is not embarrassed to make a dirty proposition to another right in the street and often in front of everyone. On the day of judgement this country will be found more guilty than Tyre and Sidon and Sodom.

For Tuesday, 11 May, 1841:

One of the neighbours of the camp got drunk and stabbed his wife in several places and escaped. That was Sunday night. The wife is still alive. They are neighbours of Neich, in the new house. We hear more women crying in the night here than birds singing in the woods during the day. I think every husband here beats his wife and I have it on good account that most of the women drink or are good for nothing and the men are drunkards. One can imagine the great harmony which reigns in these households – of which some aren't married but are living together in concubinage.

For Wednesday, 19 May, 1841:

At night we still hear the weeping and screams of the women living near Neich. Again, it's someone lording it over their wife. It's incredible what mistreatment the women suffer from their husbands in this colony, and this happens sometimes at night which is more alarming. What a country of scum this is![5]

In the circumstances, the clergy were much concerned about the Canadians' spiritual welfare. However, their temporal situation was not ignored. Father Brady wrote to a Catholic newspaper in Sydney:

The Editor,

I have just this minute returned from Longbottom, where I spent two days with the political prisoners from Canada. His Grace the Bishop has also visited them, he has given them his blessing, and has encouraged them to endure patiently their exile, and all the misfortunes which are inseparable from it.

When I consider the courage of these prisoners, and their spirit of resignation, I cannot conceive how men so gentle, so modest and so good, whose conduct arouses the admiration of all those who are witnesses of it, can deserve so terrible a punishment.

They have had the misfortune to see themselves snatched from the arms of their wives and children; they have seen their homes and their possessions given over to pillage and to destruction by fire, and after months of anguish, fear and shattered hopes, spent in the depths of prison cells, they received the terrible sentence which was to separate them from all they held dear in the world, so as to cast them into banishment in a far distant coil, where they are suffering through being deprived of the most necessary things. The food that they receive is so bad that the white Irish slave, accustomed to living on potatoes and salt, could scarcely put up with it; in spite of this the settlement at Longbottom costs the Government nearly a thousand pounds sterling per annum, an expense that could be saved by granting these men permission to seek employment in the colony, or, at least, by assigning them to good masters.

If you think that these remarks have any importance, would you be good enough to insert them in your useful and excellent newspaper; by so doing you will oblige

Your obedient servant,

J. Brady,

Missionary-Priest.

This letter, written by an Irish priest in a Catholic journal about French Canadians, resulted in an outpouring of bigotry in other papers, especially the prominent *Sydney Herald*, which claimed the Canadians' careers in their homeland had been marked by murder, pillage and arson. Its writers described them as cut-throats, worthy of a fate a hundred times worse than that inflicted on them. To sympathize with these cut-throats, the *Herald* said, was to sympathize with crime.[6]

The humane Governor Gipps, with his first-hand knowledge of the prerevolutionary period in Lower Canada, made his own inquiries about the welfare and behaviour of the French Canadians. He liked what he heard and conditions continued to improve at Longbottom, although two of the convicts, Gabriel Chèvrefils and Louis Dumouchelle, died of dysentery.[7]

The corrupt superintendent, Baddeley, who was profiting from the labours of the Canadians, also issued good reports on their behaviour. He could, of course, hardly do otherwise in case his private enterprises were revealed. So, twenty months after they had staggered weakly into the Longbottom camp, they were assigned, one by one, to work for various employers in Sydney.

The last Canadian to leave Longbottom is not named in the several remaining journals, but according to both Prieur and Lepailleur, the superintendent, Baddeley, who had been ill, died in this Canadian's arms while they were left alone at the stockade. "No other person came to be present with him in his last moments, and not a single friend followed his coffin to the cemetery," Prieur reported.

Under the convict system on the mainland, assignment to an employer was the first stage of release following a usual minimum of two years' hard labour on government projects. In the next stage a convict became a "ticket of leave" man, which meant he could work for whomever he chose, though still under government supervision, and the final stage, depending, of course, on good behaviour during all previous stages, was a full pardon, allowing the convict to become a freeman and a citizen of Australia or to return to his or her homeland if he could earn enough money for the passage.

At the time the French Canadians were assigned, the conditions were that they be employed at work commensurate with their strength, skill and previous occupations; that they should be paid seven shillings and sixpence per week, of which half was given to them and the other half deposited in a savings bank for their future; and that they were to receive as weekly rations ten pounds of fresh beef, ten pounds of wheaten flour, one pound of sugar and four ounces of black tea. They were forbidden to leave their masters' property after working hours, and had to carry a written permit when allowed out in Sundays. They were, in effect, slaves.

However, in general, the work was not too hard. Léon Ducharme, for instance, found himself assigned to a furniture maker with the duties of clerk, salesman and collector. Prieur, a merchant, and Louis Bourdon, a farmer and merchant's clerk, were first hired out to a Frenchman, a native of Mauritius, to work in his factory, but he was in the business of speculating in slave labour and almost immediately hired them out again, at a profit, to a Frenchman and a German who intended to open a confectioner's shop. They spent several months manufacturing syrups and candies but apparently were not very good at this because the store closed shortly after it opened for business. So they became gardeners.

During this period Bishop Polding visited London, where he consulted with the colonial secretary about his French-Canadian flock, pleading for better treatment of them as a special kind of convict. The result was the Canadians were given tickets of leave after only five months of assignment. So now they were more or less free to work where they wanted and for whatever wages they could get, provided they report to the police every month. The trouble was the colony was in the depths of a depression. Non-convict immigrants, the dispossessed of England seeking a better life, were arriving in large numbers. Jobs were hard to find.

There was also some discrimination among employers against the French Canadians because of their language and other differences. But this is not to say that the French Canadians were beyond reproach in their racial outlook. In a description of life in the colony, Ducharme wrote:

In New South Wales there are a large number of aborigines. The Europeans have never been able to bring them to any degree of civilization. They are the most stupid and most disgusting race of men in the world. They are divided into tribes which are ever on the move; they never sleep twice in the same place, and always in the open air without any shelter. They live on kangaroos, opossums, goannas, snakes and other animals that they catch and eat raw. They do not wear any kind of clothing. They are dirty and extremely fierce.... These degraded and useless beings can be seen prowling around towns in gangs, begging alms.... They are extremely ugly, fairly tall, but very thin and active.

However, the top echelons of the colonial establishment, including some who spoke French, found the French Canadians interesting, even exotic, and in any event superior to the run-of-the mill, often uneducated ticket-of-leave men, so there was demand in these high circles for some of them.

The chief superintendent of convicts, Captain John MacLean, employed ten of the French Canadians, Sir Thomas Mitchell, the surveyor-general, four, Samuel Perry, the deputy surveyor-general, six, Alexander Dumas, a chief clerk in the superintendent of convicts' office, six.

These Canadians employed by the establishment worked for low pay and received half of it while the other half was supposedly banked for them. Their savings, they believed, would be enough to pay their fares home, and those of some of their colleagues, once they received full pardons. But after eighteen months of service, when they asked for their discharge and the money owed to them, they were told they were free, as ticket-of-leave men, to seek work elsewhere, but they would have to come back later for the rest of their wages. They came back again and again and were always told to return later, until finally they were warned they would be put back on government work unless they stopped their pestering. Devastated and disillusioned, they appealed to Governor Gipps, who told them they could take their employers to court.

"But how, in our poverty, could we wrestle legally with rich and influential men – men who, in the issue, would have found all sorts of opportunities of injuring us?" Ducharme wrote, "Who would have believed that we would have been the dupes of these great men! … What should anyone now think of the lower classes, when the highest of all were the first to cheat you!"

They never did get the money owed to them, which they estimated at £300, enough to pay the fares of several men at least as far as London.

Ten others, later joined by a few more, started a Canadian-style sawmill in dense bushland about nine miles from Sydney.[8] They worked hard and made a small profit. At nights in their main log cabin they talked of their homes and families and often the sounds of *canadien* songs rang through the gums and pines of the distant land. After about a year, one of the great scourges of Australia struck at them. A bushfire roared and rolled through their enterprise, leaving the sleeping-hut in ashes, most of their stock of lumber burned and some of their equipment damaged. Within days they built another, skilfully repaired equipment and made the sawmill whine again.

Other French Canadians were able to find odd jobs. Despite the depression, which forced the government to house and feed hundreds of immigrants and return some assigned or ticket-of-leave convicts to the penitentiaries, the Canadians had become popular as workers and people. Although some of their jobs were poorly paid, none seemed to be unemployed.

Homesickness haunted them. François-Xavier Prieur spent every Sunday sitting on a rock in a solitary bay of Sydney Harbour. "There I dreamed of my homeland and family," he wrote. "My thoughts accompanied the wake of a [departing] ship. "With it I ranged the seas; with it I re-ascended the St. Lawrence; then the picture of the parish where I was born; then my mother's kisses, the joy of my old father, the handclasps of my friends passed through my mind, only to surrender me very soon to the harsh reality which made me find myself once again upon the wretched rock of the land of my exile.

"Then I was overcome by the anguish of unhappiness, during which I cried out ceaselessly, 'When, oh when, shall I be able to set out for Canada?'"

CHAPTER 13

Reprieve for the Human Horses

The very day we landed upon the fatal shore,
The planters they stood round us full twenty score or more;
They ranked us up like horses and sold us out of hand,
They roped us to the plough, brave boys, to plough Van
Dieman's Land.[1]

EARLY BALLAD OF VAN DIEMEN'S LAND

*W*illiam Gates, the young American from Cape Vincent captured at the Battle of the Windmill, was convinced he would not survive. In summer, the loads of stone and dirt he hauled in his cart at least ten and sometimes twenty miles a day seemed even heavier. He had no sweat left although the hot sun beat as hard as ever on his brown, withered skin and the fly bites on his body would not heal. Then, in winter, when the North Americans were moved from Sandy Bay to another station called Lovely Banks, forty miles from Hobart on the road to Launceston, it was bitterly cold. Gates recorded:

Here our work lay two miles from the station, and was mostly in the rock. Our tasks were even harder that at Sandy Bay. Our loaded carts we had to draw two miles, five times a day. At early dawn we were routed, and away at our tasks by sunrise, which we were not allowed to quit till sundown, when we were marched back in double file, and by the time we had our pint of skilly, it would be long after dark, when, to cap our enjoyments, we would be forced into the huts and locked in, where was no fire nor light, nor any convenience whatever; cold, shivering, hungry, and generally wet to the skin with the chilly rains that fall almost daily in that country during its winter months.

They were moved again to Bridgewater Station, just twelve miles from Hobart, where they worked with English convicts building a stone bridge across the wide Derwent River, and then were split into small groups and sent to nine different stations, apparently to prevent any attempt at a mass escape. It did not matter much. The rock had to be hauled at all of them. The same cruel lash caused the same horrid shrieks and bloody backs, though the North Americans were still spared the experience. Instead, for their frequent punishments they were locked in the tiny solitary confinement cells for a week or more at a time, with a piece of bread and mug of water their daily diet.

Gates's body was almost broken now and his spirit was suffering. He was forgotten, he thought, by his family and countrymen at home and now even by the stupid bureaucrats of the convict system. Two years had passed and he was still yoked to his cart. He thought he would be hauling rocks for the rest of his life.

Then one evening as he collapsed on his bunk a guard threw him a copy of the *Government Gazette*. "Read that," he ordered. "It might make you feel better."

And there it was, his name, along with those of several other Canadians, under the heading "Ticket of Leave." Maria Wait's crusade had worked and he was free, or at least free from the cart. Now he could earn a little money working for a settler, but still under government supervision. He went immediately to his friend Sherwood at Jericho Station, the English overseer who had offered to help him escape. Sherwood provided him with hot water and soap and, Gates recorded, "I

Convicts were the engine of a tramway at Port Arthur. In this old drawing they are seen transporting some officials. (National Library of Australia, Canberra)

gave my whole person a thorough cleansing, which was the first opportunity I had had since my capture at the Windmill of freeing myself from the vermin that had continually infested my person in greater or less quantities." Sherwood also gave him a new suit and, said Gates, "I felt once more like a man."[2]

Gates was seldom lucky, though. Because of the escapes of Gemmell, Wait and Chandler, he and the few others freed with him were consigned to the Oatlands district, away from the coast and its whaling ships, but there was little work available there. For three weeks he and a colleague wandered the length and breadth of the district without food or shelter. When they begged for work or food at settlers' houses, they were denounced as beggars and lazy vagabonds and invariably told to "bugger off" empty handed, empty stomached. During the nights, which were cold, they slept in the bush or were occasionally allowed to creep into the huts of other ticket-of-leave men working as farm labourers. They ate roots and sometimes stole a turnip or potato from a field. Once they found a snared kangaroo and ate it.

Finally, when Gates returned, haggard and depressed, to Oatlands township for the eighth time for his required three-day check-in with the penal authorities, he was told his friend Sherwood had recommended him to a settler named Tabart, who, when Gates knocked on his door, agreed to employ him for one year for £8 (about $40 at the time).[3]

Tabart was about fifty-five years old. He owned an estate of 4,000 acres which carried 10,000 sheep and 100 cattle. He had a staff of fifteen farm hands, four shepherds, a hostler, a butler, a cook, a gardener and two kitchen maids. He also had a wife, two sons and four comely daughters, who were affable and charming to the ticket-of-leave employees, a rarity in a land of snobbery where it was considered a disgrace for a woman even to talk with a prisoner.[4] The daughters stirred in Gates some of his almost forgotten youthful desires, but he kept a respectful distance from them while delighting in their beauty, their giggles and conversation. And he found Tabart to be a tough man if crossed, but otherwise fair and decent. In fact, Gates and Tabart got along so well that after three months as a labourer Gates was promoted to overseer of the entire establishment, a job that was easy physically and meant that he lived in the house and ate well in the kitchen with the cook, maids and butler. His small body mended and filled out. The daughters started to look even more attractive and he knew he was well again. He learned how to shear sheep and Tabart continued to give him more responsibility and more of his trust.

When the shearing was over towards the end of Gates's first year on the estate, Tabart instructed his trusted ticket-of-leave man to take the clip to market in Hobart and purchase a large quantity of supplies with some of the proceeds. Special permission had to be obtained from the authorities for a convict to make such a journey and it was granted only after Tabart guaranteed Gates's good conduct. So Gates set out on horseback in charge of three dray-loads of wool, each weighing about 3,000 pounds and drawn by three yoke of oxen, with a driver to each dray. The journey took three days.

In Hobart he made the necessary report to the local police and went for a stroll in the township. He had not gone far when he bumped into a drunken sailor who seemed to be an American.

"Hey," said Gates, "are you an American?"

"What business is it of yours, you bloody constable?" the man replied, raising his fists, ready to fight.

"Well," said Gates, "it is some business of mine because I'm not what you think I am. I'm an American too."

"The hell you are," the sailor said, dropping his arms to his side. "If you're an American how the hell did you get to this godforsaken place?"

Gates told him how he was taken prisoner in Canada and transported as a convict, about his years hauling the cart and his suffering.

"Jesus, mate," the weather-beaten sailor said. "We've got to get you out of here. Look, my ship leaves in a few days. And there's two other American ships in the harbour. You come with me now and I'll hide you on my ship."

But Gates was afraid. He was fairly sure the local police were watching him. "I'll think about it," he said.

That evening he met the sailor again with some of his shipmates, who urged him even more ardently to come with them. Gates could not sleep that night, thinking of home, dreaming of liberty.

Next day he had no trouble selling the wool for a good price. Then he purchased the supplies for the estate and found he had £1,000, the equivalent of $5,000, left in his pocket. The temptation to take the sailors' advice increased. He had more than enough capital to resume a good life in the land of the free. And when the sailors met him again they insisted they could get him aboard the ship safely.

"For, Christ's sake, man," one of them said. "If you like, we'll go back and get the mate and he'll personally promise he'll put you where the British will never find you."

Still Gates hesitated. He told the sailors he would think it over. He fingered the banknotes in his pocket but his conscience bothered him and in his journal, describing his anguish, he reverted to a language he had heard long ago as a child in some little American church. "My conscience whispered it is not thine. The owner of it hath done thee no harm; moreover, he hath put great confidence in thy integrity. Wherefore, then, shouldst thou betray thy trust and prove thyself a rogue?"

He loaded his purchases on the drays and set out for Oatlands. Twice he turned back towards Hobart, but twice again his conscience tormented him and he changed his mind. If it was government money in his pocket, he would have no compunction about it, he thought. But it belonged to someone who trusted him and had treated him with comparative kindness. Tabart was delighted when Gates led the loaded drays onto his property and handed him the money. "My God," he said. "I couldn't have done better myself."

The other North American convicts, now all parolled, scattered through the island, mostly in twos and threes, and mostly finding jobs at wages so low as to make it almost impossible to save the £100 necessary for a passage to England, once they were fully pardoned.

Some worked a farm as share croppers but made no profit. Some made shingles. Others hired themselves out as mechanics, and several helped farm production by introducing the American method of cradling wheat. From time to time, almost all of them were called upon to join official parties hunting bushrangers, the escaped "bolters" who had chosen a rough life in the bush over back-breaking work, the chains and the lash. There were many caves to hide them in the hills and there were hundreds of these outlaws – so many, in fact, that the authorities feared they might one day form a guerrilla army and overthrow the government. They crept down from the hills to steal settlers' sheep or the food and clothing from their homes. Most would just as soon shoot a human as a kangaroo, but there was also some gallantry among them and they were to become immortalized in ballad and myth, icons of the contempt of authority that is still a key part of the Australian culture.

Early in 1843, when the island was alarmed by a bigger than usual spate of murders and robberies, Governor Franklin issued a proclamation promising a pardon and free passage home to anybody who caught a bushranger, and he ordered all ticket-of-leave men to join in an organized pursuit of some of them. More than 1,500 convicts were armed with muskets, divided into groups of six to eight, headed by a constable, and sent into the bush with orders to kill.

Stephen Wright and Aaron Dresser, both Americans captured in the Battle of the Windmill, were in a posse of six which had just about given up its hunt for two desperadoes after scouring mountains and valleys for twelve days. It had rained incessantly for the last two days so they headed for a shepherd's hut to shelter for the night. A few hundred yards from the hut they saw two men emerge from it, guns in their hands, pistols danging from their belts. The constable called on them to "halt" but they ran for the woods. Wright and Dresser were ordered to follow them and Wright recorded:

> They found that we gained ground and each taking a tree, took steady aim at us from behind it; but not one of their pieces would go off, as they had been out the last two days in steady rain. One was armed with a double-barrel gun and four pistols; the other with a rifle and the same number of small arms. After finding that resistance was useless they surrendered in a very gentlemanly style. Jeffs, the younger, begged our pardon for having been taken so cowardly, and not firing; but he was pleased that what was his loss was our gain. I heard that he was a Gypsy by birth. He was what the world would call "devilish handsome;" dark eyes, long eye-lashes; and his dress was a neat and trim as a French dandy. His face was of a melancholy cast, and his form the perfection of manliness. He said death was a fate he preferred to the life of a convict. His companion, Conway, did not relish his fate quite so well.[5]

Jeffs and Conway were subsequently hanged but Wright and Dresser had earned their freedom and on July 22, 1843, they embarked for England on the brig *Areta*, loaded with wool and oil and eighteen other souls.[6] With the help of the American embassy, they sailed from London on the *Quebec*, arriving in New York in mid-February 1844, where they were entertained by William Lyon Mackenzie before returning to their families.

Linus Miller, and Joseph Stewart, convicted of attempting to escape, pleaded with Convict Superintendent Gunn to save them from their fate at Port Arthur. He was sympathetic but unable, he said, to interfere with a magistrate's decision. However, if Miller failed to survive, he promised to write to his father.

The two American convicts had good reason to worry. Port Arthur was Governor George Arthur's lasting monument. It remains in the minds of Australians today an ugly symbol of their country's cruel beginnings. Sixty miles from Hobart, on an enclosed, difficult-to-navigate inlet surrounded by high mountains, Port Arthur prison was a collection of stone barracks and solitary-confinement cells from which the only way of escape was across a narrow peninsula guarded by scores of chained wild dogs.[7] The lash used here was special. It was made of the hardest whipcord, thicker than normal. The cord was saturated in salt water then put in the sun to dry, so that it became like wire and its eighty-one knots cut the flesh like a saw. It was said that twenty-five Port Arthur lashes were worth 300 anywhere else.[8] Port Arthur was home to more than 12,000 prisoners from its founding by Arthur in 1822 to the end of transportation in 1853, almost all of them second offenders sent to be straightened out once and for all. One of the first of them was Ikey Solomons, said to be the model for Fagan, the pickpocket and fence in Charles Dickens's *Oliver Twist*.[9]

The convict population of Port Arthur was about 1,000 when Miller and Stewart were due to arrive there. There were also about 700 boys from the London slums, aged between nine and eighteen, in a neighbouring jail for juveniles at Port Puer, a dismal neck of land where tight discipline was enforced and trades were taught in a jumble of barracks and workrooms. Arthur referred to the unfortunate inmates of this awful place as "little depraved felons."[10]

Miller had been on the ice-covered *Captain Ross* on its horrible voyage across the Atlantic, Stewart on the sweltering, scurvy-stricken *Buffalo* in the Pacific, but nothing had prepared them for their three-day voyage to Port Arthur, along the coast of Van Diemen's Land, in the small brig *Isabella*.

The space between the decks was not four feet in depth and could not have exceeded six feet by ten [Miller wrote]: yet into this narrow hole, forty-six prisoners were crowded, all of whom were doubly ironed, and handcuffed in pairs. Only about one fourth of the number could enjoy the luxury of sitting upon the floor at once, for want of room, and the remainder, be it remembered, could not stand upright, but yet were obliged to support themselves upon their feet, and lean forward, at the same time clinging, with their manacled hands, to their companions. In short, all were literally wedged in, and when the vessel pitched and careened from side to side, we were thrown into heaps upon the floor; the wrenching of the irons upon our limbs producing the most excruciating pains and torture, and the weight of the uppermost crushing those beneath half to death.

The most horrid oaths and imprecations mingled with the cries and groans of the poor wretches. Nearly all were sea-sick, and the deck was literally a pool of nauseous matter, produced by vomiting. Every man was wet to the skin with it, and the stench was intolerable. The only air which we breathed was admitted through a hatchway about three feet square, and those most remote from this opening were nearly suffocated. "Water! water! for God's sake, some water!" was constantly vociferated by a dozen voices at a time; but the monsters who had charge of us would only hand down a pannikin full (less than a pint) at stated intervals. Many fainted, but it was with the greatest difficulty that they were dragged to the hatchway in order that a little fresh air might save their lives. At the end of thirty-six hours we reached Port Arthur in a state of misery which language cannot describe.[11]

After they staggered from the *Isabella*, covered in vomit, Miller, Stewart and the others remained unwashed, but their chains were removed and they were given new clothes – a sheepskin cap, striped shirt, jacket, waistcoat and shoes. The suits were black and yellow, called "magpie." Their heads were shorn of all hair. Then they were paraded before the camp commandant, Charles O'Hara Booth, read the draconian rules of the place, and set to work under a cruel overseer carrying bundles of lumber, which Miller estimated weighed between two and three hundred pounds, from a sawmill to the main camp, while the overseer whipped them along at a rate of about five miles an hour. At night they slept in small stone cells which were damp and cold.

Soon the work changed to carrying green timber, some of it eighteen inches round and forty feet long. A gang of twenty men had to shoulder such loads and the gangly Miller was always the tallest of them and had to bear the brunt of the weight. He contemplated suicide. Stewart went on strike. He threw down his load and told the overseer he could not carry it any more and was ready to die instead.

Stewart appeared before the commandant on charges of idleness, insolence and disobedience of orders, but because he was so weak and emaciated and "one of the Canadians, sent here for absconding; no other charged preferred against you," Booth spared him the lash and sentenced him to three days of solitary confinement, where he was able to recover some of his strength.[12]

Miller's miseries continued and compounded. His overseer, named Sawyer, did not like Yankees. The great loads of timber he was forced to carry became heavier. He had no socks and the insides of the shoes issued to him were roughly made. His feet became raw and bled, so he wrapped pieces from his shirt around them. When he removed them at night pieces of flesh stuck to them. A friend gave him some old rags to make pads for his shoulders.

"I am confident that I did all and suffered all which any man of the same strength could to save his life," he wrote in his journal. "Day after day I struggled on, half starved, emaciated, subject to the most horrible physical and mental torture, and praying ether for death to end my sufferings, of Heaven to grant me more strength to bear them."

Then the man the convicts called "Old Granny" visited Port Arthur. Sir John Franklin, dressed in his lieutenant-governor's finery, delivered an address to all 1,300 prisoners, lined up in rows, about twenty men deep, in front of the prisoners' barracks. According to Miller, he abused them all, but especially the most desperate characters, who were each chained to a heavy log which they had to pull with them as they worked in the gangs. He called them "vile wretches" and "worse then the devils in hell." When he had finished with them he summoned Miller and Stewart from the ranks. He told Miller he was "a vile, ungrateful, depraved man" who had misled Stewart and tried to foment revolt among the other Canadian prisoners; that his punishment would be increased and he would never leave Port Arthur. "It was not until Franklin's eyes were fixed upon me, in which I at once saw rage, malice, and I think I may add, *murder,* fearfully gleaming, that I suspected his motive in calling me from the ranks.... But before he concluded, I got rid of every feeling except pity and contempt for the poor, weak, imbecile old man," Miller wrote.

But the facts were apparently not in full accord with Miller's florid prose, because the next day he was relieved of the hard labour that was killing him and given an easy job, along with Stewart, tending the prison gardens. He attributed this to the kindness of prison supervisors, acting in defiance of Franklin's instructions, and not to what was probably an act of mercy, preceded by a stern lecture, by "Old Granny."

Soon, because of good behaviour, Miller was given another easy job in the jail's laundry, washing convicts' shirts, and after seven weeks there the prison chaplain, Rev. J.A. Manton, sought him out for the most prestigious position of clerk of the church and teacher at a night school, where some of the more privileged prisoners learned to read and write. Stewart was also given a soft job with the family of a jail official and they both regained their health.

Still, his work with the chaplain worried Miller. The rampant sodomy among the inmates upset him. His duties in helping bury the dissected bodies of the dead, at a place in the harbour called the Isle of the Dead, many of them murdered or killed by their own hand to end their sufferings, made his yearning for freedom almost unbearable.

CHAPTER 14

The French Go Home

Farewell, Van Dieman, ruin's gate,
With joy we leave thy shore;
And fondly hope our wretched fate
Will drive us there no more.

AMERICAN CONVICT SAMUEL SNOW

*T*he good Catholics of what was to become Quebec gathered con-siderable amounts of money for the sons of the Church exiled at the end of the earth. They poured their coins into the collection boxes at the cathedrals and their notes into funds organized by former rebels and their supporters. The money was meant to pay for the homeward passage of the French-Canadian *Patriotes* once they were pardoned, but the fund organizers sent it all to London, England, which made no sense at all as it left the French-Canadian convicts with their main problem – to find enough money to pay for costly passages halfway around the world from Sydney to London.

By 1844, just four years after they had started their life sentences in exile, pardons began to be granted as a result of political pleas from the bishops in Canada and pressure from Bishop Polding in Australia and a few radical politicians in England. These efforts were of limited value without the fare home.

However, the French-speaking convicts had imported the Canadian character traits of communality and survival to their prison land. Even when separated they kept in touch and helped each other. Just as they had learned to survive the bitter cold winters of their homeland, they survived the heat, flies, bugs and bushfires of New South Wales. They became popular in the colony and all found jobs as clerks, gardeners, builders, confectioners, even candlestick makers. They helped build the still-standing Victoria Barracks in the suburb of Paddington, started their own sawmill in the bush, ran a roadside store, and everywhere they went they built ovens of potters' clay and taught the Australians how to make good, risen bread to replace their heavy, pervasive damper. The few physicians among them gave their services free to poorer colonists. In one of the rare Australian stories written about the French Canadians, an early Sydney newspaper, the *Echo,* recorded: "Their good deeds, their kindness to the poor, and their general courtesy and industry are still remembered by the older residents."[1]

While still under sentence, François-Xavier Prieur went into business with a partner, Louis Bourdon, a twenty-five-year-old merchant from Saint-Césaire, making laths at the Canadian sawmill, which prospered until a depression stopped most building in the fledgling city. After their first week at the mill, the two entrepreneurs travelled to Sydney to get some provisions and there met the officers of a French whaling vessel, who offered to risk heavy penalties, including confiscation of their ship, in order to smuggle them to freedom. The ship's doctor promised to hide them in his pharmacy, to which he alone held the keys, and to take full responsibility, including a prison term, if the plot failed. The two convicts agreed, but the night before the ship sailed Prieur changed his mind. He did not want to endanger the doctor and other officers, and he worried that if he was caught he would never be pardoned and would have to spend the rest of his life away from his native land. Bourdon was hidden successfully in the doctor's quarters and became the first of the French-Canadian convicts to return home.[2]

Prieur immediately found another partner for the lath-making enterprise in Léon Ducharme, the young Montreal merchant, who also

wrote a narrative of his adventures as a convict,[3] and they worked together for a year until the business failed and they had to be fed and
clothed by their more successful colleagues at the sawmill. Prieur then
found a job as a candle salesman, but that business failed also. So he
briefly became a farm labourer. Then two of the sawmill operators,
Jean-Marie Thibert and François-Xavier Touchette, who had saved
some money, asked him to join them in building and operating a store,
bakery and blacksmith's shop at Irish Town, a village of two public
houses and three colonists' huts, about twelve miles from Sydney, but
on a well-travelled road. The business lasted just over a year. The
blacksmithery made no money at all, the shop managed to break even
but the Canadian-style bakery prospered. Then in mid-1844, the pardons started to arrive from England. At first only half the French
Canadians received them, but they included Prieur and Thibert. So
they closed the business. Thibert had enough money, mostly saved
from the sawmill venture, to pay for a passage home. But Prieur did
not.[1]

Prieur found a job as a clerk in a warehouse and waved a tearful
goodbye as twenty-eight of his companions, including Thibert, who
had negotiated a good price for passages on a merchantman as far as
England, sailed through the Sydney Heads to freedom in August 1844.
Now only seventeen remained and they met together gloomily that
evening, their only hope a promise from their departed friends to try
to have the relief funds in London transferred to Sydney.

In the next few months, three of them managed to put together
enough money for the passage to London, and ten months after the departure of the twenty-eight, Governor George Gipps, the thoughtful
administrator who had been a member of the Gosford Commission
that had investigated the discontent in Lower Canada, called Prieur to
Government House, where he happily produced an official letter from
England indicating that arrangements for transfer of the relief funds
from London to Sydney had been made and that the money would
probably arrive on the next month's mail boat. But it did not come on

that mail boat, or the next or the next or the next, and the Canadians despaired of its arrival at all.

In the meantime Prieur met a French merchant, Philemon Mesnier, who was winding up his affairs in Sydney and planned to return to Europe. By now Prieur was in a state of distress, his body weakened by worry. The Frenchman took pity on him and promised to take him with him to England, and pay his fare from there to Canada, if Prieur would help him liquidate his business. So on Shrove Sunday of February 1846, eighteen months after the first departure of the Canadian exiles, Prieur sailed with his benefactor and his wife on the *Saint George*, bound for London. The ship met violent storms while rounding Cape Horn. Ice covered the deck and hung from the rigging. After a four-month voyage Prieur stepped ashore in London. He sought out the sympathetic member of parliament John Arthur Roebuck,[5] who arranged to pay his passage to Canada from the Canadian fund, and he arrived at Quebec in the *Montreal* on September 10, 1846, seven years, less a few days, after he had been hustled below on the *Buffalo*.

Four days later, at two in the morning, he knocked on the door of his parents' home in Saint Polycarpe. Antoine and Archange Prieur threw their arms around their small son. The lights in the house went on, and then the lights in a neighbour's house, and then all along the street, despite the hour, almost all the people of the village, the children and old men, threw on their clothes and rushed to the Prieur home, shouting, "Xavier's home! Xavier's home!"

Within sixteen months of Prieur's return, all of the fifty-eight French-Canadian convicts had returned to their homeland, except the two who had died, and Joseph ("Petit Jacques") Marceau, a farmer from L'Arcadie, who decided to stay in Australia. [6]

Marceau was a thirty-three-year-old widower with three chlidren when he was shipped off in the *Buffalo*. In Sydney, he fell in love with a nineteen-year-old Lancashire lass named Mary Barrett, who had arrived in Australia at the age of three when her parents were transported for theft. They were married at St. Francis Xavier's Catholic Church in

Joseph (Petit Jacques) Marceau, a Patriote farmer from L'Arcadie in Lower Canada, and his wife, the former Mary Barrett. Marceau married Mary, the daughter of convicts, and remained in Australia to establish a farm near Dapto in southern New South Wales. There are now about 400 direct Marceau descendants in New South Wales and Victoria. (From a translation of the journal of François-Xavier Prieur by Australian historian George Mackaness)

Wollongong, near Sydney, then established a farm near Dapto, in southern New South Wales. They had eleven children, who also had many children, so that there are now about 400 direct descendants in New South Wales and Victoria. "Petit Jacques" died in 1883, aged seventy-seven.[7]

There were still no pardons in Van Diemen's Land. As the French Canadians were beginning to return home in 1844, the English-Canadian and American convicts who had survived the early brutality were still scattered throughout the evil island, attempting with great difficulty to survive economically as ticket-of-leave men, closely watched because of the escapes of Wait, Chandler and Gemmell and the attempted escape of Miller and Stewart. Despite the distances that separated them, they kept in touch as best they could, and they put together a petition for their freedom, supported by settlers and magistrates who had known them. They had little hope that this would work, however, so they planned simultaneously to take the matter into their own hands. In April 1844, just as the petition was forwarded to England with the blessing of the new lieutenant governor, Sir John Eardley-Wilmot, who succeeded Franklin in August 1843, news spread along the convict grapevine that several American whaling ships had berthed at Hobart.

Daniel Heustis and James Pierce, who were working in the Campbell Town area, obtained passes to go to the port town, where they talked with the officers of the ships and found them sympathetic. Both were offered stowaway spaces on both ships but they declined because they knew their escapes would cause additional hardship to the comrades they left behind and increased security. They insisted that one of the ships should take twenty convicts to freedom and eventually one of the captains agreed to this bold plan. Heustis and Pierce made arrangements with him to sail almost two hundred miles around the island to a place on the east coast called Wabs' Boat Harbour, which was thirty miles from any settlement. This isolated harbour was chosen because two other convicts, Garret Hicks and Riley Whitney, had gone to work on a lonely farm only five miles inland for the purpose of the mass escape that had been plotted for months.

Heustis and Pierce bribed clerks for passes to visit the farm, where they made final arrangements with Hicks and Whitney, then they travelled across the colony, notifying sixteen others of the time and place. And then they all set out on foot on long marches through the bush, from Campbell Town, sixty miles from the lonely, little harbour; from Hobart, 150 miles away; from Oatlands District, ninety miles away; and Swanport, thirty miles.

When they had all gathered at the farm, they dug up more than two tons of potatoes which Hicks and Whitney had cultivated to feed them on their voyage, loaded them into kangaroo-skin sacks and carried them on their backs the five miles to the harbour.

On the morning of the day the ship was expected to arrive they decided it would be safer if most of them remained at the farm while only three kept a lookout at the harbour because the captain had indicated he would arrive in the afternoon. But the ship arrived in the morning and the captain came ashore with two boats to find only the three men there. He agreed to come back at four in the afternoon, however, and put out to sea in the meantime, while the convicts gathered on the beach.

"How our hearts beat in view of speedy deliverance from captivity!" Heustis wrote in his journal. "In imagination we were already grasping the hands of our friends, in our dear native land! The perils of the sea were not thought of in these moments of joyful anticipation. We felt willing to endure any hardship to recover our freedom."

But it was not to be. Less than an hour after the captain pulled away from the shore, an armed government vessel loomed off the coast and remained in the area for several days. The whaler also appeared several times but sailed away when it became apparent that the government ship was there to stay.

So the convicts remained in the area, hunting and fishing, until, after eight days, three constables found them. They were charged before the police magistrate at Swanport with attempting to abscond but the witnesses against them gave confusing evidence and they were discharged and sent back to their districts. Eventually, in late 1844, because of the persistence of Maria Wait, and later some pressure from Edward Everett, the American ambassador to England, their pardons began to arrive from England.[8]

A few weeks after William Gates returned from Hobart and handed the £1,000 from the wool sale to his kindly boss, Tabart, he regretfully left him for another employer named Kimberly, who offered him an additional pound ($5) a year, which Tabart would not match. Again he was the overseer of an estate, this time of 10,000 acres with 600 in wheat and 6,000 sheep and 100 cattle. Kimberly also had two sons and four daughters, but the daughters were haughty snobs who would not even say hello to Gates or any of the convict employees. Kimberly and the sons were kind and affable although the old man (about fifty) was drunk much of the time.

Kimberly had just returned from town one evening, well into his cups and anxious to chat with Gates in the kitchen, when three of the island's most notorious bushrangers, Cash, Jones and Cavanagh, struck.[9] Gates thought he heard noises in the men's huts and told the old man he thought bushrangers were coming, but Kimberly laughed. "They wouldn't come out on such a stormy night," he said.

Soon the three bushrangers marched the men from the huts, their hands bound behind them, into the house. Jones fired a musket shot into the kitchen bedroom, barely missing the cook. Cash and Cavanagh burst into the kitchen, pointing guns, shouting, "Stand still or you're dead." They bound Kimberly, Gates, the cook, the butler, the gardener. Then, as they began to ransack the house they found the four haughty daughters and hauled them into the kitchen in a state of undress.

"It was piteous to hear their cries and entreaties and witness the anguish of their mortification," Gates wrote in his journal. "Yet I could but feel a sort of satisfaction in seeing their pride so completely humbled as it was."

There was not much money in the house, but the bushrangers collected some silver plate, clothing and a gold watch.

"Who owns the watch?" Cash demanded.

"My eldest daughter," said Kimberly.

"Where did you get it?" asked Cash, turning to the daughter.

"It was a gift from my fiancé," the shaking girl replied.

The bushranger returned the watch to its place. "I do not take the things of a woman," he said.[10]

But they did take a big sack of tea, sugar, ham and flour from a storeroom. Cash and Cavanagh disappeared into the bush with the booty while Jones untied Gates and warned him not to untie the others for two hours, while he would be watching from outside the house.

"I dared not disobey this injunction, nor did the rest either," Gates wrote, "for we well knew what desperate characters the bushrangers were, and that, defenceless as we were, one man, armed with a gun and a belt of pistols, had decidedly the advantage. So soon as the clock had struck the two hours – and they seemed long hours to us all, particularly the daughters, who supplicated and entreated me to unbind their hands, though to have spoken to me in any other situation would have been considered by them to be such a deep disgrace that no water could wash it out. I unbound them all and immediately despatched a messenger on horseback to Oatlands with the news; the constables were again in pursuit, but without success."

Gates worked on the Kimberly settlement for two years until on Thursday, September 13, 1845, the old man asked him to pick up his papers and letters at the Oatlands post office. Just as he dismounted at the post office the mail coach from Hobart arrived and Robert Kermode, a well-to-do landowner and state councillor, stepped from it.

Gates knew that Kermode was involved in government business. He also knew that some of his colleagues had recently been pardoned. So he bowed respectfully to the great man.

"I have heard that some of the Canadian convicts have been pardoned," he said, "and I'm wondering why some are pardoned and some are not when we are all supposedly guilty of the same crime."

"It's because it was thought best not to release all Canadians at the same time in case it caused troubles among other prisoners," Kermode replied. "But there have been eleven pardoned at the present sitting of the Council. What's your name?

"William Gates."

"Gates, – Gates?" Kermode said musingly. "You know I believe your name is on the list, but I'm not sure. I have the list right here in my portmanteau but I don't have time to look for it now. I've got to be going. But if you ride around to my place this afternoon I'll let you know."

In the early afternoon Gates rode the seven miles across country from Kimberly's to Kermode's, knocked on the door and stood before the councillor, trembling in both hope and fear.

"Gates, you are free," Kermode announced.

"It can't be. I don't believe it," Gates said.

"Here, look for yourself," said Kermode handing him the list.

He saw his name at the bottom of the list but still he could not believe it.

"Are you sure this is me, Mr. Kermode?" he asked.

"Of course it's you," Kermode answered, beaming with delight. Gates reined his horse directly for Kimberly's, leaping fences, logs and brushes, then burst panting into his master's house.

"It's true, it's true, Mr. Kimberly. I'm free," he shouted.

"God bless you," said the old man.

Kimberly offered to raise Gates's annual wage to £16 if he would stay for another year, but the American already had enough money for a passage to the Australian mainland, where wages were higher. So he and Riley Whitney, his countryman who had also been pardoned, set out for Hobart on foot. They covered the fifty miles quickly, but in Hobart they found no American ships on which they might work their way home.

So they went for a stroll about the town. They had not gone far when they came upon a gallows with two women on it and the hangman preparing for the drop. It was symbolic, Gates thought, that a gallows was the first thing he had seen when he arrived in the colony almost six years ago. Now a gallows was one of his last sights. He and Whitney watched as the drop fell. One of the women died almost instantly. The other dangled, still alive and struggling. The hangman jumped and grabbed the woman's feet, pulling himself clear of the ground and swinging back and forth with her for more than a minute until finally her neck snappped. The spectators cried, "Shame, shame."

"Whitney and myself turned away, sick at heart," Gates wrote in his journal, "and presently were again on the wharves. We soon found a small schooner, loaded with lumber for Melbourne, Australia.

"We went on board and that afternoon left – I trust forever – Van Diemen's Land."

CHAPTER 15

Goodbye Cruel Shores

All among the wool, boys, all among the wool.
Keep your blades full, boys, keep your blades full.
I can do a respectable tally myself, whenever I like to try.
They know me around the country as Flash Jack from
Gundagai.

AUSTRALIAN SHEARERS' SONG

*W*illiam Gates almost became an Australian. The day after he arrived in Melbourne a settler with a flock of 10,000 sheep hired both him and Whitney, and he became a shearer at a station 150 miles inland, where the soil was rich, the grass long and green, the brooks bubbling, the billabongs clear and the forests full of strange and noisy birds.

Gates was not a top-gun shearer, but Tabart had taught him well in Van Diemen's Land, and he was not bad for a new chum. At three dollars a hundred sheep he was able to save money. And when the shearing was done at his first employer's, he rode with his mates, as shearers did, to the next station to do theirs, and then to the next, a typical Aussie of the time with his calloused shearer's hands, tanned face and broad-brimmed hat, revelling in the mateship and freedom, even the hard work.

He found the birds and animals fascinating – the five-foot-tall emus, the peacocks, black swans, parrots, wallabies and platypus. "Aye, the woods are enchanting," he wrote, "with their myriads of bright plumaged birds, and the gaudy peacock – which here, in its wild state, far exceeds its domesticated kindred in size and proud bearing, and the unrivalled brilliancy of its plumes. It is indeed a country where the seeker after wealth, with a little capital, can grow rich more surely than in delving among the auriferous sands of the Sacramento. And it is a place, too, where the lover of nature and the worshipper of the beautiful may find themes worthy of their contemplation and adoration."

He marvelled as he watched aborigines hurl their ten-foot spears over a hundred yards to kill a kangaroo or wild turkey, never missing, or flick their boomerangs over wide full circles, and was awed by their magical ability to find tracks, even on the smoothest rock. "The Australians are rather tall, well-formed, with straight black hair, high cheek bones, and a colour of skin between the Negro and Indian," he recorded. "They live an easy, jolly life, hating work worse than the whites do the plague, and passionately fond of tobacco. Occasionally one can be induced to turn shepherd for a week, or even to roll fleeces for an hour or two, but never longer. They live on roots and game, and what little they can get from begging."

When the shearing season was over, he got a job as a shepherd at £26 (about $130) a year, with a weekly ration of ten pounds of flour, a pound of sugar, two ounces of tea and as much meat as he could eat. He grew strong and healthy. The clever Australian sheep dogs did most of the work. He read a lot and was content. Then, when the shearing started again, he went back to the swearing, sweating sheds with his Aussie mates.

But he was an American boy, who had risked his life in Canada to spread the American way. Thoughts of his homeland still haunted him, and after two years, when he and Whitney had saved the equivalent of $450 between them, they set off, with some regret, for Melbourne to find a ship to take them home.

There were no whaling ships in Melbourne and no indication of any arriving, so, after six weeks, with their money dwindling, they bought passages on a small vessel to Sydney, where they found the whaler *Kingston* of New Bedford, just arrived with only about 1,400 barrels of oil, and a captain so ashamed of this small cargo he did not want to go home. Instead, he sold the oil, discharged the crew and asked an elderly captain who was "on the beach" to sail the ship to America. This old man took Gates and Whitney aboard for a fare of $200 each, which was all they had.

The ship was sturdy and the ancient captain efficient. They needed to be as they rounded Cape Horn under bare poles, the decks a glare of ice, in a monstrous storm that lasted four days and four nights. Then for three days at the equator they were becalmed on a sea of glass under a burning sun. The sailors persuaded Gates to go for a swim with them. They had been in the water only a few minutes when the captain, leaning over the rail, cried, "Shark!" Gates was farthest away from the ship, but only about twenty feet. The sailors threw lines and the swimmers swam as fast as they could. Gates was the last to be hauled on board and the monster's jaws snapped beneath him just as he was pulled from the water. They did not go swimming again, but a few days later they caught a whale, and when it was lashed alongside, Gates was given the job of beating away, with a sharp, long handled spade, the ravenous sharks that attacked the carcass. He killed a few and he enjoyed that. After a voyage of four and a half months, they reached New Bedford and Gates stepped ashore onto his beloved soil. He had been away for almost ten years.

He took the stage to Watertown, then to Cape Vincent, where he arrived with half a dollar in his pocket. When he approached his family home, he found it occupied by strangers. "This was quite too much," he wrote. "I was discouraged and ready to sink down in despair. A faintness came over me; from which, however, I soon rallied."

The local people told him his parents had moved to Wisconsin, but as he had no money he could not move on, so he stayed with friends for two weeks. A "gentleman" from Kingston visited him during this time and told him of great changes the rebellions had wrought in

Canada. He said he had personally benefited from these changes and offered Gates a life of ease, with no worries about money, if he cared to live on his estate across Lake Ontario. "I thanked him very kindly indeed," Gates reported, "but assured him most decidedly that I had no inclination whatever to reside under British rule, for I had already been compelled to suffer enough of her barbarous treatment."[1]

With the help of his friends, he found a sister living about a hundred miles down the coast of Lake Ontario at Wilson, and she told him their parents had not reached Wisconsin but had settled at Aylmer, a few miles inland from Port Stanley, in what was now Canada West. Eventually, he found most of the rest of his family in the little town near the Canadian shore of Lake Erie. His aged parents took him in their arms and for a while he was content. Then he realized that after risking his life in battle for the American Way against royal persecution of the Canadians, suffering for so long in his harsh exile, and refusing a life of ease in Canada, he might still end up living in the country whose system he hated, and which was still dominated, he believed, by "the roar of the royal whelp."

Throughout 1844, most of the other convicts in Van Diemen's Land received their pardons and could hardly wait to shake the dust of the island from their shoes. John B. Tyrell, who had been branded by some of his colleagues as the traitor who warned of the planned mutiny on the *Buffalo*, was one of the first to leave. He arrived back in Elgin County, Upper Canada, in early 1845, where he eventually became a cheesemaker and a prosperous and respected citizen. Then, with the help of the American consul in Hobart, a man named Hathaway, twenty-six of them were accepted by Captain Selah Young as substitutes for an unsatisfactory crew on the whaler *Steiglitz*, which had put into Hobart for repairs. They stopped off in the Society Islands, where some of them dined with the king, while young princesses waved cocoa leaves to keep them cool, and eventually arrived at Honolulu to a friendly reception from the king there, and from American residents.

From Hawaii, they went separate ways and all eventually found their way home on whaling ships.

Others worked their way singly on vessels sailing from Hobart, but took as long as eighteen months to reach America or Canada as the ships hunted whales or took roundabout routes. And by the end of 1845, there were still thirty-three of them stuck on the island, unable to pay for a passage or sign on as crew.[2]

Linus Miller was one of them, but he continued to have an easy time at Port Arthur. He became tutor to the family of the settlement's commissariat officer, Thomas Lempriere, while his friend Stewart was given the well-paid job of signalman on Australia's first long-range communications system, which Superintendent Booth had set up to warn of escapes or other crises at the jail. It consisted of tall poles set on hilltops and islands, each carrying several sets of double arms that could be set at various angles by the use of chains. Through a relay of twenty-two such stations semaphore messages could be transmitted to Hobart within half an hour.

Both were pardoned early in 1845 and Stewart was among the twenty-six who worked their way to Honolulu on the *Steiglitz*. Miller, however, spent some months working in the office of a prominent Hobart lawyer before he left for London as a paying passenger on the *Sons of Commerce* on September 25, 1845. At anchorage in the South American port of Pernambuco, he met English and American passengers on the American barque *Globe*, bound directly for Philadelphia, and when they heard his story they offered to pay for his passage on their ship. He arrived in Philadelphia late in January 1846, then went on to New York and to his home near Stockton, where he found his family well and where he wondered in his narrative, "whether the cup of adversity, of which I have so deeply drank, has fitted me for a faithful discharge of the duties of life." His brashness broke out again as he proclaimed: "But of this I am certain, I am still blessed with a strong arm and a willing heart to wield a sword in the sacred cause of LIBERTY, either in defence of my own country, or the rights of an oppressed people."

Probably the saddest case among those left behind was that of Elijah Woodman, an American, who had lived for seven years in London, Upper Canada, where he had prospered for a while as operator of a sawmill. He had taken no part in the 1837 rebellion but sympathized with the rebel prisoners in the London jail during their trials in 1838, and tried to assist them with moral support, some extra food and by contacting defence witnesses. For these good works he was himself jailed several times, then released, apparently without trial. This treatment turned him into a rebel. He fled to Wisconsin, then to Michigan, where he became involved in the Patriot movement in Detroit and was captured in the invasion of Windsor.

He went to Van Diemen's Land on the *Buffalo* and suffered with the other convicts on the road gangs, perhaps even more because he was in his mid-forties and thus regarded by the others as an old man. But they also considered him a leader, a wise and decent old fellow who was apt to break into song to help morale in some of their most dismal situations.[3]

Woodman was pardoned on July 23, 1845, when he was forty-seven, but when he received the news he was ill and destitute. In fragmentary notes he wrote and hid, he told of being without food for as long as forty-eight hours and how he could not leave his lodgings in Hobart because he had pawned all of his decent clothes to buy food.

A kindly couple, the Wallaces, who owned the Prince of Wales Inn, invited him for meals, gave him small amounts of money, tobacco and some clothing. His eyes failed and Mrs. Wallace gave him a bed at the inn, paid a doctor to see him and provided the money for the medicine he prescribed. When Woodman was well enough to move to the lodgings of an old English convict, where four of his Canadian colleagues were already staying, Mrs. Wallace provided him with a bed, two shirts, two pairs of socks and one pound sterling. She also paid another doctor to visit him, but he used the money to buy liquor and was drunk when he arrived at the lodgings. So she engaged yet another doctor, whose treatments caused some improvement to Woodman's eyes.[4]

The American consul in Hobart also helped him with small amounts of money from his own pocket and the local Masonic Lodge set aside five pounds to be paid out in weekly doles for his support. His attempts to find a passage home on the rare American ship at Hobart Harbour came to nothing. His health worsened and he was admitted to the Colonial Hospital, where, for five months, he underwent successive operations by an assistant surgeon, of whom it was said: "The knife and the saw were his principal stock in trade and blood ran freely when he went to work."[5] The hospital was overcrowded. The attendants knew nothing about medical care. They were mostly convicts on tickets of leave, who were paid sixpence a day plus meals, or ailing convicts from the prisoners' barracks, who were too ill or weak to work in the labour gangs.

As American ships came and went, taking some of his colleagues with them, the captains still refused to accept Woodman when they learned of his condition. Then his health improved a little and in early February 1847 he was released from hospital and given lodgings at the Black Swan Inn. And his friends, the American consul and the masons, must have been active on his behalf because his diary for February 8 stated, without any previous explanation: "Captain Lathrop of the whaler *Young Eagle* has agreed to take me with him to America."[6]

Just before he boarded the ship on March 1, he mailed a letter to his family:

You will probably receive this letter three months before my arrival as the *Young Eagle* will fish some to complete her load of oil. Now, do not put too much dependence on seeing me for the All Wise Disposer of events may remove me from the shores of time before I reach my native country. I should have been home some time ago but for sore eyes and my other afflications [sic]. The cuts, the results of five operations, are about healed up and I have been able to walk about for the last three weeks. I have borne all my afflictions with patience, courage and fortitude, knowing as I do that the finger of God has touched me for my iniquities and yet at the same time He has surrounded me with His loving kindness and mercy and has blessed me by answering my prayers with mercy.

My dear wife and children, it will be nine years next August since we were all together but I have faith that I will see you all once more, so keep up good courage and think as little as possible of me. I have a mind strong enough to withstand anything the Lord sees fit to put upon me and never murmur.[7]

But by mid-April he was unable to write his daily entries in his diary and began to dictate them to the ship's second mate, Benjamin Chase. Then, on June 6, the mate wrote: "Mr. Woodman has ceased to dictate his diary. He is falling very fast, so much so that he has nearly lost the power of speech." Then the mate recorded in Woodman's diary:

June 7. Mr. Woodman not any better today.

June 8. Mr. Woodman has got a bad cough so I think he cannot last much longer. He says it will be a happy moment when the Lord takes him home.

June 9. Mr. Woodman not any better today and part of the time he is out of his head. He has to be watched all the time.

June 12. Mr. Woodman seemed more comfortable today but is very low but happy and ready to die.

June 13. The day commences with a light breeze. At seven thirty this morning Mr. Woodman died without a struggle. At eight a.m. saw the island of Juan Fernandes bearing E.N. East distant 25 miles. Henry Shew is employed in making a coffin.

June 14. Fine weather in morning but at three p.m. a heavy squall came on and we took in sail.

June 15. A light breeze from W.N. West. At four p.m. we buried Mr. Woodman in latitude 34° 54' S., longitude 77° 08' W. There was not any chance of getting into land under four or five days so we thought it best to bury him at sea rather than among the Spaniards.[8]

The *Young Eagle* was wrecked a few days later off the coast of Chile, but Chase survived wearing a jacket with the diary and Woodman's will and last letter in one of its pockets. When he finally reached Nantucket, six months after the shipwreck, he sent them, along with a personal note, to Woodman's wife.

Henry Shew, who had made Woodman's coffin, was a fellow exile, captured in the Battle of the Windmill. When he arrived home at Philadelphia, Jefferson County, New York, he found his wife had despaired of his return and married another man.

John Berry, a Canadian farmer, was the last to get away from Van Diemen's Land. He had owned 200 acres in the sixth concession of Elizabethtown, Upper Canada, but was an ardent Patriot and was imprisoned in Brockville jail when the 1837 rebellion began. When released he fled to New York State, became active in a Hunters' Lodge, and was captured in the Battle of the Windmill. After three years in a road gang in Van Diemen's Land, he was given his ticket of leave and went to work as a shepherd in a lonely part of the island. He was pardoned in 1844 but did not hear about it until 1857, thirteen years later. When he finally did get the good news, he quit his shepherd's job immediately and worked his passage on a South Seas whaler, which did not reach New York until June 1860. He crossed from Cape Vincent to Kingston, and on a steamer to Brockville he met Judge William H. Draper, the former solicitor-general who had been Crown prosecutor at his trial. The two men shook hands amicably. Berry had been away from Canada for twenty-two years.

At least three of the American convicts from New York, Moses Dutcher of Brownsville, Samuel Washburn of Oswego, and Michael Frear of Clay, married in Van Diemen's Land. According to the convict narratives, some others succumbed to the plentiful supply of raw booze and bawdy women in Hobart, and did not want to return home, or could not. A few apparently migrated to the Australian mainland and settled there, leaving no trace in history.

Altogether, of the ninety-two non-French North Americans transported to Van Diemen's Land, thirteen died and there is no record of the return of about thirty of them.

CHAPTER 16

Hello Democracy

Gae Canada's Patriot, gae, strang in your mission,
Gae bear to our sov'rein his subjects' petition;
Our despots unmask – shaw the deeds they're committin'
Pervertin' the blest institutions of Britain.

COMPOSED BY A SUPPORTER WHEN MACKENZIE
TRAVELLED TO BRITAIN IN 1832

$\mathcal{A}$s the survivors among the Canadian convicts straggled back to their homes in the late 1840s, they found their country still in political chaos. But the course of the turmoil had changed. Now, thanks to more moderate Canadian reformers and a change of government in England, the ideals for which they had sacrificed so much of their lives were suddenly more respectable.

The main catalyst of this change was a remarkable man, John George Lambton, Earl of Durham, the same man who, soon after his arrival in Quebec City as governor-general on May 29, 1838, had listened to the pleas of Maria Wait. Durham had been sent from London with dictatorial powers to investigate the Mackenzie-Papineau uprisings of 1837 and, if possible, put an end to such embarrassments in the unruly colony. He was quite a character, forty-six years old with a handsome face crowned by glistening curls. He had come from an ancient and distinguished county family but after three years in the army he ran off with an heiress for a scandalous marriage at Gretna Green.

He had fought a duel to settle an election argument and supported Britain's great Reform Bill with his father-in-law, Earl Grey. In Parliament he had earned the nickname of "Radical Jack." After he arrived in Quebec, weighed down by gold braid and mounted on a prancing white charger, it took two days to unload his masses of baggage, including his family plate and racing trophies. Despite the appearance of arrogance and vigour, he was in weak health. Second-hand smoke affected and annoyed him and he had forbidden anybody on the ship that brought him to Canada to take a single puff on pipe or cigar.

Durham found conditions in Canada even worse than he had imagined. "I expected to find a contest between a government and a people," he said in his most quoted phrase. "I found two nations warring in the bosom of a single state."

Both Upper and Lower Canada were in the depths of depression. Governments were broke, public works postponed, people desperate and angry. Farmers were emigrating by the hundreds to the United States. And the border still smouldered. The original rebellions led by Mackenzie and Papineau were over but the Battle of the Windmill, the raids into Windsor and the Short Hills area of Niagara and the uprising around Beauharnois in Lower Canada were yet to come.

One of Durham's first problems was the hundreds of rebels from the original Papineau uprising who were crowding Quebec's jails. He solved this by releasing them all except for eight ringleaders, whom he mercifully exiled to Bermuda. Then, despite his delicate health, he went to work with a frenzy, questioning witnesses, reading piles of documents, dashing around the country by boat or horseback. He developed some sympathy for the cause of the rebels and began to compile the celebrated Durham Report.

The report contained two main recommendations. First, Upper and Lower Canada should be joined together in a legislative union. Second, this united Canada and the other colonies on the Atlantic coast should be granted responsible government; that is, a government in which the cabinet would be responsible to Parliament, as Parliament was already

John George Lambton, Earl of Durham (1792-1840), politician, diplomat, colonial administrator. After the rebellions in 1837, British authorities appointed him governor general of the Canadas to investigate the rebels' grievances. He recommended responsible government. (Toronto Reference Library)

responsible to the electorate. This meant the creation of self-governing, democratic countries, no longer ruled by the British colonial office and governors appointed by the Queen.

In making these radical recommendations, Radical Jack had gone immediately to the core of the discontent that had caused so many Canadians to rebel against British domination, the family compacts and *Château Cliques*, and resulted in the transportation of the 150

Canadians and Americans to Australia. Indirectly, because other colonies would obviously demand similar treatment, he was also recommending a drastic change of course in the affairs of the British Empire, a change that would eventually result in the modern Commonwealth. The alternatives to self-government, he concluded, were more rebellion or annexation to the United States. He was certainly right about more rebellion because the Battle of the Windmill and the other Hunters' raids across the border were to come, and he was probably right about annexation. But he made another conclusion that was almost comically wrong. He believed that once the French Canadians of Lower Canada were joined with the English-speaking Upper Canadians they would be gradually absorbed into the English-speaking society and their separate language, culture and religion would disappear. He did not understand that once the French Canadians were given the power of self government, they would use it mainly to protect their separate identity, which they have been doing ever since.

There is some doubt about whether Durham actually wrote the far-reaching though somewhat flawed report because it seems impossible for one man to have performed the task in the time available. Historians believe it accurately reflected Durham's ideas but was written with much help from an interesting and unconventional trio of advisers he had brought with him. These were Thomas Turton, who had drafted the British Reform Bill in 1832, then fallen into disrepute after a scandalous divorce case, Charles Buller, his secretary, whose sharp wit often offended Canadians, and Gibbon Wakefield, who was not a member of Durham's staff but a close confidant. He had just ended a jail sentence for abducting an heiress. Lord Brougham, the inventor of a new type of carriage and a bitter enemy of Durham's, said of the report: "The matter came from a felon, the style from a coxcomb and the Dictator furnished only six letters, D-u-r-h-a-m."

Brougham, a brilliant man noted for his nastiness, also cut short Durham's stay in Canada by attacking him in Parliament for exceeding his authority in banishing the eight rebels to Bermuda, a colony outside his jurisdiction. Subsequently the British government disallowed Durham's ordinance and the Bermuda exiles were released. Durham immediately resigned after only five months in Canada and returned to England, where, at risk to his delicate health, he rushed his report into print in only two months. He died about a year later, apparently from exhaustion.[1]

The published report created a great dilemma. According to Canadian political historian Bruce Hutchison:

The practical politicians of London asked themselves whether his proposed experiment would work, whether it should be allowed to work at the risk of smashing the centralized Empire. That question was hardly less important to Americans than to Canadians. If the experiment worked, it must produce a second American nation not long hence and only such a nation could permanently secure the boundary, still unfixed in Maine and Oregon and no more than a geographical expression from the Great Lakes to the Rockies.

If the Canadian colonies could not learn to govern themselves and join together as a nation, the fate of annexation to the Republic, prepared for them by the statesmen of the Continental Congress, by Jefferson, and by the present American liberators, must ultimately ensue. Canada could not endure in separate, quarrelling fragments.

On the other hand, if the colonies governed themselves and decided to unite, how could they be compelled to serve the interests of Britain? What kind of empire would it be if several members could go their own way in great affairs? Obviously it would be no kind of empire ever known before.

In the circumstances, the British waffled. They allowed legislative union of the two colonies in 1840 but responsible government was delayed indefinitely.

Three governors followed Durham between 1839 and 1846 and they all ruled with the advice of appointed councils while the eighty-four elected members of the joint legislature, half from Upper and half from Lower Canada, continued the struggle for freedom. The elected members were backed in the mission by much more public support than the Patriots and *Patriotes* had ever had in their rebellions, but they managed only mixed success in exerting their influence. The third of these successors to Durham, Sir Charles Metcalfe, an able but stuffy civilian administrator, even began a sort of counter-revolution against the joint legislature, which was headed by Robert Baldwin of Upper Canada and Louis Lafontaine, of Lower Canada. Metcalfe had ruled over the masses of India in his previous posting and firmly believed that Canadians should be subject to the same colonial discipline as the Indians were. He made an appointment without even the usual courtesy consultation with Baldwin or Lafontaine, so they resigned in protest. Metcalfe then appointed himself leader of a loyalist party, campaigned throughout the country in an ugly, often riotous election, and managed to return a legislative majority that would not challenge his powers.

Fortunately for Canada, he was replaced, when his term was up, by a man as remarkable as Durham was. James Bruce, Earl of Elgin and Kincardine, the son of an illustrious father who had brought the Elgin marbles from Athens to England, a well-educated, devout Christian, whose mild manner belied a tough, smart core, arrived to rule over the united provinces in 1846. He was only thirty-five, though tending to stoutness and a touch of grey. He was blessed with courage and a sense of humour, and he had the backing of a new British reform government, with the Whigs under Lord John Russell in power, and the third Earl Grey, Durham's brother-in-law, in charge of the colonial office. They were ready to dabble at last with Durham's theory of responsible government in Canada.[2]

The influential economic theorists of the time, followers of Adam Smith, the father of capitalism, backed the British government. They worshipped the market as the redeemer of all economic and human problems and regarded free trade as the key to his heaven. With this philosophy, they began to regard Canada as a burden, rather than an asset, because tariff preferences on the colony's exports to Britain raised the cost of British goods.

Imperialism could not, however, be abandoned entirely. The government was not ready to go all the way by allowing annexation of Canada by the United States or granting full responsible government. Instead it instructed Elgin to follow the advice of his elected councillors but not if the advice might do serious damage to Britain. The same advice was given to Sir John Harvey, the new governor at Halifax, who faced similar demands for self-government in Nova Scotia. In both cases there was no definition of the point at which Britain might be offended.

When Elgin arrived in Montreal, then the capital of Canada, the country was still in a mess. Free trade had caused the loss of essential markets. French-English racism was rampant. The English-speaking community was divided among Tories and Reformers in the struggle for responsible government. Fierce sectarian feuds were erupting among the loyalist Church of England, the Methodists, the Presbyterians and other minor denominations. Starving, cholera-stricken Irish immigrants were dying by the hundreds on the Montreal docks and along the St. Lawrence, while the survivors imported the traditional hatreds between Orangemen and Catholics. Annexation was being invoked as the remedy for all these ills.[3]

Then the actions of the convicts and their colleagues again entered the picture. In 1849 Lafontaine introduced a piece of legislation called the Rebellion Losses Bill to award fairly generous compensation to the victims of the rebellions of 1837-38 in Lower Canada (excluding the convicts because they had been convicted of treason), in the same way that claims had already been paid for losses in the Upper Canadian uprising. The Upper Canada claims had been paid without much fuss, but in French Canada the damage had been worse, and caused almost entirely by vengeful loyalist forces. The bill passed by a two to one majority in the Assembly and created a furore among the Lower Canadian loyalists and the *Château Cliques*. It was an outrage. It betrayed them. It betrayed the Queen.[4]

The anglophone press joined in, describing the bill as "the damning insult to the loyal people of Canada, the Bill for which traitors, rebels and murderers are to be indemnified for supposed losses incurred by them in consequence of their crimes."[5]

So, once again the country erupted in riots and demonstrations. The Tories attacked the French Canadians as "aliens and rebels."[6] They castigated the despised Upper Canadian reformers and to cries of "No pay to rebels!" burned effigies of Baldwin and William Lyon Mackenzie. All-out rebellion threatened again along with the alternative – annexation by the United States. The issue became quite clear. Either Canada would manage its own affairs, accept rule by the Queen through her agent, or abandon the Empire and become part of the United States.

Elgin had tough choices. He could have dissolved Parliament but this would have resulted in rebellion. He could have "reserved" the bill and passed the buck to the British government for acceptance of rejection. Or he could sign it and thus affirm a system of responsible government in Canada.

Elgin was no coward. The responsibility, he decided, "rests and ought, I think, rest on my shoulders. If I pass the Bill, whatever mischief ensues may possibly be repaired, if the worst comes to the worst, by the sacrifice of me. Whereas if the case be referred to England, it is not impossible that Her Majesty may have before her the alternative of provoking a new rebellion in Lower Canada … or of wounding the susceptibilities of some of the best subjects she has in the province." On April 25, 1849, he drove to Montreal from his home outside the city to give Royal Assent to a new customs bill. And he had made his decision. While he was there, he would also sign the Rebellion Losses Bill.

But the word leaked out. As he left the Parliament building in Montreal, a remodelled market structure, a crowd gathered around his car-

riage. Some cheered and some jeered. The unhappy ones, mostly merchants and well-to-do people, pelted the carriage with missiles. A rotten egg hit Elgin on the cheek, but he drove on without turning his
head, and he signed the bill into law.

Mobs filled the streets of Montreal that night. With their leaders
screaming "Tyranny!" riotous gangs surged into the Parliament building carrying rocks and flaming torches. They drove members of the
Assembly out into the street and splintered the furniture. Then they
tossed balls of flaming paper about the wrecked Assembly, setting the
whole building aflame. They blocked the way of firemen as the building became an inferno. Their anger and numbers rendered the city's
seventy-two policemen helpless. All official records were burned, but a
young man rushed through the flames to rescue the Queen's portrait.[7]

Four days of civic revolution followed. Mobs attacked the houses of
Reform leaders. They burned down Lafontaine's house and stables. A
thousand armed special constables and regiments of militia patrolled
the streets, trying to keep order. Courageously, the homeless Assembly
composed an address proclaiming its loyalty to the Queen and to Elgin
and decided to present it to Elgin, not privately at his home, but pub-
licly in the heart of the city. Elgin was warned that he might be murdered on this second visit to Montreal but this did not stop him. Nor
did the howling, stone-hurling mob that met him at the building
where the presentation was to be made. His dragoons forced a passage
through the mob and he entered the building carrying a two-pound
rock that had been hurled into his carriage. After the address was read
and accepted, he left by a back street but the mob found him and followed in cabs, caleches and just about everything with wheels. The
stones they hurled broke every panel of his carriage. The commander
of his escort and the chief of police were injured and the head of Elgin's
brother, Colonel Bruce, was cut open. Elgin escaped within an inch of
his life, but he had won.[8]

The convicts who had been banished beyond the seas, though
uncredited and forgotten by history, had also won mightily, though

almost inadvertently. With the signing of the Rebellion Losses Act, Canada had thrown off the yoke of British domination. It was now a free country with its own responsible government. That was essentially what the Upper Canadian convicts had fought and suffered for, though many had favoured a republican form of democratic government. The French Canadians had also wanted independence, but a free voice in their own affairs was the next best thing.[9]

Now, belatedly, even in the Land Beyond the Seas, some small appreciation of their role in the changing of history is slowly emerging. Australian historian P.R. Stephensen, wrote recently:

The granting of what was called "Responsible Self-Government" to the Australian colonies in the 1850s was a direct result of the Canadian rebellion of 1838. The British Commissioner to Canada, Lord Durham, recommended in 1839 that responsible self-government should be granted to a Union of Upper and Lower Canada. This was done, and the same principle was later applied in Australia, New Zealand, and South Africa, thus establishing the idea of a British Empire based on willing co-operation rather than on coercion.

In that sense it was the Canadian exiles who should chiefly have been given the credit for establishing Parliamentary Democracy in Australia. The rebellion at Eureka[10] hastened a process that had begun in Canada, and it was those Canadians who gave the name of Concord [Longbottom] a special meaning for Australians who seek what is significant, and discard what is irrelevant or merely capricious, in the foundations of history in Australia.[11]

Many of the convicts became prominent and responsible citizens of Canada and the United States. Of those we have come to know best:

François-Xavier Prieur married, went into the crockery business at Châteauguay and then Beauharnois, and became a staunch conservative. As such, he moved in the high echelons of politics and became an intimate friend of prime ministers George-Etienne Cartier and Louis LaFontaine. In 1860, Cartier appointed his ex-convict friend superintendent of Lower Canada's biggest prison at Île-aux-Noix. Prieur did well at this and fifteen years later he was made superintendent of all Canadian prisons. He travelled throughout Canada, the United States and several times across the Atlantic to investigate the administration of prison systems. He did not feel the need to study the Australian system. Prieur died in 1891, aged seventy-six. Two of his convict colleagues, Jean Laberge, who had become sheriff of Beauharnois, and François-Maurice Lepailleur, who had been so shocked by the woman who lifted her skirt and patted her bum at Longbottom, were pallbearers at his funeral.

Linus Miller abandoned his legal ambitions and apparently much of his bombast. He married in 1850 and settled on the old family farm, half a mile from Stockton, New York, where he prospered quietly until his death in April 1880, when he was sixty-one.[12]

After a three-month stay with his parents at Aylmer, Canada, William Gates persuaded them to return to the United States. "I could not bear the idea of staying in Canada, to become a citizen of her most gracious majesty's government – a government that I had come to loathe with an abhorence as sincere as it was deep," he wrote.[13] He took his mother and father back to Wilson, New York, where he married a twenty-four-year-old woman, and started a butchery business with his father.[14]

Benjamin Wait moved to Michigan and, for the last twenty years of a long life, he lived in Grand Rapids, where he was in the lumber business and one of the founders of the publication *Northwestern Lumberman*. But his brave and indomitable wife was not with him. Almost nine months to the day after she took her husband into her arms on his triumphal return from the end of the earth, Maria Wait died giving birth to twins.[15]

Appendices

Appendix 1

English-Canadian and American Rebels Transported to Van Diemen's Land:

From the Short Hills Raid, Niagara

(Not all occupations and addresses are known.)

Beemer, Jacob R., 30, innkeeker, Scotland, Upper Canada.

Chandler, Samuel, 47, wagon maker, Welland County, Upper Canada.

Cooley, George, 23, farmer, an American who had been in Upper Canada for two years.

Gemmell, James, 23, a Scot who had been in the province for six years.

Grant, John, 34, wagon maker, Toronto, Upper Canada.

Mallory, Norman, 23, Scarborough, Upper Canada.

McLeod, Alexander, 24, carpenter, East Gwillimbury, Upper Canada.

McNulty, John J.,31, carpenter, Upper Canada.

Miller, Linus W., 20, law student, Chautauqua, New York.

Reynolds, William, (alias David Deal), 18, river pirate, Upper Canada.

Van Camp, Garret, 28, labourer, Burford, Upper Canada.

Vernon, John, 21, carpenter, Markham, Upper Canada.

Waggoner, James, 23, farmer, Upper Canada.

Wait, Benjamin, 24, sawmill operator and clerk, Port Colborne, Upper Canada.

From the Battle of Windsor

(Occupations and marital status unknown)

Aitcheson, James M., 28, London, Upper Canada.

Barnum, Henry V., 25, Charlotteville, Upper Canada.

Fero, James D., 25, Long Point, Upper Canada.

Gutridge, John S., 30, Cayuga County, New York.

Morin (Murray), Michael, 31, Lockport, New York.

Marsh, Robert, 25, Detroit, Michigan.

Nottage, William, 38, Halifax, Nova Scotia.

Snow, Samuel, 38, Strongsville, Ohio.

Stevens, Elizur, 27, Lebanon, New York.

Sweet, Alvin B., 22, Windfield, New York.

Sheldon, Chauncy, 57, Utica, Michigan.

Spragge, John, 23, Amherst, Ohio.

Stewart, Riley M.,31, Avon, Ohio.

Simmonds (Simons), John H., 23, Lockport and Buffalo, New York.

Tyrrell, John B., 24, St. Thomas, Upper Canada.

Williams, John C., 38, Vermont and Rochester, New York.

Woodman, Elijah C., 42, London, Upper Canada.

Williams, James P., 24, Cleveland, Ohio.

From the Battle of the Windmill (Prescott)
(From a list of participants compiled by Daniel Heustis in his *Narrative of the Adventures and Sufferings of Captain Daniel D. Heustis and His Companions in Canada and Van Diemen's Land during a Long Captivity ...*)

Allen, David, 37, Scriba, Oswego County, New York.

Blodget, Orlin, 19, Philadelphia, Jefferson County, New York.

Bradley, John, 28, Sackett's Harbour, Jefferson County, New York.

Baker, Thomas, 47, Hannibal, Cayuga County, New York.

Berry, John, 42, Oswego, Oswego County, New York.

Bugby, Chauncy, 22, Lyme, Jefferson County, New York.

Brown, George T., 23, Evans' Mills, Jefferson County, New York.

Curtis, Lysander, 35, Ogdensburg, St. Lawrence County, New York.

Collins, Robert G., 32, Ogdensburg, St. Lawrence County, New York.

Cronkite, John, 29, Jefferson County, New York.

Calhoun, Hugh, 35, Salina County, New York.

Delano (Delino), Leonard, 26, Watertown, Jefferson County, New York.

Dutcher, Moses A., 23, Brownsville, Jefferson County, New York.

Darby, Luther, 48, Watertown, Jefferson County, New York.

Dresser, Aaron, 24, Alexandria, Jefferson County, New York.

Fellows, Edom, 23, Dexter, Jefferson County, New York.

Frear, Michael, 23, Clay, Onondaga County, New York.

Gates, William, 24, Lyme, Jefferson County, New York.

Garrison, Emanuel, 26, Brownsville, Jefferson County, New York.

Goodrich, Gideon A., 43, Salina, Onondaga County, New York.

Griggs, Nelson, 28, Salina, Onondaga County, New York.

Griggs, Jerry, 21, Salina, Onondaga County, New York.

Gilman, John, 38, Brownsville, Jefferson County, New York.

Heustis, Daniel D., 32, Watertown, Jefferson County, New York.

Hicks, Garret, 45, Alexandria, Jefferson County, New York.

House (Howth), David, 26, Alexandria, Jefferson County.

Inglish (Inglis), James, 28, Adams, Jefferson County, New York.

Lefore (Leforte), 29, Lyme, Jefferson County, New York.

Liscomb (Liscum), Daniel, 40, Lyme, Jefferson County, New York.

Leeper, Andrew, 44, Lyme, Jefferson County, New York.

Loop, Hiram, 29, Scruple, Onondaga County, New York

Martin, Foster, 34, Antwerp, Jefferson County, New York.

Martin, Jehiel H., 32, Oswego, Oswego County, New York.

Matthews (Mathers), Calvin, 25, Lysander, Onondaga County, New York.

Matthews (Mathers), Chauncey, 25, Liverpool, Onondaga County, New York.

Moore (More), Andrew, 26, Adams, Jefferson County, New York.

Morriset, John, 20, Lower Canada.

Owen, Alson, 27, Palermo, Oswego County, New York.

Priest, Asa, 45, Auburn, Cayuga County, New York.

Poiley (Polly), 22, Lyme, Jefferson County, New York.

Paddock, Jacob, 18, Salina, Onondaga County, New York.

Pierce, James, 22, Orleans, Jefferson County, New York.

Reynolds, Solomon, 33, Queensbury, Warren County, New York.

Reynolds, William, 19, Orleans, Jefferson County, New York.

Richardson, Asa H., 24, Upper Canada.

Swansberg, John G., 28, Alexandria, Jefferson County, New York.

Sharp, Hiram, 25, Salina, Onondaga County, New York.

Shew, Henry, 28, Philadelphia, Jefferson County, New York.

Smith, Orin W., 32, Orleans, Jefferson County, New York.

Stewart, Joseph W.,25, Waynesburg, Miffin County, Penn.

Stockton, Thomas, 40, Rutland, Jefferson County, New York.

Thompson, Joseph, 26, Lyme, Jefferson County, New York.

Thomas, Giles, 27, Salina, Onondaga County, New York.

Wright, Stephen S., 25, Denmark, Lewis County, New York.

Whiting, Nathan, 45, Liverpool, Onondaga County, New York.

Whitney, Riley, 28, Leroy, Jefferson County, New York.

Wilson, Edwin A., 27, Ogdensburg, St. Lawrence County, New York.

Washburn, Samuel, 23, Oswego, Oswego County, New York.

Woodbury, Bemis, 22, Auburn, Cayuga County, New York.

White, Patrick, 25, Lower Canada.

Appendix 2

French Canadians Transported to New South Wales

(The main source of this list is F. Murray Greenwood's introduction to his translation of the journal of François Lepailleur, *Land of a Thousand Sorrows,* University of British Columbia Press, 1980.)

Alary, Michel, 38, carpenter and joiner, Saint-Clément (Beauharnois), married with four children.

Béchard, Théodore, 49, farmer and veterinary surgeon, L'Acadie, married with ten children.

Bergevin, also called Langevin, Charles, 53, farmer, Sainte-Martine, married with seven children.

Bigonesse, also called Beaucaire, François, 49, farmer, Saint-Cyprien, married with seven children.

Bouc, Charles-Guillaume, 48, farmer (?), clerk and "bourgeois," of Terrebonne, married with seven children.

Bourbonnais, Désiré, 20, blacksmith, Saint-Clément, single.

Bourdon, Louis, 23, country merchant, Saint-Césaire, married with two children.

Bousquet, Jean-Baptiste, 44, farmer and miller, Saint-Césaire, single.

Buisson, Constant, 30, blacksmith and bailiff, Sainte-Martine, married with three children.

Chèvrefils, Ignace-Gabriel, 43, farmer, Sainte-Martine, married with six children.

Coupal, also called Lareine, Antoine, 50, farmer, married with twelve children.

Defaillette, Louis, 49, farmer, Saint-Cyprien, married with eight children.

Ducharme, Léon or Léandre, 23, merchant's clerk, Montreal, single.

Dumouchelle, Joseph or Joson, 47, farmer, Sainte-Martine, married with four children.

Dumouchelle, Louis, 42, brother of Joseph, innkeeper, Sainte-Martine, married with six children.

Gagnon, David, 29, carpenter, Saint-Timothée, married with two children.

Goyette Jacques, 49, mason and farmer, Saint-Clément, married with three children.

Goyette, Joseph, 29, nephew of Jacques, carpenter, Saint-Clément, married with three children.

Guérin, otherwise known as Blanc Dussault, 37, farmer (?) and baker, Chateauguay, married with four children.

Guertin, François-Xavier, 44, farmer, carpenter and joiner, Saint-Césaire, single.

Guimond, Joseph, 48, farm labourer and carpenter, Châteauguay, married with three children.

Hébert, Jacques-David, 49, farmer, Saint-Cyprien, married with five children.

Hébert, Joseph-Jacques, 42, cousin of Jacques-David, farmer, Saint-Cyprien, single.

Huot, Charles, 53, notary, Saint-Cyprien, single.

Laberge, Jean, 36, farmer and carpenter, Sainte-Martine, married with six children.

Lanctôt, Hypolite, 23, notary, Saint-Rémi, married with two children.

Langlois, Etienne, 26, farmer (?) and joiner, L'Acadie, single.

Languedoc, Etienne, 22, farm labourer, Saint-Constant, single.

Lavoie, Pierre, 49, farmer, Saint-Cyprien, married with nine children.

Leblanc, David-Drossin, 36, farmer, Saint-Cyprien, married with six children.

Leblanc, Hubert-Drossin, 32, probably brother of David-Drossin, farmer, Saint-Cyprien, married with four children.

Lepailleur, François-Maurice, 33, bailiff, house painter and postal courier, Chateauguay, married with two children.

Longtin, Jacques, 59, farmer, Saint-Constant, married with twelve children.

Longtin, Moyse, 25, son of Jacques, farmer (?), Saint-Constant, single.

Marceau, Joseph, 34, otherwise known as Petit Jacques, farmer and weaver, Saint-Cyprien, widower with three children.

Morin, Achille, 25, farmer (?) and merchant, Saint-Cyprien, single.

Morin, Pierre-Hector, 54, father of Achille, ship's captain, Saint-Cyprien, married with three children.

Mott, Benjamin, 43, farmer (?), Alburg, Vermont, U.S.A, married with five children.

Newcomb, Samuel, 65, physician, Châteauguay, widower with five children.

Papineau, André, 40, also called Montigny, blacksmith, Saint-Clément, married with seven children.

Paré, Joseph, 48, farmer, Saint-Cyprien, married with no children.

Pinsonnault, Louis, 40, farmer, Saint-Rémi, married with two children.

Pinsonnault, Pascal, 27, farmer, Saint-Philippe, single.

Pinsonnault, René, 48, farmer, Saint-Edouard, married with seven children.[1]

Prieur, François-Xavier 24, country merchant, Saint-Timothée, single.

Provost, François-Xavier, 30, innkeeper, Saint-Clément, married with three children.

Robert, Théophile, 25, farmer, St. Edouard, married with no children.

Rochon, Edouard-Pascal, 39, carriage maker and painter, Terrebonne, married with one child.

Rochon, Jérémie, 36, wheelwright, Saint-Vincent-de-Paul, widower with five children.

Rochon, Toussaint, 30, wheelwright, painter and bailiff, Saint-Clément, married with two children.[2]

Roy, Basile, 42, farmer, Saint-Clément, married with six children.

Roy, Charles,52, otherwise called Lapensée, farmer, Saint-Clément, married with eight children.

Roy, Joseph, 24, farm labourer, Saint-Clément, married with two children.[3]

Thibert, Jean-Louis, 52, farmer, Châteauguay, married with three children.

Thibert, Jean-Marie, 38, farmer, Châteauguay, married with four children.[4]

Touchette, François-Xavier, 32, blacksmith, Sainte-Martine, married with four children.

Trudelle, Jean-Baptiste, 34, farm labourer and joiner, Châteauguay, married with five children.

Turcot, Louis, 36, farmer, Sainte-Martine, married with six children.

Appendix 3

The Oath of the Snowshoe
The Hunters' Lodges were Masonic-like organizations with secret signs, pass words and ranks.

Members were enlisted in four degrees:

Snowshoes – soldiers without rank.
Beavers – commissioned officers.
Grand Hunters – field officers.
Patriot Hunters – officers of the highest rank.

A candidate for induction into the lodges as a Snowshoe was blindfolded and asked to repeat the following oath:

I solemnly swear in the presence of Almighty God that I will not reveal the secret signs of the Snowshoe to any, not even to members of the society. I will not write, print, mark, engrave, scratch, chalk or in any conceivable manner make the shape or sign of the Snowshoe to any living being, not even to members of the society. I furthermore solemnly swear that I will not reveal any of the secrets of this society which may come to my knowledge through the President or Cabinet. I furthermore swear that I will give timely notice to any member or brother, if I know of any evil plot or design that has been carried on against him or the society. I furthermore solemnly swear that I will render all the assistance in my power, without injuring myself or family, to any brother or member of the society who shall at any time make the sign of distress to me. I furthermore solemnly swear that I will attend every meeting of the lodge, if I can do so without injury to myself and family.

This I swear as I shall answer to God.

Once the oath had been given, the blindfold was removed to reveal a burning candle, a naked sword pointed at the recruit's heart and two pistols flashed in front of his face. The Grand Master of the Lodge would then intone:

As you see the light, so do you also see death presented before you in the most awful shape and form, from which no earthly power can save you, the moment you attempt to reveal any of the secrets you have or which may be made known to you.

The oaths taken by recruits in the eastern U.S. states and Lower Canada required the answer: "All this I promise without reservation and consent to see my property destroyed and have my throat cut to the bone if I fail."

During the short existence of the Hunters' Lodges, at least four suspected defectors did, in fact, have their "throats cut to the bone" or were otherwise murdered.

* From *The Battle of the Windmill*, by K.F. Scott, St. Lawrence Printing, Ltd., Prescott, Ontario, 1970.

Appendix 4

In her letter describing her journey to Quebec City and back to Niagara to save her husband, Benjamin, from the gallows, Maria Wait describes the eldest daughter of Samuel Chandler, who accompanied her, only as "Miss C." My attempts to find a Christian name for her were unsuccessful. However, an old acquaintance, Terry Howes, of Etobicoke, Ontario, heard of the writing of this book and offered help. Howes is Canada's most colourful and probably most successful researcher, renowned for his discovery of money or valuables whose owners are unaware of their existence. (He has been known to ask a man if he'd like to have a million dollars, then charge him half that amount for information on how to collect it.) When I asked him if he could find the mysterious first name of "Miss C.," he at first expressed some uncharacteristic doubt, but offered to try (fortunately for me, for no charge). Within a few days, through the efforts of a colleague, Janice Wood, a genealogical research consultant, he solved the mystery. Her name was Sarah. Their research showed that Chandler had thirteen children, two by a first wife who died in the United States in 1815. He then married Ann Eliza McKelsey at Albany, New York, where Sarah, the eldest of the new family, was born. The two children of the first marriage did not come to Albany with their father after their mother's death, apparently remaining with relatives, and the members of the second family never knew the members of the first. Sarah married Jesse Wilson, of Crowland Township, Welland County, Upper Canada, in 1840 and died on their farm near Maquoketa, Iowa, on June 15, 1888.

However, the results of Howes' efforts did not end there. During his brief search for "Miss C's" first name he got in touch with Esther Summers of Fonthill, Ontario, a remarkable woman, well into her eighties, who is the official historian for the Niagara area around Thorold, where the Chandler family had lived, and she unearthed a document that told of the love of Jessie Wilson for the beautiful daughter of Samuel Chandler, whose name was Sarah. The document is an essay written from the diary of Jesse's brother, Anson Harris Wilson, and is worth recording here because it exemplifies the flight of hundreds of Canadian families to west of the Mississippi, as mentioned in Chapter Two.

The essay, in the possession of Anthony J. Phelan of Welland, Ontario, a descendant of a family named Current, who made the move westward with the Chandlers, reads:

Anson Harris Wilson was born in Lincoln County, Ontario, Canada, three miles south-west of Niagara Falls, on May 27, 1816. When the rebellion of 1837 broke out, Anson, not wishing to fight for the Queen and knowing the cause of the rebels to be hopeless, decided to leave the country. He harnessed his team to do so but was persuaded by Mahlom Brookfield and Ira Stimpson to wait until the next morning. Together the three men crossed to Buffalo, N.Y. and travelled along the south shoe of Lake Erie, crossed to the northwest corner of Pennsylvania and entered the state of Ohio. They struck the Maumee River at Perrysburg, thence across the Maumee River directly opposite and then north to Toledo. There he left his companions and went to Kalamazoo County,

Michigan where he stayed until the spring of 1839 when he was joined by his brother Jesse, and three Current brothers, William, Mark and Joseph. On 6th April, 1839, they started for the wild and far west in search of an ideal country which should be well watered, have timber in close proximity and plenty of building stone.There they intended to make their homes. A horse was used to carry their baggage.

With these aims in mind, they travelled over southern Michigan, northern Indiana, and northern Illinois which was wild and unsettled country. At last they came to Chicago, which was a small village located in the middle of a swamp. In spite of a severe storm of sleet, rain and wind, they determined to go on to Whiskey Pint, a distance of five miles. Anson obtained the point of compass from the landlord and started out ahead of the others about four p.m. As he travelled, he waded water, sometimes to his waist, and other times it was only to his ankles. He did not look back for fear of losing his course but finally came to a place that was only about two inches deep. He made a deep mark in the ground with the heel of his boot, showing the direction he wanted to take. Then he turned and looked back but none of the others were in sight so he pushed on alone and reached Whiskey Point at six p.m. He took off his blanket, which he had worn over his head, hung it up to dry and then proceeded to dry himself by turning around before the fire.

The landlord made a bed for him near the fire and, just as he was about to crawl under the blankets, William Current arrived, having been on the way five hours and only reached the place when he saw the lighted house. When Anson and William were preparing for dinner the next day, Jesse, Mark and Joe arrived. Together they resumed their journey and spent a day traversing the Dupage country without finding a satisfactory site. They started west and struck the Fox River, one side of which they looked over. After fording the stream, they found themselves between the Fox and Reeks Rivers and took time to thoroughly scour the country. They struck the Reek River at Rockford and took time to examine both sides carefully. Thence Freeport on the Pecatonica was checked but did not appeal to them. They pushed on westward and came to the Apple River near Cherry Grove. Here they spent two nights and made their headquarters at the home of a Mr. Gardner. They traversed the country without luck. The third evening found them at the site of the Apple River mill, which had been washed away. They crossed the river on the bridge stringers but could not take the horse across so

Mark elected to stay with it. William found cozy place near the road where he spent the night. Although he was tired, Anson determined to push on to Savannah three miles distance, and Joseph and Jesse declared that they would go too, even if it killed them.

The next morning they all met at Savannah, had breakfast together, and then went to the ferry to see about crossing the Mississippi. They were anxious to cross over to the Iowa shore, but found that the scow, used to take animals across, was having a [unreadable] installed and could not be used for a week. Imagine their feelings when told that they would be delayed a whole week. Seeing their sad looks, the ferryman took pity on them and suggested they he would row them across providing they could get the horse into his skiff. Someone would have to hold the horse and this job fell to Anson. The horse, being a pet, was obedient and they had no trouble coaxing him into the skiff. The ferryman placed his feet carefully and told Anson to make sure he did not move a foot or the boat would be upset. He was a bit uneasy when they pushed the skiff into the water, as it only showed about three inches above the water. Anson was not unduly alarmed as he saw an island and supposed there were a lot of them, thinking they could reach one of them if anything should happen. He said a silent prayer when they came to the open river and he learned that there were no islands and that they would have to go two miles downstream and one across before the shore could be reached at Sabula. Seeing Anson's fright, the ferryman told him he was sure they could make it but to hang onto the boat whatever happens. It was a good thing that the horse co-operated and that other boats were not operating. Even so, it was a foolish thing to take such a risk and Anson wished that he had been content to wait for the scow to be repaired.

As they neared the shore at Sabula, they saw a sizeable crowd assembled, staring wide-eyed to see a horse on the river. John Johnson had joined the crowd and, holding one hand over a sore eye, exclaimed, "My God, has Gabriel blown his trumpet?" Anson, a bit disgusted and still somewhat frightened, replied, "He can blow it till he blows his brains out, but I'll never be caught in a boat with this kind of horse as long as I live." And he never was. Seeing that it was dinnertime, he joined the crowd and managed to store away a good meal. The ferryman wasted no time in returning to Savannah for the other four and their baggage. They had eaten there and having joined Anson, they started for

Buckeye, in Iowa Territory. They scoured the area for two days, staying at night with a Mr. Ellsworth, but were not successful in their search.

The next day, having held a conference, they decided to push on in the forks of the Maquoketa River. When they reached Deep Creek, they discovered it was running high and that the banks were rather steep. They wandered up and down trying to find a crossing without luck. Anson finally suggested that they roll a log across the creek so that they could pass their baggage from one to the other as they hunched across, and again the horse presented a problem – one of them could ride him providing they could get him in the water. Jesse was elected for this job – they all pushed sand finally they succeeded, Jesse leaped on but they held their breath, hoping he would make the other side. They had some anxious moments – all they could see of the horse and rider was Jesse's straw hat which floated on the water Luck was with them – soon the horse and rider came up and were helped out by the others who had crossed on the log. After the crossing, they loaded the bags on the horse and resumed their journey towards the forks of the Maquoketa, fourteen miles distant.

On June 12, 1839, they met John E. Goodenow on the academy hill. They accepted his hospitality, spent the night with him and took breakfast with him. They accepted his offer to act as guide and set out for the forks. After dinner with Mr. Eagate, they came to the south fork where they looked at the timber. The second day they went further south and scoured between Delmar and South Grove, still looking for the right place. After a day or so, it became apparent that it would take a little time to find just the right place and Jesse, Mark and Joseph, after resting, decided home was the best place to be and started back to Canada. Jesse pined for his mother's cooking and said he just couldn't stand any more "wolley cakes." Actually he was lovesick for the beautiful girl he had left behind.

After travelling on foot for over fifteen hundred miles, Anson and William decided to remain – they found their "Eldorado." Here in this beautiful and picturesque valley, they took up claims, raised families, and remained the rest of their lives. Anson died in 1907 and William in 1881.

After Jesse, Mark and Joseph returned to Canada, Jesse married Sarah Chandler, daughter of Samuel Chandler, and by 1842, he, his parents, John and Hannah, and all his brothers and sisters had emigrated to Iowa. They took up claims adjoining Anson's claim.

Joseph and Mark Current had also returned by 1842, thus they all became pioneers.

Appendix 5

Some extracts from the newspapers of Van Diemen's Land announcing the recall of Colonel George Arthur after twelve years as lieutenant-governor of the penal colony:

From the *Trumpeter:*

GLORIOUS NEWS: – At length the happy intelligence has arrived of the removal of the most unpopular governor that ever ruled a British colony. Yes, reader, Colonel Arthur is ordered home, and *must this time obey* the orders he has received from the Secretary of State!

The downcast looks which formerly accompanied the greetings in the streets have disappeared, and the happy, the glorious intelligence has to all appearances made people ten years younger.

The colonists, to a man, rejoice – a splendid dinner is to be given on Thursday week to commemorate the happy day on which the glorious news arrived – A GRAND ILLUMINATION will also be held the same evening, and fireworks of all descriptions will be profusely let off in honour of the occasion.

A public meeting is also to be called, in order to name a petition to his Majesty, to thank him for his kindness in listening to the prayers of the people – that Colonel Arthur should be recalled.

Colonel Arthur is at last positively recalled – the official notice reached him by the *Elphinstone* prison ship on Tuesday. The successor is not named.

Never has it befallen our lot to communicate to our readers such welcome intelligence as they find this day in our first short leader. It was with feelings of joy and sincere thankfulness that we learned the joyful news brought by the good ship *Elphinstone* on Tuesday. We will teach our little ones to remember while they live and to teach their children to know the name of the ship that gladdened the hearts of many a desponding parent with the tidings that the cause of their misery and suffering, *the evil genius of the colony, was at length ordered to repair to the presence of his sovereign to answer the load of charges preferred against him by some of the unhappy victims of his oppression during the last twelve years.*

From the *True Colonist*:

A public meeting will soon be called to *thank the king* for having at length had mercy on his poor afflicted subjects in this colony, and to present a true address to Colonel Arthur from the colonists. It is proposed to have an illumination on Monday, with a bonfire and fireworks at the Battery Point. He will be wafted from these shores with the sighs, the groans, and the curses of many a broken-hearted parent and many a destitute child, which owe their misery to the foolish and wicked system of misgovernment by which the colony has been ruined. He found the colony rapidly growing to wealth and respectability – he has left it sunk in debt and misery. He has neglected the *useful* roads and ruined the agricultural interest – *he was the father of usury,* the patron of hypocrisy, falsehood and deceit – the protector of perjury – and the rewarder of perjurers. His system and the example of his government has destroyed all confidence between man and man, and sapped the very foundation of society and morals. His name will long be remembered with detestation and horror by thousands of the wretched victims of his system.

The many newspapers on the island sold out quickly so the *True Colonist* brought out a special edition:

It was with feelings of the most sincere satisfaction we announced in our last number the arrival of the "good ship" *Elphinstone* from England, bringing the very gratifying intelligence of the recall of Colonel George Arthur after an administration of twelve years; during the whole of which long period the people have been rendered wretched, unhappy, discontented and miserable by the misrule of his government.

Such was the extraordinary demand for Bent's News of Saturday last, in consequence of the intense anxiety of the people to obtain an account of the recall of Colonel Arthur, that we have, with infinite pleasure, been obliged to print a second edition, and had not the publication of our journal been unusually late, owing to the drunkenness of our printers, occasioned too by the recall of so unpopular a governor, our little, though popular News Register would have still met with a more extensive sale by several hundreds.

Appendix 6

Letter to Mr. Benjamin Miller (Linus Miller's father) from Rev. J.A. Manton, chaplain at Port Arthur Prison.

Van Diemen's Land,
Port Arthur, Oct. 24th, 1842.
DEAR SIR:- I am assured that you will pardon a stranger intruding himself upon your notice, when I inform you that the subject upon which I am to write is the welfare of your son, Linus Wilson Miller. It is now two years since Providence cast my lot at this abode of wretchedness and sin, to act in the fearfully responsible situation of Chaplain of the Station. As such the adult school came under my care. This school is open to all the prisoners on three evenings of the week. They are formed into classes, and taught by those from among their number, who may have been favoured with an education in youth. Among these teachers I observed a young man of intelligent appearance, and very steady and praiseworthy conduct. At first I said nothing to him, nor did I make any inquiry respecting him, but kept my eye upon him.

After a time I inquired his name and circumstances, when it appeared he was one of the unfortunate young men who had been sent from Canada. After some few weeks had elapsed I wanted a person to act as schoolkeeper and clerk, and made choice of your son; and I feel very much pleasure in informing you that up to the present time his conduct has been all I could wish it to be. Almost a month ago his stay at the penal settlement expired. He then obtained a situation as Tutor in the family of the Commissariat officer of the station. It will not fail to be a comfort to your minds to know that your son has passed through his probation at this severe and trying place, with knowing as little of its privations, except for a few weeks as well could be, and is now free from its restrictions, and I trust *forever.*

You will be pleased to know that his health has been good; and his way thus made plain; and it will give you greater pleasure to be acquainted with the fact that though a prisoner, your son has commended himself to us as a CHRISTIAN. We all regard him as a good man, walking in the fear and love of God, and in the comfort of the Holy Ghost; and should he in the course of a few years be permitted to return to his home, I trust that you will find that his afflictions have yielded the peaceable fruits of righteousness. In the course of a few months we are in hopes that with the recommendations he will be able to get from this place, he will obtain a partial freedom, and afterwards there can be little doubt of his getting a free pardon. May God in his good providence restore him to your aged arms.

Linus knows nothing of my writing to you, but I have thought that a line respecting him from another party would be acceptable to you; and from the high regard I bear toward him, and the fervent wishes I entertain for his present and eternal welfare, I would take this liberty. I trust the God whom you serve will afford you all that consolation which you need under your afflictions. To lay our sons in the grave, I know to be a sad and trying dispensation; but to lose them under such circumstances as yours, even worse. But you know the promise is "as is thy day, thy strength shall be," and you have this comfort also that your son has not forgotten his father's God. So look up, and urge your way to a better world.

I am, yours sincerely, the unknown,

J.A. Manton

Appendix 7

Letter to the *New York Tribune* written by Aaron Dresser and Stephen S. Wright following their release from Van Diemen's Land as a reward for capturing bushrangers:

New York, February 17th, 1844.

To the Editors of The Tribune:
The undersigned were engaged with Col. Von Schoultz in the affair of the Windmill, near Prescott, in November, 1838. They were tried by a militia court martial at Kingston, Canada, and sentenced to death but sent to Van Diemen's Land as convicts; where after a residence of nearly four years, they were forgiven and allowed to return to their native country by Sir John Franklin, the British governor.

On our voyage out, we doubled the Cape of Good Hope; on our voyage home, we doubled Cape Horn – performing, in all, a journey of upward of thirty thousand miles, and sailing once, at least, around the world.

As there are fifty-four of our comrades who were under Von Schoultz still in captivity, we think it is a duty to them and their relatives to offer the public an account of their present circumstances, so far as the same are known to us. To do this in the most satisfactory manner, we here name them severally. They are all in tolerable health, except Thomas Stockton, who is in a consumption. Severe treatment and other causes, which it would only excite unkind feelings for us to dwell upon, have made great inroads into many constitutions, once very strong; and should it be the pleasure of the British Government to release them, seeing that it is on the most friendly terms with ours, and perfect peace prevailing on this continent, their wives, sisters, parents and other relatives may expect to meet with men broken down, careworn, or in many, if not most, cases, friends who have endured a very heavy, and, as some think, most unmerited bondage.

Their names are: David Allen, Orlin Blodgett, George T. Brown, Robert G. Collins, Luther Darby, William Gates, John Morriset, James Pearce, Joseph Thomson, John Berry, Chauncey Bugby, Patrick White, Thomas Baker, John Cronkite, John Thomas, Nathan Whiting, Riley Whitney, Edward A. Wilson, Samuel Washburn, Bemis Woodbury, John Bradley, James Inglish, Joseph Lafore, Daniel Liscomb, Hiram Loop, Calvin and Chauncey Matthews, Andrew Moore, Jehiel H. Martin, Hugh Calhoun, Leonard Delano, Moses A. Dutcher, Elon Fellowes, Michael Frier, Manuel Garrison, Gideon A. Goodrich, Nelson and Jeremiah Griggs, John Gillman, Daniel D. Heustis, Garret Hicks, David House, Hiram Sharp, Henry Shew, Orin W. Smith, Joseph W. Stewart, Foster Martin, Ira Polly, Jacob Paddock, William and Solomon Reynolds, Asa H. Richardson and John G. Swansburg. Also T. Stockton, who is ill in health.

The following Prescott prisoners are dead: Anson Owen, Asa Priest, Lysander Curtis, John Stuart of Ohio, William Nottage and Andrew Leaper.

The above are nearly all Americans. The prisoners from Windsor and the Short Hills, partly Canadian and partly from the United States, are in tolerable health, except Robert Marsh, who is consumptive. Their names are Chauncey Sheldon, Elijah C. Woodman, Michael Murray, John H. Summons, Alvin B. Sweet, Simeon Goodrich, James M. Acheson, Elijah Stevens, John C. Williams, Samuel Snow, Riley M. Stewart, John Sprague, John B. Tyrrell, James DeWitt Fero, Henry V. Barnum, John Varnum, James Waggoner, Norman Mallory, Horace Cooley, John Grant, Lynus W. Miller (student at law) and Joseph Stewart.

Of these, L.W. Miller and Joseph Stewart are at Port Arthur, a place of additional punishment. They attempted to recover their freedom and suffer accordingly.

The prisoners were in hopes that when President Tyler and Mr. Webster concluded the late Treaty with Britain, through Lord Ashburton, and when Canada got a new constitution, their hard fate would be remembered; but no one of these on the island knows of any steps taken for a release. Mr. Everett, our minister at London, told us he was doing what he could for his unhappy countrymen, but thought it was very doubtful whether they would be allowed again to see their native land. We were five months on the passage from Van Diemen's Land to London, and Mr. Everett got us a ship to New York.

We say it with truth and sincerity, that we would not *of choice* pass the rest of our lives on Van Diemen's Land, if the whole island were given to us freehold as a gift; and as there can be no fear that our unfortunate friends who remain there will ever again desire to interfere with Canada, we would entreat the generous and humane to exert themselves to procure their release. We have not to complain of unusual harshness toward ourselves and yet both of us have often wished to be relieved by death from the horrid bondage entailed on those who were situated as we were. To be obliged to drag out an existence in such a convict colony, and among such a population, is, in itself, a punishment severe beyond our power to describe.

Several parties, in all about one thousand five hundred men, were placed last May under proper officers by the governor, for the purpose of securing four criminals guilty of murder, etc. We were in one of these parties by whom the criminals were secured; and this and general good conduct procured several persons their liberty, among whom we two were so fortunate as to be included.

Morriset, Murray, and Lafore, are, we think, from Lower Canada.

We can speak more decidedly as to our comrades from Prescott, Windsor and the Short Hills, above named, because when we got our freedom, we visited most of them, though scattered through the interior of the country, following their several trades or occupations. One of us, Aaron Dresser, resides in Alexandria, Jefferson county – the other, Stephen S. Wright, lives in Denmark, Lewis county, both in New York State. We will be happy to reply to any post-paid letters from the relatives of our comrades, and to give them any further information in our power.

Endnotes

Preface

1. A few Canadian and Australian academics have picked away at parts of this story, but their work does not appear to have reached the general public, and none have attempted to put together the full story. Canadian historian Edwin C. Guillet made the best attempt in his *Lives and Times of the Patriots*, published by Thomas Nelson in 1938. However, his scholarly and readable work deals only with the rebellion in Upper Canada and its aftermath, and therefore omits the large number of French Canadians involved. University of Western Ontario historian Fred Landon's *An Exile from Canada*, published by Longmans, Green and Company in 1960, tells the story of Elijah Woodman, a transportee from the London area of Ontario, and also provides an overview of what happened to others from Upper Canada and America. And more recently, in 1978, Concordia University professor George Rude included the Canadians and Americans in a social study of all groups of political prisoners transported from various parts of the world in the last century (*Protest and Punishment*, Oxford at the Clarendon Press). Entries by contemporary historian Colin Read in the *Dictionary of Canadian Biography* provide brief backgrounds of several of the Canadian convicts, but by nature the dictionary does not put the story together. Read and a colleague, Ronald J. Stagg, have also published interesting pieces on the 1837 rebellion in Upper Canada. Robert Hughes mentions the Canadians briefly in *The Fatal Shore* (Alfred A. Knopf, New York, 1987). And writer Beverley C. Boissery and historian F. Murray Greenwood, both of White Rock, British Columbia, have done work on the French Canadians, as have several Quebec historians. Australian historian George Mackaness has provided important insights in introductions to his reprints of two of the Canadian convicts' journals. But these examples of academic interest are rare.

Chapter 1: The Rebellions

1. Gerald M. Craig, *Upper Canada: The Formative Years*, McClelland and Stewart, 1963.

2. Randall White, *Ontario, 1610-1985: A Political and Economic History,* Dundurn Press, 1985.

3. William Kilbourn, *The Firebrand, William Lyon Mackenzie and the Rebellion in Upper Canada,* Clarke, Irwin & Company Limited, 1956.

4. The story of Head's mistaken appointment was circulated in the Canadas by Sir Francis Hincks, one of the founders of the Reform Party, and in England by prominent liberal lawyer J.A. Roebuck.

5. Bruce Hutchison, *The Struggle for the Border,* Longmans, Green & Company, 1955.

6. Most of the students of Upper Canada College offered their services to the militia, but after entertaining them to refreshments, Bond Head advised them to go home.

7. For stories of the Yonge Street Rebellion see William Kilbourn's *The Firebrand, The Yonge Street Story, 1793-1860,* by F.R. Berchem, McGraw-Hill Ryerson Limited, 1977, and *A Military History of Canada,* by Desmond Morton, Hurtig, 1988.

8. Mackenzie, the grandfather of future Canadian prime minister William Lyon Mackenzie King, spent eleven months in jail at Rochester as a result of the Navy Island incident, and a long period of further exile in which he and his family suffered much poverty. He was eventually pardoned in Canada, however, and returned home to be elected again to Parliament and end his days as a loyal subject of the Queen.

9. Many histories state that the flaming *Caroline* hurtled over the falls but others state a bridge at Goat Island would have prevented such a dramatic end. In fact, the greater part of the ship sank in the rapids above the falls where her engine could be seen for some years afterwards. Some parts of the ship did go over the falls, however, and the figurehead was picked up near Lewiston.

Chapter 2: Retribution and Revenge

1. Edwin C. Guillet, *The Lives and Times of the Patriots,* Thomas Nelson, Toronto, 1938.

2. *Ibid.*

3. Matthew Josephson, *Edison,* McGraw-Hill, 1959.

4. According to Guillet in *The Lives and Times of the Patriots,* all who escaped on the *Industry* later returned to Canada, where many eventually occupied prominent positions. Sixty-one years after the event, Thomas Conant, son of the ship's owner, said he still thought it imprudent to divulge the names

of the Patriots involved. The patriarch of the ship-owning, reform-minded Conant family, also named Thomas, was foolish enough during the repression to accuse a despatch rider of drinking on duty. The rider drew his sword and cut open Conant's skull. He was tried for murder but acquitted because the only witness could not positively identify him.

5. Duncombe differed with William Lyon Mackenzie on the future they wanted for Canada. American-born Duncombe regarded annexation to the United States as the proper road to liberation of the country. Mackenzie was prepared to accept American aid, but insisted that the rebel movement be Canadian directed and its aim an independent Canada. Mackenzie went so far as to accuse Duncombe of being a paid agent of the United States government. (Michael Cross, in an afterword to Press Porcépic's 1976 reproduction of the letters of Benjamin Wait.)

6. Dr. Duncombe was eventually pardoned, but returned to Canada only briefly. He spent the rest of his life in Sacramento, California, where he died in October 1867. His friends erected a monument over his grave with the inscription "A Friend of Liberty."

7. George Rudé, *Protest and Punishment,* Oxford at the Clarendon Press, 1978.

8. The third person to be executed in this period, after Samuel Lount and Peter Matthews, was James Morreau, a tanner from the Niagara District, who was captured at the time of the Short Hills invasion. He was hanged at the end of July.

9. Until the erection of the Lunatic Asylum in Toronto in 1846, there was no other place to send the insane.

10. Robert Marsh, *Seven Years of My Life, or Narrative of a Patriot Exile,* Faxton and Stevens, Buffalo, 1847.

11. By no means all of these insurgents were American. At least twenty-nine were British subjects, including eight French Canadians. Twelve had lived in Upper Canada, eight had close relatives in Upper Canada and thirteen were European immigrants. Some of the Upper Canadians were regarded as leaders of the assault.

12. Bruce Hutchison, *The Struggle for the Border.*

13. The defence council for Von Schoultz and others at court martials at Fort Henry was a twenty-three-year-old Kingston lawyer named John A. Macdonald, who later became Canada's first prime minister.

14. Guillet, *The Lives and Times of the Patriots.*

15. Fernand Ouellet, *Lower Canada, 1791-1840: Social Change and Nationalism.*

16. Montgomery's diary tells how a group of the escapees, who helped him

hobble along on his injured leg, found a boat and rowed it to Long Island (now Wolfe Island). They carried the boat across the island, relaunched it, but were unable to navigate across the water to Cape Vincent on the American shore. So they headed for the nearest land. "We pulled her up and went to a house near the shore, and there learned that we were on American ground," he wrote. "We asked a woman whom we saw there to get us a carriage to take us to Cape Vincent; but she refused and sent to the field for her husband who consented for $1.50 to take us in the boat.

"We asked him if he had heard of the escape from the fort; he said, 'Yes, that day at noon,' adding, 'I wish I knew where the poor fellows are, I would tell Bill Johnson (the river pirate) and have them safe off before I sleep. When we told him who we were he earnestly requested us to take the money back, and on landing threw up his hat and gave three cheers for the Patriots."

17. Guillet, *The Lives and Times of the Patriots*.

18. *Ibid.*

19. *Ibid.*

20. Historian J.M.S. Careless, a leading Canadian expert on the 1837 rebellion and its aftermath, describes Arthur as "a conscientious, experienced public servant [who] was no bloody-minded reactionary but a good deal more moderate than many of his provincial Tory officials." But Careless fails to bridge the gap between Canadian and Australian history. Phillip Buckner does this skilfully in the *Dictionary of Canadian Biography,* but most Canadian historians have concentrated only on Arthur's Canadian experience and his various lives have remained as distant as the countries in which he served.

Chapter 3: A Remarkable Woman

1. Mary Brown, of the University of Western Ontario, in an introduction to a collection of letters written by Benjamin and Maria Wait, first published in Buffalo by A.W. Wilgus in 1843, rediscovered by Brown and published by Press Porcépic in 1976.

2. Michael S. Cross, of Dalhousie University, in an afterword to Mary Brown's collection of the Wait letters.

3. *Ibid.*

4. Wait, in a letter written from Ashgrove, near Oatlands, Van Diemen's Land, April 1840. His letters were written at monthly intervals "to Thaddeus Smith, Esq., of Canada West," who apparently assisted his family during its troubles.

5. A fourth leader of the Short Hills raiders, Jacob Beemer (or Beamer), a twenty-nine-year-old innkeeper and carpenter from Oakland township near London, Upper Canada, was later sentenced to the gallows for the same crime of high treason. Wait regarded him as an ignorant and brutal man.

6. Maria Wait's exact relationship to Randall is vague. She is mostly described merely as his "heir."

7. Wait said the hangman was kept around the jail as a precaution by the sheriff to prevent the necessity of having to perform the executions himself. This he had had to do in Morreau's case after a hundred dollar bribe had failed to induce a "black man" to act for him.

8. Letter from Maria Wait written at Niagara, Upper Canada, on October 15, 1838, and addressed to "My Dear Friend." Benjamin Wait carried a copy of the long letter throughout his imprisonment and transportation.

9. Maria Wait's letter of October 15, 1838.

10. *Ibid.*

11. *Ibid.*

12. *Ibid.*

13. *Ibid.*

14. *Ibid.*

15. *Ibid.*

16. Wait, in his second letter from Ashgrove, dated April 1840.

Chapter 4: Uprisings and Invasions

1. The surnames of the others were Wixon, Watson, Parker, McLeod, Chandler, Walker, Alves, Bedford, Malcolm, Brown, Anderson, Waggoner, Vernon, Miller, Reynolds, Grant, Mallory, Gemmell, McNulty, Cooley, Van Camp and Beemer.

2. Benjamin Wait's letter from Ashgrove, near Oatlands, Van Diemen's Land, dated June 1840.

3. Wait's letter from Van Diemen's Land dated August 1840.

4. Linus Miller, *Notes of an Exile to Van Diemen's Land*, pp. 56-57. The full title of Miller's memoir, published in 1846 in Fredonia, New York, by "W. McKinstry, printer," is *Notes of an Exile to Van Diemen's Land: comprising incidents of the Canadian rebellion in 1838 ... also, an account of the horrible sufferings endured during a residence of six years in that land of British slavery, together with sketches of the island, its history, productions, inhabitants, etc. etc.*

5. *Notes of an Exile to Van Diemen's Land*, pp. 67-84.

6. For details of Prieur's life see *Prieur l'Idealiste*, by Dr. Emile Falardeau, Montreal.

7. Australian historian Dr. George Mackaness, in an introduction to his 1949 translation of Prieur's journal, *Notes of a Convict of 1838*. A new edition of the journal was published in French by Librairie Saint-Joseph in 1884.

8. See Prieur's journal.

9. *Ibid.*

10. William Gates, *Recollections of Life in Van Diemen's Land*, published by D.S. Crandall, Printer; Office of the *Lockport Daily Courier*, New York, 1850. Part 1, ch 1.

11. *Ibid.*

12. Gates' journal, ch. 2.

13. *Ibid.*

14. *Ibid.*

Chapter 5: Rough Ships and Prison Hulks

1. The nine "ex post facto" prisoners were Paul Bedford, Finlay Malcolm, John G. Parker, Randal Wixon, Leonard Watson, Ira Anderson, William Alves, James Brown and Robert Walker.

2. Benjamin Wait, in a letter from Van Diemen's Land dated September 1840.

3. Wait, in a letter from Van Diemen's Land dated November 1840.

4. *Ibid.*

5. Benjamin Wait in a letter from Van Diemen's Land dated December 1840.

6. Linus Miller, *Notes of an Exile to Van Diemen's Land*, p. 135.

7. Facts of the trial are taken from a long description by Linus Miller. The description contains none of his usual bombast and seems to have been taken from an official transcript which he may have obtained before his journal was published in 1846.

8. Benjamin Wait, in a letter written from Van Diemen's Land dated February 1841.

9. *Ibid.*

10. The nine were Benjamin Wait, Samuel Chandler, Alexander McLeod, John Vernon, John J. McNulty, James Waggoner, Norman Mallary, George Cooley and Garret Van Camp.

11. Benjamin Wait in a letter from Van Diemen's Land dated May 1841.

12. Benjamin Wait in a letter from Van Diemen's Land dated July 1841.

13. Linus Miller, the young American law student, became obsessed by McLeod's death and the treatment of his remains. After his parole he spent much of his spare time searching for his grave. And he wrote this poem:

I sought the grave of my friend,
Amid the slumb'ring dead;
In the yard where outcast men
Are doomed to lay their head.
Where the wrong'd and injured lie,
Neglected and forgot;
And the raven's mournful cry
Alone bewails their lot.

Where the felon finds at last
An end to sin and crime;
His weary pilgrimage pass'd.
And sorrow healed in Time.

Where the free and bond both sleep,
In earth's cold, dismal cell;
And the gaoler, Death, doth keep
And 'tend his pris'ners well.

I sought in vain the place
Where they had made his bed;
The sexton had left no trace
Of the forgotten dead!

Stranger! wouldst thou wish to hear
Why I thus sought that grave,
To mingle a comrade's tear
With ashes of the brave?

It was to bid him sweetly rest,
Though in a foreign land;
And plant a rose on his breast,
Cull'd by a comrade's hand.

To erect an humble stone
In honour of the brave,
With this inscribed thereon:
"This is a Patriot's grave."

14. *Ibid.*
15. Linus Miller, *Notes of an Exile to Van Diemen's Land.*
16. *Ibid.*

Chapter 6: The Voyage of the Buffalo

1. But Dr. Perrigo, the war of 1812 veteran who led the rebel charge at Beauharnois, was an exception. He gave a secret Masonic sign when he entered the courtroom and never came to trial.
2. Prieur's journal, *Notes of a Convict of 1838,* was translated by Australian historian George Mackaness in 1949 and published privately by Review Publications Pty. Ltd., a small company in the small town of Dubbo, New South Wales. The edition was limited to 125 copies for sale and ten for presentation in Australia and 100 copies for distribution in Canada. Between 1935 and 1962, Mackaness, who was president of the Royal Australian Historical Society for several years, edited and privately published forty-six historical monographs, mostly involving previously unpublished material. All were limited editions with some as small as thirty copies. They are now rare collectors' items.
3. The sentences were couched in these terms: That [François-Xavier Prieur] be hanged by the neck until he be dead, at such time and place as His Excellency the Lieutenant General, Commander of the Forces in Lower and Upper Canada, and Administrator of the said Province of Lower Canada, may appoint.
4. Prieur's journal.
5. *Ibid.*
6. From the journal of William Gates, *Recollections of Life in Van Diemen's Land.* This was also privately printed in two volumes by Mackaness in 1961.
7. *Ibid.*
8. Seventy-eight of the prisoners on the *Buffalo* were captured during the invasion of Windsor and the Battle of the Windmill at Prescott. One, Horace Cooley, was arrested in June 1838 and convicted of participation in a raid on St. Clair. Four others were common criminals. They were Edwin Merrit, John McMunegall (or McMuligan) and John Dean, all convicted of murder, and William Highland, a deserter.

   Of the fifty-eight in the French-Canadian group, one was an American, Benjamin Mott, who had been captured after wandering across the border from Vermont.

9. This is probably John Tyrrell, one of the prisoners from Upper Canada. He returned to his farm near Vienna in southwestern Ontario in 1845 and became a prosperous cheesemaker and respected citizen.

10. Highland, a deserter, was one of the four common criminals on the *Buffalo*.

11. The story of the voyage of the *Buffalo* is taken from the journals of William Gates, François-Xavier Prieur and Léon Ducharme. Ducharme gives a day-to-day account. Gates and Prieur are much more descriptive. There are some differences in the accounts but they are on minor points.

Chapter 7: Botany Bay

1. Robert Hughes, *The Fatal Shore*, pp. 19-24.

2. *Ibid.* pp. 31-42.

3. *Ibid.* pp. 40-42.

4. Historical Records of New South Wales, Phillip to Evan Nepean, under-secretary to Lord Sydney, March 18, 1787.

5. *Ibid.* pp. 71-74

6. *The Journal of Arthur Bowes Smyth, surgeon, Lady Penrhyn, 1787- 1789.* Australian Documents Library, Sydney, 19/9.

7. *Ibid.*

8. Robert Hughes, *The Fatal Shore*, pp. 120-128.

Chapter 8: The Cruel Shores

1. Robert Hughes, *The Fatal Shore*, pp. 120-128.

2. Alexandre Dumas illustrated the pervasiveness of the convict presence in Van Diemen's Land in his *The Journal of Madame Giovanni*, published in 1856. When Madame Giovanni arrives in Hobart she asks where the convicts are and is told, "everywhere and nowhere." She is not satisfied with this and presses for a more explicit answer. Then she is told:

> The porter who brought your luggage is a prisoner; the maid who waits on you is a prisoner; the man in the street from whom you enquired the way is a prisoner; the police agent who inspected your entry papers is a prisoner; I myself who have the honour to serve you am a prisoner; but as you see, we are prisoners without a prison.

3. For a positive report on both Franklin and Lady Jane, see Kathleen Fitzpatrick's *Sir John Franklin in Australia, 1837-1843*, Melbourne University Press, 1949.

4. Phillip Buckner, in the *Dictionary of Canadian Biography.*

5. *Ibid.*

6. Robert Hughes, *The Fatal Shore,* p. 385.

7. Evidence by Arthur to a select committee of the House of Commons in 1837.

8. Morrell lived in Hobart for twelve years. His testimony is quoted in the Welland County Historical Society's *Papers and Records, Volume V,* edited by Louis Blake Duff and published in 1938. Australian historian George Mackaness and Canadian historian Edwin C. Guillet both accept his figure (1,508 hangings, or an average of almost three a week) as fact. In any event, there were a lot of hangings. At one single sitting of the Criminal Court in Hobart in 1825, seventy-one persons were sentenced, twenty-five of them to death on the gallows.

9. Clive Turnbull, *Black War: The Extermination of the Tasmanian Aborigines,* F.W. Cheshire, Melbourne, 1948. pp. 28-29.

10. *Ibid.* p. 40. At an Aborigines' committee in 1830, evidence was given that a man named Harrington had procured ten or fifteen native women, placed them on different islands of Van Diemen's Land and left them to procure kangaroo skins for him. If, on return, they had not procured enough he would punish them by tying them to trees for twenty-four to thirty-six hours, flogging them at intervals. If they were stubborn, he killed them in cold blood. Among a litany of other horrific evidence, one Gilbert Robertson testified: "Great ravages were committed by a party of constables and some of the 40th Regiment sent from Campbell Town; the party consisted of five or six; they got the natives between two perpendicular rocks ... has heard and does believe that seventy of them were killed by that party ... the party killed them by firing all their ammunition upon them, and then dragging the women and children from the crevices in the rocks and dashing out their brains."

11. Robert Hughes, *The Fatal Shore,* p. 422.

12. Clive Turnbull, *Black War,* p. 100.

13. A government surveyor, G. Woodward, who was working on the island when the first natives arrived, told other government officials: "When they saw from shipboard the splendid country which they were promised, they betrayed the greatest agitation, gazing with strained eyes at the sterile shore, uttering melancholy moans, and, with arms hanging beside them, trembling with convulsive feeling."

14. Clive Turnbull, *Black War,* p.163.

15. *Ibid.* pp. 235-35. The death and burial of Lanney, his resurrection and muti-

lation, are described in *The Mercury*, of Hobart, of March 8, 1869, and succeeding issues.

16. There is much academic ambivalence about Arthur, as illustrated by Phillip Buckner in his long portrait of the man in the *Dictionary of Canadian Biography*. With the backing of some recent historians, particuarly A.G.L. Shaw, author of *Sir George Arthur, Bart., 1784-1854* (Melbourne University Press, 1980), Buckner paints Arthur as a narrow, evangelistic, anti-responsible government autocrat, who, nevertheless, was not to blame for the difficult situations he was supposed to solve, and an efficient administrator, capable of some mercy. He says his reputation was "blackened by hostile and exaggerated accounts of his activities in Van Diemen's Land and Canada circulated in North America by Patriots who had been exiled to Australia," and describes William Lyon Mackenzie's biographer Charles Lindsey and Edwin Clarence Guillet *(The Lives and Times of the Patriots)* as "apologists of the Patriots."

"None the less," Buckner adds, "while he [Arthur] was neither bloodthirsty nor completely reactionary, he remains a rather unattractive figure. He was frequently petty and vindictive and he could be self-serving and hypocritical... He condemned land speculation and nepotism in Upper Canada but had been guilty of both in Van Diemen's Land. In the midst of a severe financial crisis in Upper Canada he spent more than 2,000 pounds on improvements to Government House and asked for another 1,000 pounds for furniture."

Australian-born Robert Hughes *(The Fatal Shore)* describes Arthur as "certainly a martinet, and sometimes a suffocatingly pious one," but he also gives Arthur an occasional passing mark, mainly for his efforts to reform his criminal charges. Today's Australians, Hughes says, would regard Arthur as "a God-bothering, blue-nosed wowser."

There is no such academic ambivalence, however, on the fact that Arthur was extremely unpopular, among both convicts and free settlers, during his long rule in Van Diemen's Land.

17. Most of the information on Arthur's financial activities is taken from Kathleen Fitzpatrick's *Sir John Franklin in Australia*, Melbourne University Press, 1949. She says *The Colonial Times* reported (July 4, 1837) that a sale of Arthur's landed property in Van Diemen's Land had realized £40,154 3s. The *True Colonist* stated (July 7, 1837) that Arthur would receive a permanent income of three thousand pounds a year from his colonial property. There is confirmation of this figure in Arthur's own hand in a letter to Coutts &

Co., bankers, telling them that he expects to have annual remittances from Van Diemen's Land "to the extent of about three thousand pounds" (Arthur Papers, December 23, 1837).

18. A year after he returned to England from Canada in 1841, Arthur was appointed governor and commander-in-chief of the presidency of Bombay. In 1846, he was nominated to succeed Lord Hardinge as governor-general of India in the event of an emergency, but he became ill and was forced to resign. He died in retirement in London in September 1854.

Chapter 9: Convict Life – and Death

1. Lieut. Ronald Campbell Gunn, F.R.S. (1808-1881) was appointed Superintendent of Convicts, Van Diemen's Land, in 1829, and later Police Magistrate.
2. Robert Hughes, *The Fatal Shore*, pp. 232-34.
3. *Ibid.*
4. *Ibid.*
5. Linus Miller, *Notes of an Exile*.
6. The North American convicts, whether American or Canadian, were all called "Canadians" because that was where they came from. They are still called "the Canadian convicts" in Tasmania today.
7. William Gates, *Recollections of Life in Van Diemen's Land*.
8. Quoted by Janet Carnochan in a 1905 essay titled *A Canadian Heroine of 60 Years Ago*.
9. *Ibid.*
10. Letter from London to a friend, dated December 30, 1839.
11. *Ibid.*
12. Letter written by Maria Wait in London, dated July 2, 1840.
13. Letter from Maria Wait, dated September, 1840.
14. Daniel D. Heustis, *A Narrative of the Adventures and sufferings of Captain Daniel D. Heustis and His Companions in Canada and Van Diemen's Land During a Long Captivity …* – Redding and Co., Boston, 1847.

Chapter 10: The French-Canadian Convicts

1. One man did try to get away from Norfolk Island at the turn of the nineteenth century. He stole a door, cut two leg-holes in it and paddled out over the reefs in the hope of floating a thousand miles to the Australian mainland.

2. Robert Hughes, *The Fatal Shore,* pp. 113-119 and 460-484.

3. *Ibid.*

4. For some bureaucratic reason, Benjamin Mott, the American who had strayed across the border from Vermont to Lower Canada, was not kept in Van Diemen's Land with his fellow Americans and the Upper Canadians.

5. From the journals of François-Xavieur Prieur and Léon Ducharme.

6. Polding, a Benedictine, was consecrated the first Bishop of Australia in London on June 29, 1834. He was forty-one years old when he arrived in Sydney in September, 1835. He was a deeply religious, cultured and urbane man whose work with Catholic convicts in the colony was credited by the authorities for a decrease in crime and a general improvement in law and order. He died in March 1877, aged eighty-three.

7. Prieur says Brady spoke French "with the greatest of ease." Brady was educated in France and was for nineteen years a missionary on the French-speaking island of Bourbon (Reunion). In 1837 he visited Rome where he was persuaded by the convict system reformer William Ullathorne to offer his services for the Australian mission. He was detailed for Norfolk Island but when he arrived in Sydney on February 24, 1838, Bishop Polding saved him from that fate and kept him in New South Wales. Brady was an expert linguist. He studied the languages of the Aborigines and after he became Bishop of Perth in 1845 he published a short *Descriptive Vocabulary of the Native Language of West Australia.* He died in France in 1871.

8. Fernand Ouellet, *Lower Canada, 1791 1840: Social Change and Nationalism,* McClelland and Stewart Ltd., 1980.

9. A few months later, on July 26, 1841, the *Buffalo* dragged her anchors and ran aground while sheltering from a gale in Mercury Bay, New Zealand. She broke up within a few hours and was a total loss. Except for one seaman and a boy, the crew survived.

Chapter 11: Escapes

1. Robert Knopwood, like many of the colony's officials, had an interesting background. He was a hard-drinking, hard-swearing parson, accused in England of being a frequenter of the establishment of "Old Mother Dillywater and her lovely, fair crew." It was said that he had blown a fortune of £90,000 at London's gaming tables before people of great influence obtained him a chaplaincy in the navy, which brought him to the banks of the Derwent.

2. The stories of Mary Bryant and Alexander Pearce are condensed from *The Fatal Shore*, by Robert Hughes. Pearce's confession can be found in the British Committee on Transportation report of 1838, pp. 313-16.

3. Stephen S. Wright's and Linus Miller's narratives.

4. Linus Miller's *Notes of an Exile to Van Diemen's Land.*

5. *Ibid.*

6. *Ibid.*

7. *Ibid.*

8. Robert Hughes, *The Fatal Shore.*

9. Chandler related the story of his and Wait's escape to friends and neighbours in Maquoketa, Iowa, where he eventually settled. It was recorded by local historian Harvey Reid in a newspaper series titled *In the Shadow of the Gallows, a True Story of a Maquoketa Pioneer.*

10. Chandler died in Colesburg, Iowa, on May 25, 1866. He was seventy-six.

11. Benjamin Wait, in a short Conclusion to his *Letters from Van Diemen's Land,* Press of A.W. Wilgus, Buffalo, New York, 1843.

Chapter 12: The French-Speaking Slaves of Sydney

1. Three little bays near the site are now called Exile Bay, Canada Bay and France Bay. There is now a golf course on the shore of Exile Bay and a chemical factory on France Bay. At the head of France Bay there are streets of pleasant suburban homes and the boat shed of the prestigious King's School.

2. Prieur's journal, written some time after the event in 1864, gives Baddeley's amorous attentions towards the policeman's wife as the reason for the fight but the more immediate diary of François-Maurice Lepailleur says Baddeley tried to stop the policeman who was assaulting his wife.

3. Prieur's journal.

4. *Ibid.*

5. Lepailleur's diary was translated from fairly primitive French only recently (1980) by F. Murray Greenwood, an assistant professor of history at the University of British Columbia.

6. Prieur's journal.

7. Louis Dumouchelle, of the Parish of Sainte-Martine, in Montreal, was an innkeeper, aged forty-two at the time of his arrival in Australia, a married man with six children; he was tried on January 11, 1839, for treason and, with his brother Joseph, transported for life. Ignace Gabriel Chèvrefils, a farmer

of the same district, aged forty-seven, also with six children, was also sentenced to transportation for life for treason.

8. The site is now Balmain, a suburb of Sydney.

Chapter 13: Reprieve for the Human Horses

1. For some unknown reason early ballads and all of the Canadian convicts' narratives wrongly spell "Diemen's" as "Dieman's."

2. William Gates, *Recollections of Life in Van Diemen's Land*, Australian Historical Monographs, privately printed in Sydney, 1961.

3. *Ibid.*

4. The offspring of the free settlers were called the "sterling." Those of convict parentage were called the "currency."

5. Wright's *Narrative and Recollections of Van Diemen's Land*, J. Winchester, New World Press, New York, 1844.

6. Wright reported that Jeffs made a remarkable defence at his trial and "died as he had lived, a fearless dare-devil."

7. Only two prisoners are known to have escaped from Port Arthur. One died in the woods and the other was recaptured. Robert Hughes tells a story in *The Fatal Shore* of a former actor named William Hunt who disguised himself as an enormous "boomer" – a male kangaroo – and tried to sneak away along the narrow isthmus that connects Port Arthur to the mainland. Two guards, who thought he really was a kangaroo, gave chase and levelled their muskets. "Don't shoot, I'm only Billy Hunt," the frightened kangaroo shouted.

8. This description of the Port Arthur lash comes from John Frost, the Chartist who was an acquaintance of Linus Miller at the prison. Frost was sentenced to be hanged, drawn and quartered for leading a band of rebel miners against the English town of Newport after the mass arrests of Chartist leaders in 1839. His sentence was commuted to transportation for life.

9. Ikey Solomon went to Van Diemen's Land on his own volition to join his wife, Ann, who had been transported for receiving stolen goods and taken their four children with her. He had been tried and sentenced for theft in 1827 but escaped from the Black Maria on his way to Newgate jail. (The van was conveniently driven by his father-in-law). He fled to Denmark, then to the United States, then Brazil and finally to Hobart under an alias to join his family. He started a business which flourished, but everybody, including Lieutenant-Governor Arthur, knew who he was and Arthur eventually got

a warrant from England for his arrest. Solomon was said to be a major contributor to the building of Tasmania's first synagogue, but this proved to be untrue.

10. *Puer* is Latin for "boy." The first sixty-eight boys arrived at Point Puer in 1834, all drunk after breaking into a crate of wine on the ship that carried them.

11. Linus Miller, *Notes of an Exile to Van Diemen's Land*, Fredonia, New York, W. McKinstry, printer, 1846.

12. Charles O'Hara Booth had been commandant at Port Arthur since February 1833, shortly after the prison opened. He was a tough and strict disciplinarian, quite prepared to follow Arthur's instructions to make the prison a place that would take "the vengeance of the Law to the utmost limits of human endurance." He had no illusions about reforming the convicts in his care, but he also had a human side. He loved puns and cracked jokes. He detested the lash, though it was used often, and had a reputation for justice among his subordinates. At one point in his narrative, Miller describes him as "really an excellent man."

Chapter 14: The French Go Home

1. Annals, Australia, April 1992.

2. François-Xavier Prieur, *Notes of a Convict of 1838*, translated from the original by George Mackaness in 1949.

3. Ducharme's narrative, *Journal of a Political Exile in Australia*, was also translated from the original by Australian historian George Mackaness and privately printed in 1944.

4. Prieur's narrative. Prieur and Thibert tried to sell their business and buildings, but found no buyers.

5. John Arthur Roebuck was born in Madras in 1802, but brought up in Canada. He was MP for Bath in 1832, and for Sheffield in 1849, 1868, and 1874-79. The well-known Canadian politician Arthur Wentworth Roebuck, who served in the Ontario Legislature, the House of Commons and the Senate, was John Arthur's grand-nephew.

6. None of the convicts' narratives mention Benjamin Mott, the American who was captured after wandering over the Vermont border, was convicted of treason and included in the group of fifty-eight French Canadians on the *Buffalo*. But Prieur accounts for the return of fifty-five of them, two having died and one remaining in Australia. This indicates that Mott must have served his time with them in Sydney and returned with those who came back.

7. According to Sydney journalist and author Alan Gill, who researched the Marceau family for me, six of the seven Marceau families in the Sydney telephone directory are descended from Joseph and Mary. Most of the other four hundred direct descendants are scattered in rural areas.

   The original Marceau apparently became ashamed of his convict background and did not relate any of his tales of woe to any of his five sons and six daughters. Instead, he told them he was descended from a French general, François Severin Desgraviers Marceau, whom he described as having served under Napoleon. But this Marceau, though a national hero, died before Napoleon came to power, never married and is not known to have had any illegitimate children.

   The family now recognizes their convict background and is proud of it. Many of them are prominent citizens of Australia. A spokesman for the family, Kevin Marceau, a great-great-grandson of convict Joseph, is a very senior civil servant whose home in a posh Sydney suburb is named "Richelieu," after the valley where his ancestor lived. Gill reports that Kevin is anxious to visit Quebec to look further into his family's background, but is embarrassed because he cannot speak a word of French.

8. Everett made several informal but apparently effective pleas on behalf of the American convicts to British leaders, in particular to Lord Aberdeen, a former secretary of state for the colonies. He later became president of Harvard University.

9. Cash was the leader of the gang and something of a dandy. He was the son of well-to-do but dissolute English parents and was sent to Australia for shooting a man he discovered with an arm around the waist of his mistress.

10. Martin Cash was eventually captured and tried in Hobart for the murder of a policeman. When a Mr. Kerr and his wife were called to identify him, both denied having seen him before. "I could see a smile on the lady's countenance and was perfectly satisfied I was no stranger to her," Cash wrote in a memoir. He said he learned subsequently that the lady was one of Kimberly's daughters, probably the one whose watch he had returned.

    Cash was convicted anyway, but spared the rope and sent to Norfolk Island. He was released when the penal settlement was closed in the mid-1850s and returned to Van Diemen's Land where he was placed in charge of government gardens. Later he bought a farm at Glenorchy, five miles from Hobart. He died, a well-respected and popular citizen, on August 27, 1877.

Chapter 15: Goodbye Cruel Shores

1. Gates's journal.
2. Linus Miller, in an appendix to his *Notes of an Exile*, says thirty-three Canadian exiles remained in the island in 1845. His list differs from some in other narratives, but he wrote:

Of the ninety-one Canadian State prisoners transported to Van Diemen's Land [he didn't count Asa Priest, who died on the way], thirty-three remained on the island in September 1845. Joseph Stewart, Solomon Reynolds, Elijah C. Woodman, Robert G. Collins, John Berry, Joseph Leforte, Moses A. Dutcher (married in the colony), J.S. Gutteredge, Jacob Paddock, John Vernon, John C. Williams, and James M. Aitcheson were pardoned, but had no means of paying their passage home. Orlin Blodget, Asa H. Richardson, Hugh Calhoun, John Sprague, Henry Shew, Hiram Loop, Thomas Baker, George B. Cooley, Michael Fraer, Chauncey Mathews, Calvin Matthews, Andrew Moore, William Reynolds, John Bradley, Patrick White, Riley M. Stewart, James Ingles, Horace Cooley, Samuel Washburn and Norman Mallory, held tickets of leave, but were not pardoned. Jacob Beemer was at a road party, Robert Marsh, J. Cronkhite, Leonard Delano, Luther Darby, Elon Fellows, Nelson Greigs, Gideon Goodrich, John Gillman, David House, Daniel D. Heustis, Ira Polly, Orin W. Smith, Elijah Stevens, Samuel Snow, John G. Swansburg, Alvin B. Sweet, Chauncey Sheldon, Joseph Thompson, John Thomas, Beemis Woodberry, Edward A. Wilson, Nathan W. Whiting, John Grant, James D. Fero, Riley Whitney and Henry Barnham left Hobart Town in January 1845 for the Sandwich Islands, per American whaling vessel "Steiglitz."

David Allen, John B. Tyrel (cc), John Morrisette, were pardoned and left the colony for the United States in 1844.

Aaron Dresser and Stephen S. Wright were pardoned for capturing bushrangers in July, 1843.

George T. Brown left on an American whaler in January, 1845, and arrived home in the spring of 1846.

Emanuel Garrison, Garret Hicks and Daniel Liscombe left Sydney in the American merchant vessel "Eliza Ann," June, 1845; the two former intending to work their passages home in that vessel.

Michael Murray left Van Diemen's Land in the United States whaling vessel "Fame" in June, 1845.

Hiram Sharp left in the United States whaling vessel "Belle" for a whaling voyage in the South Seas, August, 1845.

Jehial H. Martin and james Pearce left for Sydney in a colonial vessel, September, 1845.

Benjamin Wait, Samuel Chandler and James Gemmell made their escape from the island in 1842.

Alexander McLeod, John James McNulty, Garret Van Camp, J.P. Williams, Asa Priest, Andrew Leper, Lysander Curtis, Foster Martin, William Notage, John Simmons, Alson Owen and Thomas Stockton were dead; nearly all these men died in consequence of bad treatment.

Emmanuel Garrison, Garret Hicks and Daniel Liscombe.

3. See Linus Miller's narrative. Woodman's favourite song was *The Hunters of Kentucky*.

4. Fred Landon, *An Exile from Canada*, pp. 242-43.

5. *Ibid*, p. 250.

6. *Ibid*, p. 254.

7. *Ibid*, p. 256. Woodman concluded this letter with a list of Canadian prisoners still on the island. The list is almost certainly incomplete, but it is the last to be compiled by a prisoner from Canada as all of the authors of other exile narratives had already left. Woodman wrote: "All of our party have left here but 25 of us and thirteen of this number are still in bondage. Their names are Asa Richardson, Wm. Reynolds, Calvin Matthews, Chauncey Matthews, John Goodridge, John Bradley, Patrick White, Hugh Calhoun, James English, Horace Cooley, George Cooley, James Waggoner, Jacob Beemer. Three have married and settled here, M.A. Dutcher, Samuel Washburn and Michael Frears. Jas. Aitchison has gone to the continent of New Holland (Australia). I do not think he will ever reach America."

8. *Ibid*, p. 261. Professor Landon's work is based on letters written by Woodman to his family and relatives from Van Diemen's Land which were in the possession of Woodward's great-grandson, Colonel Ibbotson Leonard, of London, Ont. The original Woodman diary has disappeared, but ancient copies were made of some extracts.

Chapter 16: Hello Democracy

1. Bruce Hutchison, *The Struggle for the Border*, pp. 299-313.

2. J.M.S. Careless, *The Union of the Canadas*, p. 115.

3. Bruce Hutchison, *The Struggle for the Border*, pp. 306 07.

4. J.M.S. Careless in *The Pre-Confederation Premiers*, pp. 137-38.

5. Quoted by Gilbert Tucker in *The Canadian Commercial Revolution, 1845-1851*, Ottawa, 1970, p. 131.

6. The Tory-Orange attitude towards French Canadians in both Eastern and Western Canada was quite fervid at the time. In his *Union of the Canadas, 1841-1857*, J.M.S.Careless quotes Tory William Boulton warning that Reformers would sacrifice Tory interests to "tobacco-smoking, dram drinking, garlic eating Frenchmen ... foreign in blood, foreign in race and as ignorant as the ground they stand upon."

7. Bruce Hutchison, *The Struggle for the Border*, pp. 310-11.

8. *Ibid.*

9. Nova Scotia achieved responsible government fifteen months before Elgin signed the Rebellion Losses Bill in the Province of Canada. The Nova Scotian Reformer Joseph Howe, who had been advocating responsible government since 1836, finally achieved his goal after an election on August 5, 1847, which focussed on that single issue. It came into effect when his Reform administration took office late in January 1848. Prince Edward Island was granted responsible government in 1851, New Brunswick in 1854, and Newfoundland in 1855.

The majority of Canadian historians who are expert in the rebellions of 1837-38 in Upper and Lower Canada believe that the two rebellions in combination, the threats of invasion or annexation by the United States and the simultaneous, strong political efforts of moderate reformers, in particular Dr. William Warren Baldwin and his more famous son Robert Baldwin (who probably converted Durham to the idea of responsible government) led to responsible government in the Canadas and that Elgin's signing of the Rebellion Losses Bill into law marked its beginning. However, two modern historians, Colin Read and Ronald J. Stagg, have doubted that the Upper Canadian rebellion, by itself, had much of an effect on the introduction of responsible government. See Read's pamphlet, *The Rebellion of 1837 in Upper Canada*, published by the Canadian Historical Society in 1988 and an introduction to a collection of documents relating to the rebellion in Upper Canada, co-authored with Stagg and published in 1985 by the Champlain Society and the Ontario Historical Society.

10. In December 1854, a group of Australian miners working the Eureka gold lead near Ballarat, Victoria, angrily protested the often-brutal collection of licence fees which entitled the holder to work a single, tiny, twelve-square-foot claim. The monthly fee of thirty shillings was payable regardless of the amount of gold recovered.

The government in Melbourne responded to the miners' protests by sending troops to the area and increasing the rate of collections. Some miners burned down the Eureka Hotel. Others burned their licences, unfurled a rebel flag and built a flimsy stockade on about an acre of ground near the Eureka lead.

At 3 a.m on December 3, a party of 276 police and soldiers opened fire on the stockade, which contained about 200 miners. After a brief exchange of gunfire the miners were easily routed and twenty-two of them were killed. Casualties on the government side were four killed and twelve wounded.

Thirteen of the stockaders were tried for treason in Melbourne early in 1855 and all were acquitted to great public acclaim. A subsequent commission of enquiry into the administration of the goldfields was scathing in its critisism of the government, and in the folowing months most of the miners' demands were met. The miners' licence was replaced by an export duty on gold and a Miners' Right which cost a small annual fee. The pace of reform was so rapid that within a year, the rebel leader Peter Lalor was representing Ballarat in the Legislative Council. After the establishment of the Legislative Assembly in 1856, he was elected to that chamber, of which he later became speaker.

The Eureka affair has been mythologised by the left wing in Australia as a revolt of free men against imperial tyranny, of labour against a privileged ruling class, and by the right wing as a victory of independent free enterprise against burdensome taxation. It is regarded by many as the cradle of the country's democracy.

11. P.R. Stephensen, *History and Description of Sydney Harbour,* A.H. & A.W. Reed, Sydney, 1980.

12. Fred Landon, *An Exile from Canada,* p. 307.

13. *Ibid.*

14. Wilson census, 1850 and 1860.

15. Edwin C. Guillet, *The Lives and Times of the Patriots,* p. 221.

Appendices

1. Whether Louis, Pascal, and René Pinsonnault were related is unknown.
2. The three Rochons were brothers.
3. Charles Roy was the uncle of Basile and Joseph.
4. The relationship of the Thiberts is unknown.

Bibliography

Ballstadt, Carl (with Elizabeth Hopkins and Michael Peterman). *Letters of Love and Duty: The Correspondence of Susanna and John Moodie*. University of Toronto Press, 1993.

Bateson, Charles. *The Convict Ships, 1787-1868*. Brown, Son & Ferguson, Glasgow, 1959.

Berchem, F.R. *The Yonge Street Story, 1793-1860*. McGraw-Hill Ryerson , 1977.

Bonwick, James. *The Lost Tasmanian Race*. S. Low, Marston, Searle, and Livingstone, London, 1884.

Brebner, J. Bartlet. *Canada*. University of Michigan Press, Ann Arbor, 1960.

Bumsted, J.M. *The Peoples of Canada: A Pre-Confederation History*. Oxford University Press, 1992.

Careless, J.M.S. *The Union of the Canadas: The Growth of Canadian Institutions, 1841-1857*. McClelland and Stewart, 1967.

Careless, J.M.S. (editor). *The Pre-Confederation Premiers, 1841-1867*. University of Toronto Press, 1980.

Carnochan, Janet. *A Wife's Devotion: A Canadian Heroine of 60 Years Ago*. Pamphlet, 1905.

Cash, Martin. *Martin Cash, the Bushranger of Van Diemen's Land in 1843-4*. J.Walch, Hobart, 1940.

Craig, Gerald M. *Upper Canada: The Formative Years, 1784- 1841*. McClelland and Stewart, Toronto, 1963.

Creighton, Donald. *Dominion of the North*. Macmillan of Canada, Toronto, 1957.

Cruikshank, E.A. *The Insurrection in the Short Hills in 1838*. Papers and records.

Ducharme, Léon (Léandre). *Journal of a Political Exile in Australia*. Translated from the original, with introduction and notes by George Mackaness. D.S. Ford, Sydney, privately printed, 1944.

Duff, Louis Blake. *Welland County Historical Papers and Records*. Welland, Ontario, 1938.

Evans, Lloyd (with Paul Nicholls). *Convicts and Colonial Society, 1788-1853*. Cassell, Australia, 1976.

Fitzpatrick, Kathleen. *Sir John Franklin in Australia, 1837-1843*. Melbourne University Press, 1949.

Forsyth, William Douglas. *Governor Arthur's Convict System, Van Diemen's Land, 1824-36.* Longmans, Green, London, 1935.

Franklin, Sir John and Lady Jane. *Some Private Correspondence of Sir John and Lady Franklin (Tasmania, 1837-1845),* with an introduction, notes and commentary by George Mackaness. D.S. Ford, Sydney, 1947.

Gates, Lillian F. *After the Rebellion: The Later Years of William Lyon Mackenzie.* Dundurn Press, Toronto, 1988.

Gates, William. *Recollections of Life in Van Diemen's Land.* With an introduction, notes and commentary by George Mackaness. Privately printed, Sydney, 1961. Two volumes. Australian Historical Monographs, No. 40.

Greer, Allan. *The Patriots and the People: The Rebellion of 1837 in Rural Lower Canada.* University of Toronto Press, 1993.

Guillet, Edwin Clarence. *The Lives and Times of the Patriots: An account of the rebellion in Upper Canada, 1837-1838, and the patriot agitation in the United States, 1837-1842.* Thomas Nelson, Toronto, 1938.

Head, Sir Francis Bond. *The Emigrant,* 3rd ed. John Murray, London, 1846.

Heustis, Daniel D. *A Narrative of the Adventures and Sufferings of Captain Daniel D. Heustis and His Companions in Canada and Van Diemen's Land during a Long Captivity, with travels in California and voyages at sea.* Published by Redding and Co. for Silas W. Wilder, Boston, 1847.

Hughes, Robert. *The Fatal Shore.* Alfred A. Knopf, New York, 1987.

Hutchison, Bruce. *The Struggle for the Border.* Longmans, Green, Toronto, 1955.

Jackman, S.W., *Galloping Head.* Phoenix House, London, 1958.

Josephson, Matthew. *Edison.* McGraw-Hill, 1959.

Kilbourn, William. *The Firebrand: William Lyon Mackenzie and the Rebellion in Upper Canada.* Clarke, Irwin, Toronto, 1956.

King, Jonathan. *The First Fleet: The Convict Voyage that Founded Australia, 1787-88.* Secker & Warburg, London, 1982.

Landon, Fred. *An Exile from Canada, being the story of Elijah Woodman, transported overseas for participation in the Upper Canada troubles of 1837-38.* Longmans, Green, Toronto, 1960.

Lee, David. *The Battle of the Windmill.* Parks Canada, 1974.

Lepailleur, François. *Land of a Thousand Sorrows, the journal of François Lepailleur,* translated and edited by F. Murray Greenwood. University of British Columbia Press, 1980.

Levy, M.C.I. *Sir George Arthur: A Colonial Benevolent Despot.* Georgian House, Melbourne, 1953.

Lower, Arthur. *Colony to Nation*. Longmans, Green, Toronto, 1946.

Lyon, Caleb. *Narrative and recollections of Van Diemen's Land during a three year captivity of Stephen S. Wright together with an account of the Battle of Prescott*. J. Winchester, New World Press, New York, 1844.

Marsden, Arthur Reginald, *The Origins of Democracy in Canada*. Canadian Historical Society, 1930.

Marsh, Robert. *Seven Years of My Life, or Narrative of a Patriot Exile ... with a true but appalling history of ... five years of unmitigated suffering on that detestable prison island ... with a concise account of that island*. Faxton and Stevens, Buffalo, 1847.

Melville, Henry Saxelby. *The History of Van Diemen's Land, From the Year 1824 to 1835 inclusive, During the Administration of Lieutenant-Governor George Arthur*, edited with an introduction by George Mackaness. Horwitz-Grahame, Sydney, 1965.

Miller, Linus Wilson. *Notes of an exile to Van Diemen's Land: comprising incidents of the Canadian rebellion in 1838 ... also, an account of the horrible sufferings endured ... during a residence of six years in that land of British slavery, together with sketches of the island, its history, productions, inhabitants, etc.* W. McKinstry, printer, Fredonia, New York, 1846.

Moir, John S. *Rhymes of the Rebellion* (collection). Ryerson Press, Toronto, 1965.

Morton, Desmond. *Military History of Canada*. Hurtig, Edmonton, 1988.

Mowat, Farley. *Ordeal by Ice*. McClelland and Stewart, Toronto, 1960.

Mowat, Farley. *The Polar Passion*. McClelland and Stewart, Toronto, 1967.

Mowat, Farley. *Tundra*, McClelland and Stewart, Toronto, 1973.

Murison, Barbara Cresswell. *Sir George Arthur in Upper Canada: Politics and Administration, 1838-1841*. University of Western Ontario thesis, 1977.

Neatby, Leslie H. *The Search for Franklin*. Hurtig , Edmonton, 1970.

Ouellet, Fernand. *Lower Canada, 1791-1840, Social Change and Nationalism*, McClelland and Stewart, Toronto, 1980.

Prieur, François-Xavier. *Notes of a Convict of 1838*, translated from the original, with an introduction and notes by George Mackaness. D.S. Ford, printer, Sydney, 1949.

Robson, L.L. *A History of Tasmania*. Oxford University Press, 1983.

Robson, L.L. *The Convict Settlers of Australia*. Melbourne University Press, 1965.

Read, Colin. *The Rebellion of 1837 in Upper Canada*, a collection of documents, edited with an introduction by Colin Read and Ronald J. Stagg. Champlain Society in cooperation with the Ontario Historical Society.

Read, Colin. *The Rebellion of 1837 in Upper Canada*. Canadian Historical Association, Ottawa, 1988.

Rude George. *Protest and Punishment*. Oxford at the Clarendon Press, 1978.

Ryan, Lyndall, *The Aboriginal Tasmanians*. University of Queensland Press, 1981.

Ryerson, Stanley B. *The Birth of Canadian Democracy*. Francis White, Toronto, 1937.

Sage, Walter. *Sir George Arthur and His Administration in Upper Canada*. Jackson Press, Kingston, 1918.

Scott, K.F. *The Battle of the Windmill*. St. Lawrence Printing, Prescott, Ontario, 1970.

Shaw, A.G.L. *Convicts and Colonies*. Melbourne University Press, 1978.

Shaw, A.G.L. *Sir George Arthur, Bart, 1784-1845*. Melbourne University Press, 1980.

Smyth, Arthur Bowes. *The Journal of Arthur Bowes Smyth, Surgeon, Lady Penrhyn, 1787-1789*. Australian Documents Library, Sydney, 1979.

Snow, Samuel. *The Exile's Return, or Narrative of Samuel Snow, who was banished to Van Diemen's Land for participating in the patriot war in Upper Canada in 1838*. Smead and Cowles, printers, Cleveland, 1846.

Taft Manning, Helen. *The Revolt of French Canada, 1800-1835*. Macmillan of Canada, Toronto, 1962.

Travers, Robert. *The Tasmanians: The Story of a Doomed Race*. Cassell, Melbourne, 1968.

Turnbull, Clive. *Black War: The Extermination of the Tasmanian Aborigines*. F.W. Cheshire, Melbourne, 1948.

Wait, Benjamin. *Letters from Van Diemen's Land, written during four years of imprisonment for political offenses committed in Upper Canada: Embodying, also, letters descriptive of personal appeals on behalf of her husband ... by Mrs. B. Wait*. Press of A.W. Wilgus, Buffalo, New York, 1843.

Wait, Benjamin. *Letters from Van Dieman's Land, written during four years' imprisonment for political offenses committed in Upper Canada. 1843*. Introduction by Mary Brown and afterword by Michael Cross. Press Porcépic, Erin, Ontario, 1976.

White, Randall. *Ontario 1610-1985: A Political and Economic History*. Dundurn Press, Toronto and London, 1985.

Wilson, Keith, *Benjamin Wait*. Faculty of Education, University of Manitoba, Winnipeg, 1992.

Index

About the author

JACK CAHILL was born and educated in Australia, but has no convict ancestors. After service in the Royal Australian Air Force in World War II, he became a cadet reporter in 1946 and eventually chief crime reporter for the *Sydney Daily Telegraph*. He immigrated to Canada in 1957 to join the *Vancouver Sun*, where he worked on the crime beat and then became chief of the paper's legislative bureau in Victoria and eventually its Ottawa bureau chief. In 1965 he moved to the *Toronto Star*, where he became bureau chief at Queen's Park, national editor and then Ottawa bureau chief. Through the 1970s he was the *Star*'s Asian bureau chief, based in Hong Kong. Toward the end of his forty-five years in the frontlines of journalism, he was a senior feature writer for the *Toronto Star*, specializing in national and international affairs. When he retired in 1991, the *Star* described him as "the reporter who has been everywhere and done everything."

Jack Cahill has won many awards for journalism, including a National Newspaper Award in 1975 for his coverage of the Vietnam War. He is the author of four earlier books: *If You Don't Like the War, Switch the Damn Thing Off!* (General Publishing, 1980), *Hot Box: The Story of the Mississauga Disaster* (Paperjacks, 1980), *John Turner – The Long Run, a Biography* (McClelland and Stewart, 1984) and *Words of War* (Deneau, 1987). He lives in Toronto with his wife, Marie.